MEN OF MAIZE

Books By
MIGUEL ANGEL ASTURIAS
(in English translation)

El Señor Presidente
Mulata
Strong Wind
The Green Pope
The Eyes Of The Interred
Men Of Maize

MIGUEL ANGEL ASTURIAS

translated from the Spanish by Gerald Martin

MEN OF MAIZE

A Merloyd Lawrence Book
Delacorte Press/Seymour Lawrence

Originally published in Spanish by Editorial Losada, S.A.,
Buenos Aires, Argentina, under the title: HOMBRES DE MAIZ

Library of Congress Cataloging in Publication Data

Asturias, Miguel Angel.
Men of maize.

Translation of Hombres de maíz.
"A Merloyd Lawrence book."
I. Title.
PZ4.A843Me   [PQ7499.A75]   863   75-6629
ISBN 0-440-05583-0

Aquí la mujer,
yo el dormido.

CONTENTS

MEN OF MAIZE

GASPAR ILÓM

I

"Gaspar Ilóm is letting them steal the sleep from the eyes of the land of Ilóm."

"Gaspar Ilóm is letting them hack away the eyelids of the land of Ilóm with axes . . ."

"Gaspar Ilóm is letting them scorch the leafy eyelashes of the land of Ilóm with fires that turn the moon the angry brown of an old ant . . ."

Gaspar Ilóm shook his head from side to side. To deny, to grind the accusation of the soil where he lay sleeping with his reed mat, his shadow and his woman, where he lay buried with his dead ones and his umbilicus, unable to free himself from a serpent of six hundred thousand coils of mud, moon, forests, rainstorms, mountains, birds and echoes he could feel around his body.

"The earth falls dreaming from the stars, but awakens in what once were green mountains, now the barren peaks of Ilóm, where the guarda's song wails out across the ravines, the hawk swoops headlong, the giant ants march, the dove sighs, and where sleeps, with his mat, his shadow and his woman, he who should hack the eyelids of those who fell the trees, singe the eyelashes of those who burn the forest, and chill the bodies of those who dam the waters of the river that sleeps as it flows and sees nothing until trapped in pools it opens its eyes and sees all with its deep water gaze . . ."

Gaspar stretched himself out, curled himself in, and again shook his head from side to side to grind the accusation of the

1

earth, bound in sleep and in death by the snake of six hundred thousand coils of mud, moon, forests, rainstorms, mountains, lakes, birds and echoes that pounded his bones until they turned to a black frijole paste dripping from the depths of the night.

And then he heard, with the hollows of his ears he heard:

"Yellow rabbits in the sky, yellow rabbits in the forest, yellow rabbits in the water will fight with Gaspar. Gaspar Ilóm will go to war, compelled by his blood, his river, the blind knots of his speech . . ."

The word of the earth turned to flame by the sun all but set fire to the maize-leaf ears of the yellow rabbits in the sky, the yellow rabbits in the forest, the yellow rabbits in the water; but Gaspar was once again becoming earth that falls from where the earth falls, which is to say, sleep that finds no shade in which to dream in the soil of Ilóm, and the solar flame of the voice could do nothing, tricked by the yellow rabbits that set to suckling in a papaya grove, turned into forest papayas, that fixed themselves against the sky, turned into stars, and faded into the water like reflections with ears.

Bare earth, wakeful earth, sleepy maize-growing earth, Gaspar falling from where the earth falls, maize-growing earth bathed by rivers of water fetid from being so long awake, water green from the wakefulness of the forests sacrificed by the maize made man the sower of maize. The maize planters beat their way in with their fires and their axes, into forests that were grandmothers of shade, two hundred thousand young silk-cotton trees each a thousand years old.

In the grass was a mule, on the mule was a man, and in the man was a dead man. His eyes were his eyes, his hands were his hands, his voice was his voice, his legs were his legs and his feet were his feet for taking him to war as soon as he could get away from the snake of six hundred thousand coils of mud, moon, forests, rainstorms, mountains, lakes, birds and echoes that had curled itself around his body. But how could he get away, how could he untie himself from the crops, from his

2

woman, the children, the rancho; how could he break free
the cheery companionship of the fields; how was he to dra
himself off to war with the half-flowered bean patch about hi
arms, the warm chayote tips around his neck, and his feet
caught in the noose of the daily round.

The air of Ilóm was heavy with the smell of newly felled
trees, the ashes of trees burned down to clear the ground.

A whirlwind of mud, moon, forests, rainstorms, mountains,
lakes, birds and echoes went round and round and round and
round the chief of Ilóm, and as the wind beat against his face
and body and as the earth raised by the wind beat against him
he was swallowed by a toothless half moon which sucked him
from the air, without biting him, like a small fish.

The air of Ilóm was heavy with the smell of newly felled
trees, the ashes of trees burned to clear the ground.

Yellow rabbits in the sky, yellow rabbits in the water, yellow
rabbits in the forest.

He didn't open his eyes. They were already open, piled up
among his eyelashes. He was shaken by the thudding of his
heartbeats. He didn't dare move, swallow saliva, touch his
naked body, for fear he would find his skin cold and inside his
cold skin the deep ravines dribbled in him by the serpent.

The brilliance of the night dripped copal resin between the
canes of the rancho. His woman scarcely showed up on her
petate. She was breathing face down as though she were blowing on the fire in her sleep.

Gaspar dragged himself off on his hands and knees, full of
empty ravines, to search for his bottle gourd, making no sound
other than the joints of his bones, which ached as if by an effect
of the moon, and in the darkness, striped like a poncho by the
firefly light of the night filtering in through the canes of the
rancho, his face, that of a thirsty idol, could be seen sucking
away at the gourd, drinking down great gulps of cane liquor
with the greed of a baby too long deprived of the breast.

A flash of maize-leaf flame caught his face as he finished the
gourd. The sun that beats down on the sugar plantations

burned him inside: it burned his head till his hair no longer felt like hair, but like a pelt of ashes, and it burned the flittermouse of his tongue in the roof of his mouth, so he couldn't let the words of his dreams escape as he slept, his tongue that no longer felt like a tongue, but like a maguey rope, and it burned his teeth that no longer felt like teeth, but like freshly sharpened machetes.

His half-buried hands clawed at the ground, the ground sticky with cold, his fingers glued to it, deep, hard, without resonance, his fingernails heavy as shotgun slugs.

And he went on digging around himself, like an animal that feeds on corpses, searching for the body he felt had become detached from his head. He felt his head, full of liquor, like a gourd hanging from one of the wooden uprights of the rancho.

But the liquor didn't burn his face. The liquor didn't burn his hair. The liquor didn't decapitate him because it was liquor but because it was the water of war. He drank to feel himself burned, buried, beheaded, which is how you have to go to war if you want to go unafraid: no head, no body, no skin.

That is what Gaspar thought. That is what he said, his head separated from his body, babbling, burning, wrapped in a bundle hoary with moonlight. Gaspar grew older as he talked. His head had fallen to the ground like a potsherd broken into fragments of thought. What Gaspar was saying, now that he was old, was forest. What he was thinking was forest remembered, not new hair. His thoughts passed out of his ears to hear the cattle going by above his head. A herd of clouds on hoofs. Hundreds of hoofs. Thousands of hoofs. The booty of the yellow rabbits.

Piojosa Grande struggled beneath Gaspar's body that was damp and warm as young maize shoots. He carried her with him in his pulsations, ever further away. The spasm took them far beyond him, far beyond her, to where he ceased to be just himself and she ceased to be just herself, to become species, tribe, a stream of sensations. Suddenly he held her tight. Pi-

4

ojosa cried out. Shouts, boulders. Her sleep spread over the petate like her matted hair combed by Gaspar's teeth. Her pupils of grieving blood saw nothing. She shrank back like a blind hen. A handful of sunflower seeds in her entrails. The smell of the man. The smell of breath.

And the next day:

"Look, Piojosa, the ruckus'll be starting up any day now. We've got to clear the land of Ilóm of them who knock the trees down with axes, them who scorch the forest with their fires, them who dam the waters of the river that sleeps as it flows and opens its eyes in the pools and rots for wanting to sleep . . . The maizegrowers, them who've done away with the shade, for either the earth that falls from the stars is going to find some place to carry on dreaming its dream in the soil of Ilóm, or they can put me off to sleep forever. Get some old rags together to tie up my things, and don't forget the cold tortillas, and some salt beef, and some chili, all a man needs to go to war."

Gaspar scratched the anthill of his beard with the fingers on his right hand, took down his shotgun, went down to the river and fired on the first maizegrower who passed by, from behind a bush. Name of Igiño. The next day, in another spot, he brought down the second one. Fellow called Domingo. And from one day to another Igiño, Domingo, Cleto, then Bautista and Chalío, until the forest was clear of the planters.

The matapalo is bad, but the maizegrower is worse. The matapalo takes years to dry a tree up. The maizegrower sets fire to the brush and does for the timber in a matter of hours. And what timber. The most priceless of woods. What guerrillas do to men in time of war the maizegrower does to the trees. Smoke, flames, ashes. Different if it was just to eat. It's to make money. Different, too, if it was on their own account, but they go halves with the boss, and sometimes not even halves. The maize impoverishes the earth and makes no one rich. Neither the boss nor the men. Sown to be eaten it is the sacred sustenance of the men who were made of maize. Sown to make money it means famine for the men who were made of maize. The red staff of the Place of Provisions, women with children and men with women, will never take root in the maize plantations, try as they will. The earth will become exhausted and the planter will take his little seeds off somewhere else, until he too begins to waste away like a discolored seed fallen in the midst of fertile lands ripe for planting, lands that could make him a rich man instead of a nobody who wanders around ruining the earth everywhere he goes, always poor and finally losing all pleasure in the good things he could have had: sugar cane on the hot low-lying slopes, where the air grows thick over the banana groves and the cacao trees shoot up like rockets in the sky to explode silently in sprays of almond-colored berries, not to mention the coffee, in rich soils spattered with blood, and the wheatfields ablaze beyond.

Creamy skies and butter rivers running low, turning green, merged together in the first downpour of a winter that was pure wasted water on the barren black fields, and nothing anyone could do about it. It was a crying shame to see all those crystals falling from the sky onto the burning thirst of the abandoned plots. Not a seed, not a furrow, not a planter. Indians with rainwater eyes spied on the houses of the Ladinos from the mountains. There were forty houses in the town. Only rarely did anyone set foot in the cobbled streets in the early morning air, for fear of being killed. Gaspar and his men could make out their forms and if the wind was right they could hear the grackles squabbling in the silk-cotton tree down in the square.

Gaspar is invincible, said the old folk of the town. The rabbits with maize-leaf ears protect Gaspar, and for the yellow rabbits with maize-leaf ears there are no secrets, no dangers, no distances. Gaspar's hide is mamey skin and gold his blood —"great is his strength," "great is his dance"—and his teeth, pumice stones when he laughs and flint stones when he bites or grinds them, are his heart in his mouth, as his heelbone is his heart in his feet as he walks. Only the yellow rabbits know the mark of his teeth in the fruits and the mark of his feet along

6

the paths. Word for word, that is what the old folk of the town said. You can hear them walking when Gaspar walks. You can hear them talking when Gaspar talks. Gaspar walks for all who have walked, all who walk and all who will walk. Gaspar talks for all who have talked, all who talk and all who will talk. That is what the old folk in the town told the maizegrowers. The storm beat out its drums in the hall of the blue doves and beneath the sheets of cloud over the savannahs.

But one day after a day, the knotted speech of the old folk announced that the mounted patrol was on its way again. The countryside sown with yellow flowers warned danger to the one protected by the yellow rabbits.

At what hour did the troop enter the town? To the Ladinos under threat of death from the Indians it seemed like a dream. They neither spoke nor moved nor saw anything in the shadow that was as hard as the walls. The horses passed before them like black worms, and they sensed the riders had faces of burned almonds and honey. It had stopped raining, but there was a stupefying smell of sodden earth and the stench of skunk.

Gaspar changed his hiding place. In the deep blue of the night of Ilóm tiny twinkling rabbits hopped from star to star, a sign of danger, and the mountains smelled of yellow marigolds. Gaspar Ilóm changed his hiding place with his gun fully loaded with seeds of darkness—that's what gunpowder is, deathly seeds of darkness—his machete dangling at his waist, a gourd full of liquor, a cloth with his tobacco, his chili and his salt beef, two bay leaves stuck with saliva to the panicky senses, a jar of bitter-almond oil, and a small box of cameline ointment. Great was his strength, great was his dance. His strength was the flowers, his dance was the clouds.

The balcony of the Council House was up above. Down below the square looked heavy with water. The saddled horses were tossing about in the smoky dampness of their breath, with their bridles tied to the stirrup leathers and their girths loosened. Ever since the troop arrived the air smelled of soaking wet horses.

The leader of the mounted troop wandered in and out of the gallery, a lighted cigar in his mouth, uniform unbuttoned, a white crape kerchief at his neck, and faded trousers hanging over his leggings and combat boots.

By this time the town had eyes only for the forest. Those who had not already fled were decimated by the Indians who came down from the mountains of Ilóm, led by a cunning and treacherous chief, and those who stuck it out in the town stayed holed up in their houses and when they crossed the street they scuttled like lizards.

The news of the proclamation brought all out of their houses. It was read out on every corner. "Colonel Gonzalo Godoy, Leader of the Army Expeditionary Force in the Field, wishes to inform that having regrouped his forces and received orders and supplies, he entered Pisigüilito last night with one hundred and fifty riflemen on horseback and another hundred men on foot armed with machetes, and every one just waiting to throw lead and steel against the Indians up in the mountains."

Shadow of dark clouds. Distant sun. The mountains an olive green. The sky, the air, the houses, everything the color of prickly pear. The man reading the proclamation, the little group of townspeople listening from corner to corner—almost always the same group—the soldiers escorting him with pipe and drum, seemed to be made not of flesh, but of green tomatoes, vegetables, edible things.

After the proclamation the elders of the town paid Colonel Godoy a visit. No sooner was it over than a delegation of them arrived. Don Chalo, without removing the bar from his mouth, sitting in a hammock hanging from one of the beams of the gallery, fixed his round blue eyes on everything about him, except the delegation, until one of them, after much hesitation, took a step forward and made as if to speak.

8

The colonel looked him over. They had come to offer him a serenade with marimba and guitars to celebrate his arrival in Pisigüilito.

"Seeing as we've butted in on you, colonel," said the one who had spoken, "see what you think of our program. 'Too Much Mustard,' first tune of the first part; 'Black Beer,' second tune of the first part; 'Baby's Died,' third—"

"What about the second part?" the colonel cut him short.

"Ain't no second part," said the oldest of the serenaders, taking a step forward. "Here in Pisigüilito these are the only tunes we've played in a long while, and every one of them my own composition. The last one I wrote was 'Baby's Died,' when our Crisanta's little girl was taken up to heaven, that's its only merit."

"Well, my friend, you'd better start writing a song called 'I Was Born Again,' because if we hadn't arrived here last night the Indians would have come down from the mountains this morning and not one of you slobbering bastards would be alive to tell the tale. They'd have trampled over the lot of you."

The composer, with his skin like old bark, his hair sticking out over his forehead like the tip of a sucked mango, and his eyes scarcely visible between the slits of his lids, stood looking at the colonel in the silence, which was like a spreading creeper through which everyone could feel the Indian bands gliding, the Indians who under Gaspar Ilóm had lost none of their taste for the things they lacked, still hankering after cattle, after liquor, after dogs, and the patchouli in the apothecary's store that would disguise their sweat.

The Indian warrior smells of the animal that protects him and the aroma he puts on: patchouli, aromatic water, magic ointments, fruit juices, help him rub out that magic presence and put those who seek to harm him off the scent.

The warrior who smells of peccary disguises his trail and adorns himself with orrisroot. Heliotrope water hides the odor of the deer and is used by the warrior who gives off little

9

deer-drops of sweat. Still more penetrating is the spikenard, most suitable for those who are protected in war by night birds, frozen and perspiring. Likewise the essence of the gardenia is for those who are shielded by snakes, those who have scarcely any odor at all, those who do not perspire in combat. The fragrance of rosewood conceals the warrior whose smell is of the mockingbird. The morning-glory hides the warrior who smells like the hummingbird. Arabian jasmine he who reeks of kinkajou. Those who give off the sweat of the jaguar must smell of forest lilies. Of rue those who give off the odor of the macaw. Of tobacco those who clothe themselves in parrot cackle as they sweat. The tapir warrior is concealed by the fig leaf. The bird warrior by rosemary. The crab warrior by orange-blossom water.

Gaspar, yellow flower in the wind of time, and his Indian bands, heelbones that were hearts within the stones, continued to pass through the spreading creeper of silence woven between the colonel and the old musician of Pisigüilito.

"Even if they'd murdered the lot of you," the colonel's voice began to rise, "even if they'd trampled all over you there'd have been no loss, and that's a fact. What kind of town is it where you can't even have a horse shod, for Christ's sake?"

The colonel's men, curled up among the horses, jumped to their feet all at once, shooing away a kind of waking dream they had subsided into through crouching for so long on their heels. A dog dyed red with ringworm was running round the square like a firecracker, its tongue hanging out, its eyes staring, snorting and dribbling.

The men lapsed back into their brooding, sitting back on their heels to stay silent for hours and hours in their waking doze. If a dog's after water it ain't got rabies and the wretched animal rolled about in the puddles, then jumped, black with mud, to rub itself against the walls of houses which looked onto the square, against the silk-cotton tree, and the badly worn wood of the straypost.

"What's wrong with that mutt?" asked the colonel from his

10

hammock, the same agave net which seemed to catch him in every town at siesta time.

"Had some kind of accident," said the orderly, without taking his eyes off the dog. He was sitting on the verandah of the Council House with his feet wedged heel to toe against one of the posts by the colonel's hammock. He fell silent and then, without changing position, he said, "I reckon he's eaten a billbug and sent himself crazy."

"Go find out, it could be rabies."

"Where can I find out?"

"In the apothecary's, fuck it, there's nowhere else here."

The orderly put on his rope sandals and ran to the store, just across the square from the Council House. The dog was still raging. Its barks splintered the silence of the horses tossing their long-maned heads, and the half-conscious dozing of the men crouching among them. Suddenly it ran out of steps. It scrabbled at the ground as if it had buried them and was looking for them now that it had to be off again. Then a shake of the head, another, then another, trying to wrench out whatever was stuck in its throat. The animal spat foam, dribble, and a whitish substance which flew from the back of its throat to the ground without touching either tongue or teeth on the way. It wiped its muzzle, barking furiously, and set off on the scent of some medicinal herb which in the snaking confusion of its run became a shadow, a stone, a tree, retching and vomit, mouthfuls of quicklime on the ground. Then off again, running like a jet of water the wind curved up and outwards, then let drop to the ground once more. Urged on by its body, it managed to stand again, eyes flecked, tongue hanging, tail thrashing between rigid legs, shivery and brittle. But in trying to take the first step forward it stumbled, as though it were hobbled, and the death spasm wheeled it round and threw it to the ground with its legs pawing the air, fighting with all its strength not to leave this life.

"It's stopped tearing about at last . . . ," said one of the men crouched among the horses. Their looks were striking. The

11

one who had spoken had a face the color of vinegar scum with a machete scar right on his eyebrow.

The dog shook its teeth into chattering like a wooden rattle and then lay trapped in its own rib cage, ringworm, penis, entrails, anus. Funny how life clings hardest to the basest parts of the body in the desperation of dying, when everything begins to grow dim in the dark pain without pain that is death. Or so thought another of the men curled up among the horses. And he couldn't contain himself and said, "It's still moving a bit. It's even a job to put an end to this goddam life. Good thing God made us so we could die without beating about the bush—what reason could he have found to make us live forever? It turns my guts over just thinking about it."

"That's why I say it's no great punishment to be shot," added the man with the scar on his eyebrow.

"It ain't a punishment, it's a cure. It'd be a punishment if they could leave you alive forever, just imagine."

"Yes, that would be real hell."

The orderly returned to the gallery of the Council House. Colonel Godoy was still mounted in his hammock, moustachioed, eyes open wide, just like a fish swelling a net.

"Apothecary says he gave it something to eat, colonel, on account of it's filthy with ringworm."

"Didn't you ask him what he gave it to upset it like that?"

"Something to eat, he said—"

"Something to eat, yes, but what did he put in it?"

"Ground glass mixed with poison."

"What sort of poison?"

"Just a moment, I'll go ask him."

"Better do it yourself, Chalo old boy," the colonel muttered to himself, as he climbed out of his hammock, his pale blue eyes like ground glass, and in his thoughts poison for the chief of Ilóm.

"You," Godoy ordered the soldier, "go find me those musicians who came about the serenade and tell them to be here tonight."

12

The afternoon turned deep yellow. The mountain of the deaf ones was sawing up the great rain clouds soon to be burned by the storm like maize-ear dust. Weeping of the spines on the cactuses. Moans of parrots in the ravines. Ay, and what if the yellow rabbits fall into the trap! Ay, and what if the perfume of the chilca, color of the stars by day, fails to cover Gaspar's smell, the mark of his teeth in the fruits, the mark of his feet along the paths, known only to the yellow rabbits!

The dog kicked out its legs in the death frolic, unable to raise its head, urinating fitfully, swollen belly, bristling backbone, erect penis, foaming muzzle. You could hear the stampeding rainstorms in the distance. The animal closed its eyes and then lay fast against the earth.

With one violent kick the Leader of the Expeditionary Force knocked over the three bamboo legs holding up an earthenware flowerpot in which someone had just lit a torch pine in front of the Council House, to advertise the serenade. The man who had lit it took part of the blow and the orderly, who was just coming down from the gallery with a lighted paraffin lamp, received a lash on the back. This gave the town elders something to think about. Shouts of "put out that light," "throw earth on it." And once the colonel's goodwill had been retrieved, arms waved about like roots to salute him. They introduced themselves. The one standing nearest to the colonel was Señor Tomás Machojón. Standing between the colonel, the military authority, and his wife, the supreme authority, Vaca Manuela Machojón.

Machojón and the colonel moved off, speaking in low voices. Señor Tomás had formerly been one of Gaspar Ilóm's band. He was an Indian, but his wife, Vaca Manuela Machojón, had turned him into a Ladino. Ladino women have iguana's spittle, which hypnotizes men. Only by hanging them by their ankles can you extract those viscous mouthfuls of flattery and servility which allow them to have their way in everything. That was how Vaca Manuela won Señor Tomás over for the maizegrowers.

It was raining. Mountains under the rain in the night give off the smell of dampened embers. The rainstorm thundered on the Council House roof like the lament of all the planters murdered by the Indians, shadowy corpses scattering handfuls of maize down from the sky in torrents of rain which could be heard above the sound of the marimba.

The colonel lifted his voice to call the head musician. "Listen, maestro, that tune of yours, the one you call 'Black Beer,' change its name, will you? Call it 'Holy Remedy' instead. And I'll dance it with Doña Manuelita here."

"If that's what you want, it's agreed, so dance: 'Holy Remedy' coming up."

Vaca Manuela and Colonel Godoy jigged in and out of the darkness to the sound of the marimba, like the ghosts that come up from the rivers when it rains in the night. And in his partner's hand the Leader of the Expeditionary Force in the Field left a small bottle, a holy remedy, he said, for Indian ringworm.

II

The sun let down its hair. The summer was received in the domain of the chieftain of Ilóm with comb honey rubbed on the branches of the fruit trees, so the fruit would be sweet; with headdresses of immortelles on the heads of the women, so the women would be fertile; and with dead raccoons hanging from the doors of the ranchos, so the men would be potent.

14

The firefly wizards, descendants of the great clashers of flint stones, sowed sparkling lights in the black air of the night to be sure there would be guiding stars in the winter. The firefly wizards with their obsidian sparks. The firefly wizards, who dwelt in tents of virgin doeskin.

Then they lit bonfires, to speak with them of the heat that would parch the earth if it beat down with its yellow might, of the ticks that made the cattle thin, the locusts that dried out the moisture in the sky, the empty streams, where the mud gets more wrinkled year by year, like an aging face.

Around the fires the night was like a dense flight of small birds with black breasts and blue wings, the same ones the warriors took as tribute to the Place of Abundance. Men, crisscrossed with cartridge belts, their haunches pressed against their heels. Without speaking, they were thinking, it's always more difficult for those who live in the mountains to fight in summer than it is for the horse soldiers; but next winter it will be the other way round, and they feed the fires with thorny branches, because in the fire of the warriors, which is the fire of war, even the thorns weep.

Close by the blazing fires other men cleaned their toenails with their machetes, the machete edge inside the nail hardened by long days of mud, and the women counted their beauty spots, laughing and laughing, or counted the stars. The woman with the most beauty spots was the mother of Martín Ilóm, the newborn son of chief Gaspar Ilóm. The one with the most beauty spots and the most fleas. La Piojosa Grande, the Great Fleabag, the nana of Martín Ilóm.

In her lap that was warm as a baking dish, in her rags worn smooth with age, her son slept like a new clay pot and beneath the coxpi, the delicately woven net that covered his head and face to protect him from evil eye, you could hear the sound of his breathing like water falling on porous earth.

Women with children and men with women. Heat and light from the fires. The women far away in the firelight and close by in the shadows. The men close by in the firelight and far away in the shadows. All of them in the roaring tumult of the flames, fire of the warriors, fires of war that will turn even the thorns to weeping.

So said the oldest Indians, with the senile nodding of their heads beneath the wasps. Or they said, without losing their old men's motion: Before they plaited the first maguey rope they plaited the hair of the women. Or again: Before men and women intertwined from the front there were those who were intertwined from the other side. Or: Alvarado ripped the gold rings from the ears of the lords. The lords cringed in the face of such brutality. And precious stones were delivered up to that man who ripped the gold rings from the ears of the lords. Or: They were savages. One man for one woman, they said. One woman for one man, they said. Savages. Beasts were better. Snakes were better. The worst animal was better than the man who denied his seed to the woman who was not his wife and kept his seed cool as the life he denied.

Adolescents with faces like unpainted tortilla gourds played among the old people, among the women, among the men, among the bonfires, among the firefly wizards, among the warriors, among the cooks sinking calabash ladles into great pots of pulique, sancocho, chicken stew and pipian, to fill the glazed earthenware bowls the guests kept passing and passing and passing and passing, without ever confusing the orders, whether pipian, stew or pulique. The women in charge of the red chili sprinkled drops of huaque chili like spots of blood into bowls of tawny soup swimming with spiny chayote halves, skins intact, chunks of meat, pacayas, melting potatoes, and tender guicoy squashes shaped like shells, and handfuls of stringbeans, and strips of root chayote, all with coriander, salt, garlic and tomato to taste. And they sprinkled red chili over bowls of rice and chicken stew, seven chickens, nine white chickens. The tamale-makers, blackened by the smoke, took banana-leaf bundles tied with reed strands out of bubbling earthenware tubs and opened them in a trice. Those who served the open tamales, the ones ready to eat, were sweating as though exposed to the sun, after standing so long taking the blistering steam from the boiled maize dough full in their faces, those brilliant red packages with meat inside, snares set for folk who eat the tamale and end up sucking their fingers and exchanging confidences with their neighbors. Guests are put at their ease as they eat their tamales, so much so they soon have no qualms about trying their companion's or asking for another, like Gaspar's brash guerrillas as they asked the serving women, slipping in a pinch or two, only to have their hands brushed aside or answered with slaps, "Let's have another one, missy . . . !" Large tamales, red ones and black ones, the red ones salted, the black ones filled with turkey, sugar and almonds; and smaller ones like acolytes in white maize-leaf surplices, and others of purple amaranth, pink choreque flowers, loroco seeds, or pita and pumpkin flowers; and tamales with aniseed and tamales with green maize-ears, like the soft unhardened flesh of little maize boys. "Let's have another one, missy . . . !" The women were eating things that looked like roseapples of maize dough brushed in milk, little tamales colored with cochineal and subtly perfumed. "Let's have another one, missy . . . !" The cooks wiped the backs of their hands across their foreheads to push their hair away. Now and then they used their hands to wipe their noses, streaming with the smoke and the tamales. Those serving the roasts savored the first smell of the meat smoking nearby: dried beef seasoned with sour oranges, lots of salt and lots of sun, meat contorted in the fire as though the animal had come back to life and were being burned alive. Other eyes were devouring other dishes. Roasted calabashes. Yucca with cheese. Oxtails with chili sauce, so sweet it seemed like calabash honey. Meat fritters sweating with red-hot chili. Those drinking chilate finished off their gourds as though they were putting them on as masks, so eager were they to taste the last salty dregs. The atole was served in round bowls, slightly mauve, slightly acid. The atole made from whey and maize tasted like eloatole, and the ground atole tasted like cane sugar. The boiling fat made rain bubbles in tortilla dishes steadily losing the glory of fried bananas, served whole and covered in mead to women who were already flocking and twittering to taste the cinnamon-flavored milk and rice, plums in syrup and coyoles in honey.

Vaca Manuela Machojón heaved herself up from the mound of clothes on which she was seated, she wore lots of skirts and lots of petticoats ever since she went down with her husband, Señor Tomás Machojón, to live in Pisigüilito, whence they had traveled to be at Gaspar's celebration. She rose to thank Piojosa Grande for the invitation, Piojosa still with Gaspar Ilóm's son in her lap.

Vaca Manuela Machojón made a slight bow and hung her head as she said, "Beneath my armpit I shall place you, for you have the white heart of a dove. I shall place you on my fore-head, where the swallow of my thoughts has flown, and I shall not slay you on the white mat of my fingernail even if I catch you in the black mountain of my hair, because my mouth has eaten and my ears have heard pleasant things in your company of shade and water, of grain-bringing stars, of the tree of life that gives color to our blood."

Beaten in gourd cups you couldn't hold in your fingers, so hot was the liquid smelling of pinole they contained, rose water in tumblers, coffee in small wooden cups, maize beer in chocolate beaters, and cane liquor by the bowlful kept each gullet clear for the chattering conversation and the food.

Vaca Manuela Machojón did not repeat her words of grati-tude. Like the outline of a mountain, with her child in her arms, Piojosa Grande disappeared into the night.

"Piojosa's made off with your son," Vaca Manuela Ma-chojón ran to tell Gaspar, who was sitting eating among the firefly wizards, those who dwelt in tents of virgin doeskin and fed on the flesh of the paca.

And the man who saw in the dark better than a forest cat, whose eyes were yellow in the night, got up, and left the conversation of the firefly wizards, which was like a silver-smith's tiny hammer, and—

"By your leave," he said to Señor Tomás Machojón and

Vaca Manuela Machojón, who had come up to the feast with news of Pisigüilito.

With one bound he caught up with her. Piojosa heard him leaping through the trees like her heart inside her clothes, to drop into her path of black honey with his fingers like arrowheads to put her to death, seeing her closed eyes from whose seams, badly sewn by her eyelashes, butterflies emerged—he was not dead, and her caterpillar tears had turned to butterflies —speaking to her with his silence, possessing her with a tooth and cactus-tree love. He was its tooth and she its cactus-tree gum.

Piojosa Grande made to take the gourd that Gaspar held in his hands. By now the firefly wizards and guerrillas had caught them up. But too late, for her fingers were paralyzed in the air as she saw the chief of Ilóm's mouth wet with that vile liquor, that liquid with the weight of lead in which two white roots were reflected, and she set off again, running like cascading water.

The horror of it extinguished their words. Faces of men and women trembling like the leaves of trees hacked by machetes. Gaspar raised his gun, rested it against his shoulder, took aim —and did not fire. A hump on his woman's back. His son. Something like a little worm curled on Piojosa's back.

When Vaca Manuela Machojón had come up to declare her affection Piojosa had remembered a dream, from which she awoke weeping just as she was weeping now that she could wake no more, in which two white roots moving like reflections in troubled waters penetrated from the green earth down to the black earth, from the surface of the sun to the depths of a dark realm. Beneath the earth, in that dark realm, a man seemed to have been invited to a meeting. She could not see the faces of the other guests. They were cracking whips, jingling spurs, spitting. The two white roots dyed the amber liquid the man at the underground feast held in his hands. He did not see the reflection of the white roots and when he drank from it he turned pale, gesticulated, and fell writhing to the ground, feeling as though his intestines were ripping him open, his mouth foaming, his tongue purple, his eyes staring, his nails almost black against his fingers yellow in the moonlight.

Piojosa Grande could not get away fast enough, could not break the paths fast enough, the stalks of the paths, the trunks of the roads stretching out in the heartless night that was already swallowing up the distant glow of the festive fires, the voices of the guests.

Gaspar Ilóm appeared at dawn after drinking down the river to extinguish the thirst of the poison in his intestines. He washed out his entrails, washed his blood, cast off his death, pulled it over his head, away from his arms, like dirty clothing, and let it float away downstream. He vomited, spitting and weeping as he swam, head down among the stones, beneath the water, head up again, recklessly, sobbing. How disgusting was death, his death. The intolerable cold, the paralysis in his stomach, the itching at his ankles, at his wrists, behind his ears, on the slopes of his nostrils, which were like terrible defiles along which the sweat and tears flowed toward the ravines.

Alive, erect, his face of yellow clay, his hair of gleaming black varnish, his teeth of granular white coconut, shirt and breeches clinging to his body, dripping liquid maize-ears of muddy rainwater, river weeds and leaves, Gaspar Ilóm appeared with the dawn, triumphant over death, triumphant over poison, but his men had been taken by surprise and massacred by the soldiers.

In the soft blue glow of the morning, the sleeping moon, the moon of disappearance with the yellow rabbit on its face, father of all the yellow rabbits on the face of the dead moon, the saffron-colored mountains, bathed in turpentine down to the valleys, and the morning star, the Nixtamalero.

The maizegrowers returned to the mountains of Ilóm. Their iron tongues could be heard cutting at the trunks of the trees. Others set fires to clear the ground for planting, little fingers of an obscure will which still struggles, after thousands of years, to free the prisoner of the white hummingbird, the prisoner of man in the stones and in the eyes of maize grains. But the captive can escape from the entrails of the earth in the blazing heat of the clearing fires, or of warfare. The prison is fragile and if the fire escapes, what fearless manly heart can fight against it, if it makes all men flee in terror?

Gaspar, seeing that he had lost, threw himself into the river. The water which gave him life against the poison would give him death against the soldiers who fired on him and missed. Then all that could be heard was the buzzing of the insects.

MACHOJÓN

III

 Machojón said goodbye to his father, an old man long since out of harness, and to his godmother, a well wrinkled lady who lived with his father, and whom they called Vaca Manuela.

"So long, mind how you go, be seeing you," shouted Señor Tomás drily, without getting up from the leather stool on which he sat with his back to the door. But when he heard his son move off with his spurs jingling he shriveled up as though all the heat had gone out of his body, and he forced back the tears in his eyes with his heavy-nailed fingers.

Vaca Manuela kissed Machojón just as though he were her own son—he was her stepson and her godson—blessed him with the sign of the cross, and advised him that if he was to marry he should be a good husband, which in a word means a man who is neither sour nor syrupy, neither a madcap nor a milksop.

And from the outer gate of the house she added, "Seeing that you've broken in more than three hundred stallions you ought to know how to treat your woman right. Bridle of angel's-hair, spurs that don't dig too deep, and thick blankets so she won't do herself harm. Not too tight with the girths nor too much freedom with the rein, because if you're too tough on 'em you wear 'em down, and if you're too soft they just turn skittish."

"I'll remember that, ma'am," replied Machojón, putting on his wide-brimmed sombrero, the size of the square in

23

Pisigüilito. Friends and rancheros with baked puff-pastry faces were waiting to see him off. None of them could figure out why the boss was letting his one and only son go some other place to plant his seed. A man who has seen the turning of the seasons, like Señor Tomás Machojón, shouldn't let his son go roaming. The rancheros confined themselves to saying it didn't seem right to see the Macho going away like that, and stayed at their doors, while his friends joked with him and whacked him with their hats.

Machojón was going to ask the hand of his intended. She was the daughter of Cheba Reinosa, one of the Reinosas from beyond Sabaneta way, on the road you take for the Candlemas pilgrimage. Soda water and crisp cheese tortillas in his saddle-bags, a kerchief filled with herbs to tie round his forehead for he might have to sleep out in the open, and his hat, with that smell that would keep on smelling for eight days wherever he left it in his sweetheart's house. His friends rode as far as Juan Rosendo's fields to see him on his way.

"There he goes," shouted one of the rancheros, as he faded from sight of the big house, followed by his escort, mid the dust, the barking of the dogs and the bobbing of the horses, the most macho of the Machojones.

Señor Tomás smoked all afternoon to ease the pain. After the death of Gaspar Ilóm the firefly wizards went up onto the mountain of the deaf ones and wept. Five days and nights they wept, with their tongues crossed through by spines, and on the sixth day, on the evening before the day of curses, they kept a silence of dried blood in their mouths, and on the seventh day they made the auguries.

One by one the curses of the firefly wizards exploded in Don Tomás' ears the day his son went away, and he was gripped by the cold. "Light of the sons, light of the tribes, light of the progeny, before your countenance let it be said, here before you let it be said that the carriers of the white-root poison shall have the pixcoy bird to their left along the trails; that their sunflower seed shall be as dead earth in the bellies of their women and daughters; and their descendants shall embrace the spinebushes. Here before you let it be said, before your countenance we extinguish in the carriers of the white poison and in their children and their grandchildren and all their descendants, generation through generation, the light of the tribes, light of the progeny, light of the sons, we, the yellow heads, we, summits of flint stone, who dwell in moving tents of virgin doeskin, beaters of storms and drums, we are taking the eye of the fire hummingbird from the maize, before your countenance let it be said, because they murdered the one who succeeded in throwing the noose of his word round the fire running wild in the mountains of Ilóm and took it to his house, tied it down in his house, to stop it doing away with the trees for the benefit of the maizegrowers and their business."

Señor Tomás felt the glow of the maize-leaf cigarette between the tips of his fingers. A little ash worm which his old man's cough blew away. The hoarse, melodic voices of the cowhands came up from the ranchos, seeming to falter as they changed key. Vaca Manuela must be having them drink the health of Machojón.

Señor Tomás sighed. Vaca Manuela was tall, strong, lean-limbed and healthy. But like a she-mule. The curse was being fulfilled. The pixcoy to the left along the trails, Vaca Manuela barren, all that remained was for the glow of the firefly wizards to fall on his son. The cowhands sang on, sometimes just voices, sometimes to guitar. Maybe he should talk to them. Yes, maybe he should. Tell them the curse of the mountain of the deaf ones was hanging over Machojón. Yes, maybe he should talk to them. Tell them to fetch his son back.

Señor Tomás went to the door—his old man's buttocks sagged—and round at the back of the house, where no one could see him, he saddled a stallion whose hairs were falling out and set off down the trail.

The ranchero song followed him in the distance. Rising and falling. Words that meant so much to whoever was singing them. Who was it that was singing them?

25

There is a lily
that time doth consume,
and there's a fountain
that keeps it e'er young;

You are the lily,
come give your perfume,
I am the fountain,
pray bid me yet run.

There is a songbird
that nightly doth moan,
and there's an angel
who comes to console;

You are the angel,
my true love, my own,
I am the songbird,
pray come and console.

"Where are you going so late in the day, Señor Tomás?" It was Juan Rosendo, owner of the irrigated lands they called Juan Rosendo's fields. Señor Tomás reined in his horse and confided in this friend who had stepped into his path. The outline of a man he could scarcely see in the darkness.

"I'm going after Machojón—you seen him go by? After him or a woman to have another son by . . ."

The outline of the owner of Juan Rosendo's fields moved closer to Señor Tomás. "Well, if you're going far in search of a woman, you'd best get down from that horse right now, 'cause we got plenty hereabouts."

They both laughed. Then Rosendo told the old man, "Don Macho went by here early, didn't even say hello. I found out later he was off to ask the hand of one of Cheba Reinosa's girls. Why would you be wanting more sons, Señor Tomás, with all the grandsons coming your way . . . ?"

Señor Tomás' face puckered up. A sob chilled his nostrils.

26

His son would have no children. The firefly wizards were cut to pieces by machetes on the mountain of the deaf ones; but from the pieces of their bodies, from the tatters of their blood-stained garments, from their owlish faces, from their beaklike tongues, the curse continued to be uttered whole, untouched, intact. The machete blades could not cut the curse to pieces.

"Don't think about it, Señor Tomás, why not dismount and have a bite to eat here with us. Tomorrow is another day."

The house smelling of calabash honey, in Juan Rosendo's fields, the voices of the women, the weight of his gold chain and silver watch on his thick woolen waistcoat, boots that pinched his toes, food on white plates, plenty of it, dressed with radishes and lettuce, cool water in pitchers, and a horde of begging dogs, crawling children and warm legs. Señor Tomás forgot about the mountain of the deaf ones, the pixcoy to the left along the trails, and his son. Machojón was a man, and his fears were just that, the tremors of an old fool who, because of his age, was starting to be afraid of everything.

The torrent of people coming down that way on the pilgrimage of Our Lady of Candlemas had run dry. Crosses wreathed with faded paper flowers, names written on rocks in charcoal with pitchpine tips, the ashes of fires extinguished beneath the shade of the amates, stakes to which animals had been tethered, shoals of corn shucks and dried maize leaves, nothing more remained of the pilgrims who passed by year after year, as the yucca fences bloomed like a procession of white candlesticks.

The most macho of the Machojones had come down that way in February, on the rising swell of pilgrim folk, eve of Candlemas, when the stream of faithful come from afar meets the rivulets of local folk joining the highway from other roads. Morning stars, rockets, chants. Hymns, lemon sellers, wet nurses, dogs, squalling children and men and women with their hats decked out in yellow chichita berries and swathes of long moss round their palm-leaf hatbands, staff in hand, the day's victuals on their backs, and their bedding stored away in cane baskets with their candlesticks.

Down he had come with his intended bride, Candelaria

Reinosa, her barefoot, him with boots on, her short and fair-skinned and him dark and swarthy, her with nance dimples in her cheeks and him with his straggling moustache falling either side of his mouth, her with her fresh-water perfume and him rank with the smell of billy goat and crumble-baked tortillas, her chewing on a leaf of rosemary and him smoking his ceegar with his eyes drowsy with contentment, slow of hearing and sluggish of touch, so he could drink in the joy of having her near.

Thronging crowds. Shawls. Candlemas flowers. Candy "rosaries" like sugared cartridge belts around young bosoms. Little figures dressed in huipiles sculpted in colored icing sugar in boxes of candy delights. Sweet loaves with sesame seeds. Machojón remembered he'd had to untie the knot in his handkerchief many times to take out the pesos for all Candelaria Reinosa's fripperies and tidbits.

From the shoulders of the rider to the shoes of the stallion he was riding to ask the hand of his sweetheart was but one mass of shadow trotting across the savannah. The horse carried two stars at its flanks, quivering in time with its gait, and the rider had all the spurs in the sky on either side of his eyes, in his senses, which are the spurs of the mind. Only they weren't stars, but fireflies, tiny spurs of greenish light, like small, full choreque flowers.

A swarm of locusts on fire, Machojón thought, and he bowed his head to hide his face from the downpour of luminous insects. The fireflies beat against the straw hat pulled down around his ears, like golden hailstones with wings on. The stallion snorted like the bellows in a forge, to force a path through the rising storm of sparks. Machojón caught a glimpse of the pixcoy to his left and crossed himself with the hand in which he held the rein.

"Out, pixcoy, away!" The sad echo of the wood doves. The rain-lashed, disjointed flight of birds in the skeleton light of fireflies like clouds of grasshoppers. The unrequited howling of coyotes. The calls of nightjars drilling the air. Hares bounding. Deer like lunar sawdust in the fragile light.

28

Machojón eyed the flying storm of sparks. It was still grow-ing heavier. He was bent over like a crooked stick to protect his face. But now his neck was aching. The horse, the packsad-dle, the sheep-skin cover, the bags he was using to carry his gifts to Candelaria Reinosa, everything was on fire, without giving off either flame, smoke, or any smell of burning. The candle glow of the fireflies streamed down from his hat, behind his ears, over the collar of his embroidered shirt, over his shoulders, up the sleeves of his jacket, down the backs of his hairy hands, between his fingers, like frozen sweat, like the light at the beginning of the world, a brightness in which everything could be seen, but without definite form.

Machojón, anointed with light and water, felt his jaw trem-bling like a loose horseshoe. But the shaking of his hands was worse. He sat himself upright, with his face uncovered, to confront the enemy who was dazzling him, and was blinded by a lash of white fire. He dug the spurs into the horse with all his might and made a run for it, as long as he stayed astride, encrusted in the saddle, groping . . .

As long as he stayed in the saddle he would be a star up in the sky. The darkness streamed out of the anthills.

IV

 Vaca Manuela, the friends from Juan Rosendo's fields, Candelaria Reinosa's brothers, the mayor of Pisigüilito, all together to keep up their courage.

Señor Tomás closed his eyes when they told him Machojón had disappeared. He sat as if crushed. Without saying a word he started bleeding away inside.

Every so often Vaca Manuela would wipe her handkerchief against her flat nose, with her eyes all swollen from weeping. The mayor of Pisigüilito raised little grains like sand from the brick floor with the point of his shoe. Someone took out a roll of maize-leaf cigarettes and they smoked.

"Swallowed up by the earth," said the mayor, keeping down his voice so as not to hurt Señor Tomás too much, adding, as he blew out all the cigarette's fig-perfumed smoke through his nose, "There's no place left to look, nowhere you could say we haven't looked, even under the stones, and that's not counting the ravines, and we even searched behind the waterfall out across the white stone plains."

"All we can hope is he's gone off to see the world," broke in one of Candelaria Reinosa's brothers. "I knew a man who went off like that, half naked, with a beard and hair as long as a woman's. He ate salt like the cattle do, and was always starting from his sleep, because even when you're sleeping it must feel strange when the earth you're lying on isn't your own earth, and surely you can't rest easy like when you bed down in your land, where you can go off to sleep for good, stretched out for always on the earth where they'll bury you by-and-by."

"All that's just idle talk," Señor Tomás interrupted. "My son's been gunned down, and what needs to be done now is find out where the buzzards are landing or where it stinks of dead flesh, and bring home the body."

"That's what Colonel Chalo Godoy thinks," agreed the mayor, moving a staff with black tassels on it, like the authority he was, and taking on a certain extra aplomb in his speech as he mentioned the name of the Leader of the Expeditionary Force in the Field. "I sent a message from here in Pisigüilito to where he is, to inform him of what happened to Machojón, and he sent back a warning to take good care because the war with the Indians goes on."

"It goes on and will keep going on," confirmed Señor Tomás, only to be cut short by Vaca Manuela, drowning her sobs in her handkerchief as she broke in, "Oh my God, sweet Lord of Mercy . . . !"

"It goes on and will keep on going, but not with us anymore. The Machojones are finished. The war is finished for the Machojones. My son the Macho, as you all well know, was the last of the Machojones, the very last—," and as his voice turned flesh and blood in the cartilage of his nose, mid sobs and thick snuffles, he added, "The seed is finished, they have castrated the machos, because one of the machos didn't act like a macho, and that's why the Machojones are finished."

From the verandah came the sound of maize kernels dropping on a cowhide spread out on the floor, as a harelipped boy shed them from the maizecobs using a young green cob as a corn knife. It made the same noise rubbing against the other cobs as the clippers his godfather Señor Tomás used to cut his hair made on his head. The loosened grains rattled against the hide, mingled with the grunting of the pigs and the wild fluttering of the hens frightened off by the shouts of the boy, whose teeth protruded beneath his torn lip:

"Fuhin pigs . . . chihins . . ."

Vaca Manuela went out to shut the boy up and the house fell silent, as though uninhabited. Their friends, Candelaria Reinosa's brothers, the mayor, all went away, without taking their leave of Señor Tomás, who sat on his leather stool and sucked in his tears, with his back to the door.

With a blood sausage in her left hand and the knife she would use to cut it from the string in her right hand, Candelaria Reinosa stood on the small porch that looked out from her house onto the road, where, whenever her brothers did some slaughtering, they improvised a pork butcher's stall on a counter made of canes.

Other parts of the animal were dripping blood hanging from a rope stretched between two poles, the crude fat was in a sugar mold and the lard in a tin bucket.

The boy Candelaria Reinosa was supposed to be serving saw

her just standing there without cutting the sausage, because she was listening to a woman speaking to her from the roadside. Her black face, her tangled hair and greasy clothing contrasted with her teeth, which were white as lard.

"Yes, child, the men who went out to burn saw Don Macho riding through the flames. They say he was dressed all in gold, they say. Gold from his hat and coat right down to the horse's saddle and hoofs. A real sight to see. They say they knew it was him from his wild way of riding. You remember how he was on a horse. What a man he was, Holy Mary, what a man! Two days ago I went and told Señora Vaca Manuela, but she took it amiss. Only you, she told me, could get it in your head that Machojón appears when they burn the forest to plant maize. That's what she said, it's the liquor talking, and she said a quick prayer. Well, that may be, child, but I went into the forest, too, and I saw that dead man there in the flames, in the dense smoke of the fires. Goodbye, he said, holding out that hat of his, and then he put the spurs to his horse. Gold all over. And the fire followed on behind with a rush, like a shaggy dog wagging its tail of smoke at him."

"Was all this near here?" asked Candelaria Reinosa, still not cutting the sausage for the boy, pale, her lips as white as yucca blooms.

"Well, no, it was a long ways off. But afterwards I seen him close by, too. There's no near or far for a dead man, child. Anyway, I come to tell you so's you could say a prayer for him, on account of the deceased meant, maybe still does mean, something to you."

The blade of the knife in her left hand sliced through the greasy cord tying the string of sausages. She served it in a strip of banana leaf to the boy who stood there waiting, with a copper coin in his hand.

The color of the road, white earth as fine as ash that the wind sometimes lifted in blinding clouds, was the color of Candelaria Reinosa, ever since Machojón disappeared.

If she saw only through the eyes of Machojón, why did she

still see without those eyes? Alone now, she liked to spend her Sundays by the roadside with her eyes closed all day, and open them suddenly when, after listening to horse hoofs approaching, she heard them grow near, with the faint hope that one of these days it would be Machojón, since, like some folk said, he might have gone off round the world, gone off riding over every road in the world.

"God bless you, you did right to come and tell me," she said to the woman, after taking the money from the boy's hand. He set off from the improvised meat stall kicking up a great cloud of dust, followed by a dog, and Candelaria Reinosa went back indoors, until another voice said, "Ave Maria, ain't no one serving out here . . .?"

The other woman had disappeared down the road with her hair all awry, her dirty black dress, and her teeth white as lard. Candelaria Reinosa served half a pound of that ghostly woman's teeth in the form of white lard, and a bit of crackling.

She put the weight made up of shotgun slugs on one side of the basket balance, and the lard on the other, on a banana leaf. And as the woman buying was pretty well known to her, she told her, as she picked out her crackling, how Machojón was appearing where they were setting fires for clearing, mounted on his stallion, all in gold from the top of his hat to the shoes of his horse. And you know what, they say he looks real handsome, like the Apostle Santiago himself.

The other woman lapped saliva over her crackling before crunching on it, and as it's dangerous to contradict what lunatics or lovers say, she just nodded, without moving her lips.

The maizefields were blazing high up in the mountains as evening fell. It was a blue vein in the sky, and it made the clearing fires look the color of the sun. Candelaria Reinosa closed her eyes on the porch where she sold the pigmeat. The road eventually faded away that night as it did every night, not quite completely. Roads of white earth are like the bones of all roads that fall dead at night. You can see them. They are roads which have lost the life of their flesh, which is the passage over them of pilgrims, flocks, herds, people marching, mule-trains, and horsemen, and they remain unburied to give passage to souls in torment, men who go wandering the earth, criminals, the mounted patrol, the Christian Princes, the kings and queens from packs of cards, the Saints of the Litany, military escorts, shackled prisoners, evil spirits . . .

Candelaria Reinosa closed her eyes and dreamed, or saw, Machojón riding down from the mountain gullies where the fires were, on his unbroken stallion, with soda water and cheese tortillas in his saddlebags, and that fierce-smelling sombrero she used to lay over her knees so her body would smell of it for eight whole days.

V

 The peons hacked their way into the abandoned over-growth with machetes, to break the continuity of the forest vegetation, with spaces of up to three arm's-lengths, which by tradition were used to halt the advance of the clearing fires. The rounds, as they called these cleared spaces, looked like the ropes of enormous pulleys stretched out from peak to peak, from one field to another, between the trees condemned to the flames and the trees that would merely look on, as horrified witnesses.

Señor Tomás could not stay still in his house, so engrossed was he in the clearing of the land he'd given over without much discussion to the planters for sowing their maize, ever since he'd heard that his son appeared at the height of the blaze, mounted on his horse, all in gold, jacket of lunar gold, hat of lunar gold, and his shirt, and his boots, and his stirrups, with spurs like stars and eyes like suns.

On his two feeble legs, beardless, ragged, wrinkled, a maize-

34

leaf cigarette butt in hand or mouth, Señor Tomás went back and forth like a possum, finding out who was going to set a fire, and where, and when, so he could stand among the men who went out to watch over the wall of flame in the rounds, ready with branches to put out any sparks the wind sent flying over the cleared spaces, the danger being, if the sparks weren't put out, that the whole forest would catch fire.

Señor Tomás' bulbous eyes trembled like the eyes of an animal caught in a trap, in the glow of fires that washed in restless rivers of gold enraged by the currents of wind among the brushwood thickets, pinnates, and other trees. Fire is like water when it flows, no one can cut it off. Foam is the smoke of water as smoke is the foam of fire.

The billowing smoke rubbed Señor Tomás out for moments at a time. Not even his form could be seen, as the old man looked for his son among the glowings of the fire. He might have been burned up. But there or somewhere else, nearer or further away, he would reappear, stock still, staring fixedly at the flames, with his face toasted by the red glow of the fire, eyelashes and hair singed blond, sweating at the dead of night or in the early morning, as though he had been in a steambath.

Señor Tomás went home at dawn and upended himself to drink water from the trough where the cattle drank. The liquid glass reflected his bony face, his eyes, all red and swollen from staring into the fire, and his cheekbones, and the tip of his nose, and his chin, and his ears, and his soot-blackened clothes.

Vaca Manuela always greeted him with the same question, "Did you see anything, Tata?"

And Señor Tomás, after rubbing his teeth with a finger and swilling out a mouthful of fresh water, would shake his head from side to side.

"And have the others seen him, Tata?"

"Have you seen him, I ask them every morning. And they tell me they have. The only one that doesn't is me. It's pure castigation. To think I agreed to take part . . . Better if I'd drunk that poison myself . . . Yours was the evil heart, Gaspar was my friend . . . What was wrong in defending the earth to stop them bastard maizegrowers burning it . . . Good thing he gunned down a stack of the sons-of-bitches . . . The wizards were cut to pieces, and even that made no difference: the curse is being fulfilled. Even the harelip saw him last night. Look, it him, he said, Señor Macho'ón! And he jumped up and down pointing him out to me among the flames and shouting, Gold! Gold! All gold! As wide as I opened my eyes, as much as I singed my face, as much as I swallowed smoke, I saw only the fire, the trees falling in their hundreds, the smoke swirling like milk, the great senseless blaze . . ."

The old man tumbled into his armchair and in a while his head would slump on his chest or roll against the back of the chair, and he would fall asleep, like a man escaped from the fire, black with soot, smelling of singed hair, and with black holes in his clothes, where sparks had flown on top of him, which the peons beat out with branches, handfuls of earth, or doused with water from their gourds.

Truly it was a relief when the time for burning the ground for sowing was past. Señor Tomás busied himself about the hacienda: there were heifers to be branded, some of the timbers of the house to be replaced, some children to be godfathered, and the morning star to be shouted at in good time, so it wouldn't be idle.

The water of the first rains caught them all sowing. They had burned too much and there weren't enough hands to do the work. New land, real virgin land, it was a joy to see the way the hoe went in. The maize'll shoot up in no time, and how, they kept telling one another, as they sowed. If we don't make it this time, well, we never will. And what simpletons they'd been at the beginning to contradict the crazy old fool. Them saying they couldn't see Machojón among the flames, because the truth was they couldn't, and the old man insisting they could, and giving away land so they would burn more and more of the forest. At first they nodded their heads out of kindness, and there it all began: the old man urged them on to burn more, gave them permission to set fires without pity or prudence where no one had ever set foot before, and finally paid no attention to them, neither measured their acreage nor signed any agreements. Just keep sowing, he told them, and we'll settle up afterwards.

Machojón, according to what this cloud of maizegrowers said, rode through the smoke and flames of the clearing fires like the little bull once the powder starts to burn, dressed all in gold, in little twinkling lights, with the face of a statue, eyes of glass, the brim of his hat turned up, and they said he sighed, that his sigh dropped from the tips of his spurs like tears, almost like words.

A maizegrower by the name of Tiburcio Mena was run out of camp because he kept threatening to go tell Señor Tomás they were fooling him, that they saw no more than he did, a heap of lovely trees turned to torches of gold, firebrands of blood, and plumes of smoke.

Pablo Pirir confronted Tiburcio Mena, machete in hand, and at the height of their quarrel he told him, "Look here, you heap of shit, you better clear out, 'cause if you don't you'll bite the dust right here."

Tiburcio Mena turned the color of wormseed, fell into a cold sweat, and that same night he collected his things and disappeared from the camp. Better gone than dead. Pablo Pirir had three deaths to his credit already, and to avoid trouble is no disgrace.

The damnedest thing was sitting waiting for it to rain. The great clouds clambered over the mountaintops, and the dark mass of water, greenish up there—there's nothing men can do about it, the green just falls from the sky—hung over the earth, but didn't fall. The water threatened, but that was all. The men, eyes worn from gazing up above the hills, started to stare at the ground, like dogs after a bone, trying anxiously to guess, through the earth, whether the seeds had dried up. It was even whispered among them that this was God's punishment for having deceived old Machojón. And they even thought of going down to the big house to kneel in front of Señor Tomás and ask his forgiveness, if that would make the rains come, make him understand once and for all that they had not seen Machojón in the fires, and that if they had told him different it was so as not to upset him and so he would give them good lands for planting. If we tell him, the old man will take away half our crop. Instead of losing it all we'd lose half. As long as he stays wronged it won't rain, and if many more days go by we'll be ruined. That's what they said. That's what they told one another.

The rain caught them sleeping, wrapped in their ponchos like mummies. At first they thought they were dreaming. Their desire was so great it must be deceiving them. But they were awake, with their eyes wide open in the darkness, listening to the lightning lash the sky, the roar of the thunder, and they could sleep no longer, waiting only for daylight to see their rain-soaked fields. The dogs fled into the ranchos. And the water ran into the ranchos, too, like a dog into its kennel. The women pressed up against them. Even asleep they were afraid of the storm and the lightning.

Gratitude must smell, if it has a smell, of rain-soaked earth. They felt their breasts swollen with gratitude, and every so often they would say to themselves, "God bless God." When men have sowed and there's no rain they start turning mean, and the women have to put up with their evil moods, which was why the sound of water falling in abundance was joy to the women's ears. The skin of their breasts the same color as the rain-washed earth. The black part around the nipple. The nipple moist with milk. The breast weighing down, to give suck like the rain-soaked earth. Yes, the earth was a huge nipple, one enormous breast to which every peon was fastened, hungry for harvest, for milk with the real taste of woman's milk, the way the maize stalks taste when you chew them young and tender. A miraculous crop, the way they all shot up with the first downpours. Something unheard of. Ninety bushels each, they'd be getting. That's what they reckoned. Maybe more.

Certainly not less. And as for beans, how could they not grow
well here from the seeds they'd brought with them, since they
even grew wild. Why, those seeds of theirs were famous. And
the pumpkins would be a joy to behold. Enough to chuck
away. And maybe they'd even sow a second crop. They'd be
fools not to take their chances now while they could. It showed
that God hadn't taken it amiss, them cheating the old man. To
deceive the rich is the poor man's law. The proof was this
splendid winter. They hadn't asked for that much. Someday
we'll be roasting the corn. That's what they'd said, thinking it
would be a long time coming, and now here they were roasting
away, over a gentle flame, because if you cook it too fast it's
no good. "We really got it made here, compañero," said Pablo
Pirir, his teeth thick with grains of young tender-roasted maize,
Pablo Pirir, the man who made Tiburcio Mena move on.

The sun, blear-eyed, could hardly see. It was the devil's own
job to get the clothes even half dry. But who cared. Not they.
Whereas the fact that it was raining steadily meant a lot. Plenty
of water to quicken the laugh of those who could only laugh
with maize teeth once a year.

"What news down there, you, Catocho?"

"Nothing to speak of . . . No, nothing. Señor Tomás is still
half crazy, some maizegrowers were gunned down in the Cattle Pass on their way to Pisigüilito, and the patrol set off again
to throw lead at the Indians of Ilóm. The leaders seem to be
called Tecún or something; but no one knows for sure."

"And what about the price of maize, did you find out?"

"Scarce. It's fetching plenty at the moment."

"Where'd they tell you that?"

"I went to several different places to ask if they had any, and
how much they were asking for it."

"That was smart, because that way you made sure. You're
a sly one, you are, compañero. The great thing is that the maize
should fetch a good price this year. I'm going to wait until it's
real high before I sell mine, and I advise you to do the same,
because you only get a crop like this once in a lifetime, and

even if it did happen again, we'd never get another where we didn't have to go halves with Señor Tomás Machojón, 'cause rich people don't hardly ever lose their senses."

"There was a fiesta at Juan Rosendo's place."

"Tell me more. Those folks really know how to enjoy themselves. Their celebrations are famous."

"Ain't much I can tell you. I just saw some people knocking back San Gerónimo and the women shaking themselves this way and that, all wiggling and dancing to the phonygraph."

"I'll bet you dived straight in there."

"Didn't even get down from my horse."

"Why, you should have gone over and got yourself a drink. You didn't find anything out, then?"

"They may have been celebrating a christening. Someone I did see there was Miss Candelaria Reinosa, Don Macho's intended. She's let herself go a bit, but she's pretty, and I wouldn't say no to her."

"Well, if the maize sells good I'll let you have her. No one ever says no to a rich man. With plenty of pesos in your pocket and a couple of brandies inside you, you'll talk her into it right away."

"Do you think so?"

"I'd bet my life on it."

"Trouble is they say she vowed not to marry, to remain faithful to her dead love."

"But she's a woman, and between the mortar and the pestle she grinds a lot of maize grains every day, to make her brothers' tortillas, and sooner or later that promise to the dead man you're talking about will fall among the maize grains, and she'll break it."

Among the maizefields pushing up corncobs just as fast as they could, appeared dolls made of old clothes to crucify the revelries of maize-eating birds and stubble-scouring pigeons. Stones from agave slings hummed through the razor-sharp air in the sun-toasted silence of the ripened fields, to cut through flocks of thrushes, jackdaws and grackles in search of seeds for nest and crop alike.

MACHOJÓN

The harelip took the old man to see the scarecrows. The boy led Señor Tomás Machojón by the hand as he walked round the maizefields to laugh like an idiot at the rag dolls, greeted at a distance by the suspicious planters. The old man was up to something. Funny he should go on a tour round the fields just to look at scarecrows. Maybe he was measuring the crop by sight, on the sly, or by paces, as he walked. So many paces, so many acres, from so many acres so many bushels, and half of it for him. And them having already agreed among themselves not to give him his half of the crop.

The old man went on chatting to the harelip, in gasps, asking what was the meaning of those maizefield Judases, without faces, without feet, some of them made just from a hat and coat.

"Dolls!" shouted the harelip, showing his teeth under the torn lip, as though his child's laugh had been slashed in two forever.

"Go sniff their arses."

"Ugh! Nirty!"

"What do you think this one with the big hat is called?" the old man asked him, with a certain intention.

The harelip picked up a stone and threw it at the rag doll, which looked like a Mexican on account of its big sombrero.

"Fink it called . . . ," the boy hesitated, his harelip contracted like that of a fish caught on the hook, but seeing the old man was so foolish he blurted out what he was thinking, "fink it called Macho'ón." Through the tattered lip his incisors, like two enormous nose drippings, thrust forward a ridge of cold laughter.

Señor Tomás stood transfixed by the boy's face, staring at him. As the poor old man breathed he sucked in his cheeks, which were salty with all the weeping that passed over them. He had no teeth. Only the gums nailed down with stumps. And the skin inside his mouth became glued right down inside his gums whenever he was displeased or distressed. Madmen and children speak the truth. The Machojón of gold, for these simple folk, had become a scarecrow. Two crossed sticks, an

41

old hat, a coat with no buttons, and a pair of breeches with one leg intact and the other ripped off at the knee.

The harelip helped him up from the stone on which he had been sitting and they went back to the big house in the darkness, keeping clear of the sarespino bushes, which by day seem to keep their spines hidden, like jaguars, and bring them out as it grows dark to wound those who pass by.

"I see they've already started wringing out up here," the old man said. In the thick yellow evening light they could see a sudden change in the height of the maize plants, upright before and now bent over halfway up, "wrung out" so they would finish drying off.

"Tomorrow they'll be wringing again," added Señor Tomás, and as he said the word "wringing," in the maize-grower's sense of the word, wringing out the fields to get them dry, it made him remember the echo of the bells that toll for the dead down in the town until they make everyone dizzy, tilan-tilon, tilan-tilon, tilon, tilon, tilon.

He stopped, turned and looked behind him several times to remember the way, then sighed, before repeating ominously, "Tomorrow they'll be ringing again . . ."

The hands of those who snap the maize plant so the cob will finish ripening are like the hands that break the sound of bells in two, so the dead person will ripen.

The old man did not sleep. Vaca Manuela went without making the smallest sound to the door of Machojón's room, where Señor Tomás had moved his bed, and as she saw no light she put her ear to the door. The old man's breathing, in feigned tranquility, filled the room. She made the sign of the cross and blessed the darkness in which her man was sleeping. "May the Lord Jesus and the Blessed Virgin watch over him and keep him from harm," she whispered, and went to her room. Before she got into bed she looked for a towel to cover her face in case the rats ran over her. The house was so neglected ever since the disappearance of Machojón that the rats, cockroaches, bedbugs and spiders had become part of the

42

family. She put out the oil lamp. Into the hands of God and the
Holy Trinity. The snuffy snoring of the harelip and the running of the rats, real persons to judge from the noise they
made, as though they were moving furniture, were the last
things she heard.

A shadow with spurs, a big hat and a riding jacket emerged
from Machojón's room. He wasn't as tall as the Macho, but he
was like him all right, he could certainly pass for him. Out in
the stable he saddled a horse and—away. The mount scarcely
made a sound as it set off, guided by the strips of earth that
skirted the cobbled yard. Without stopping, like a shadow, the
old man rode through Juan Rosendo's fields, and the streets of
Pisigüilito, where Candelaria Reinosa now lived. Now and
then he would hear voices. See shapes. Let them see, let them
hear. Then he headed into the dry maizefields and set fire to
them. It was madness. Señor Tomás' lighter sneezed sparks as
the flint struck the steel. Not to relight the dead maize-leaf
cigarette in his mouth, but to light up the whole of the maizelands. And not out of malice, but to ride the stallion in and out
of the flames so they'd think he was Machojón. He slapped his
face, hat, clothes, to put out the sparks that sailed at him, as
others flew like little partridge eyes to set alight the gold-
starched clothes of dry sun and dry moon, dry salt and dry star,
of the maizefields. In the beards of the cobs, in the dusty axils
of the mauve leaves and stalks, as they matured, in the thirst
of the earth-covered roots, among flowers like doomed flags
crawling with insects, the fire sprung from those sparks went
about, releasing flames. The night woke up fighting to trap, in
its web pearled with water, the flies of light falling from the
spark-maker. It awoke with all its articulations asleep in corners
of darkness and cast its webs of weepy silver turpentine over
the sparks, which were already small conflagrations making
contact with new centers of violent combustion, beyond all
strategy, in the most skillful of skirmishing tactics. Drops of
nocturnal water could be heard falling with a resonant rain
patter from the withered leaves, blood red in the glow of the

flames, clinging with mist, hot with smoke, down to the very marrow of dead stalks swathed in porous tissue which thundered like dry powder. One enormous firefly, the size of the plains and the mountains, the size of everything that was painted with sun-roasted maize ready for threshing. Señor Tomás reined in the stallion to gaze at his golden hands, his golden clothes—just like they said Machojón's looked. By now the sky was one vast flame. The headlong rush of fire that respects neither fence nor door. Trees curtsied before falling in flames on dense wooded vegetation which resisted, in the midst of the suffocating heat, the advance of the fire. Others entirely forgot they were vegetable matter and burned like torches of feathers. So many birds lived in them that now they became birds, birds of brilliant feathers, blue, white, red, green, yellow. Streams of ants poured up from the thirsty earth to do battle with the glow of the fire. But the darkness running out of the earth in the form of ants was in vain. What is already lit cannot be put out. Stalks, flashes of fire, teeth of maize on cobs snapping at teeth of maize on cobs. Snakes like the threads of severed stitches, leaping in pieces. Tumorous roots of chayote vines. Pumpkin plants with dried-up flowers. The yellow flowers of the forest withering away. Strings of beans on their way to the lard in the pot in the heat of the fire, the fire dancing in the kitchen. And to think it was that same docile friend of the hearthstones now running amuck like an enraged bull through the smoke. Señor Tomás rode back and forth at the whim of the unbroken white-eyed stallion, wherever it took him, without putting away his flint stone, that insignificant object from which had leaped, no larger than the eye of a maize plant, the spark for the lightning now spilling around the tortilla-smooth soil of the flatlands, the liana-strewn beds of the brooks, and the slopes rising to the mountains up in the clouds. Living gold, like golden pollen, like golden air climbing up to the fresh heart of the sky from that great lustful firebrand which was slowly covering the maizelands with the skins of red lizards. Not for nothing was he and no one else the one to

44

singe the ears of the yellow rabbits, which are wrapped round
the cobs in bundles. That is why they are sacred. They are the
protectors of the milk of the young maize, the seminal sustenance of the bee eaters with long black beaks and dark blue
plumage. Not for nothing was he and no one else the accursed
man who through some obscure mandate of his dark misfortune conveyed the poison roots to that treacherous liquor, that
brew which has always been frozen and still, as if in its clear
mirror it held the blackest treachery known to man. For man
drinks down only darkness in the clear light of liquor, a luminous liquid which coats everything inside you black as you
swallow it, dresses you in mourning inside. Señor Tomás, who,
ever since Machojón disappeared, died, ran away, who knows,
had been turning to moss, always downcast, with no interest,
no taste for anything, was now a living whipcord clawing youth
out of the night air. Head erect beneath the huge sombrero,
his body seemingly corseted to the waist, his legs treading the
emptiness of the air down to the firmness of the stirrups, and
the spurs speaking to the stallion in a telegraphic, starlike
language. Breathing keeps the fire of blood pumping through
the veins, which are tunnels full of ants from which the night
emerges to envelop those who die in the blackest of betrayals.
Death is the dark betrayal of the liquor of life. Only now the
old man seemed to be living on without breathing, rider and
horse one mass of gold, like Machojón himself. His sweat
tormented him. Smoke filled his nose and throat. He was
drowning in excrement. And a crumbling vision, a suffocating,
fissile atmosphere, blinded him. All he saw were the flames
scuttling about like the ears of yellow rabbits, in twos, in
hundreds, basketfuls of yellow rabbits fleeing from the fire, a
round-shaped beast with nothing but a face, no neck, a face
turned to the ground, rolling, a beast whose face looked like
the swollen skin of an inflamed eye among the thick eyebrows
and beard of the smoke. The ears of the yellow rabbits passed
through sandy pools of deep water, unextinguished, fleeing
from the fire which stretched out the skin of its dreadful eye,

skin that had no touch, skin that consumed what could be touched just by seeing it, that consumed what would be impossible to use up in centuries. Through the flailing paws of furry flames of red gold passed jaguars dressed in eyes. The fire spews jaguars dressed in eyes. The dry, foolish moon, sterile as ash, like the curse of the firefly wizards on the mountain of the deaf. It took a lot to convince the maizegrowers, who were cutting rounds here and there in an improvised fashion, risking their lives, aided by their womenfolk, by their little children, that it was useless to try to stop the blaze. They were convinced, yes, when they fell exhausted to the ground, writhing in the sweat that kept pouring off them, that burned the erect fibers of muscles hot with rage against fatality, without clearly grasping what it was they saw only too clearly, half prostrated, prostrated at times and at times reviving to fight the fire. The women chewed on their plaits and tears rolled down the dark, unkneaded dough of the older women's cheeks. The children, naked, scratched the base of their backs, at the doors of their ranchos, as the dogs barked in vain. The fire was taking hold of the forest now and was starting to light up the mountainside. Everything began to set sail in the smoke. Soon the maizefields on the other side of the gorge would be alight. Up on the skyline they could see tiny human figures silhouetted in black against the living flesh of the sky, battling to save those other maizefields, destroying part of the toasted plantations, as a break against the fire, leaving nothing but the bare earth itself in the breaches. But there wasn't time. The fire climbed up and went running down the other side. Many were unable to escape, blinded by the violent dazzle or scorched from the feet up, and the flames devoured them without a sound, without a cry, because the smoke took good care to cover their mouths over with its asphyxiating handkerchief. Now there was no one to defend the canefields of the hacienda. The peons who arrived from Juan Rosendo's fields wouldn't risk it. The wind is against us, they said, and with their shovels and picks and hoes in their hands they stood gaping at the burning of everything:

46

maizelands, canefields, woodland, forest, trees. The patrol arrived from Pisigüilito. All brave men. But they didn't even get down from their horses. Who's been playing with fire, said the one in charge, and Vaca Manuela, who was standing nearby, wrapped in a woolen shawl, said: Colonel Godoy, your leader, was the one who played with fire, when he made me and my man poison Gaspar Ilóm, the fearless male who had succeeded in throwing the noose of his word round the fire running wild through the mountains, and took it to his house, and tied it to his door, to stop it going out doing any more damage. I shall tell that to the colonel, so you can repeat it to his face, said the other. If he had any face, Vaca Manuela spat the word back at him, he'd be here helping us combat the misfortune he brought us through the favor he did us. Hero that he is, he thinks that by keeping well away he's going to save himself from the curse of the firefly wizards. But he's mistaken. Before the seventh fire, before the seven years are completed, he will be soot, soot like this tree, soot like the whole of the land of Ilóm that will burn until only the naked earth remains, part due to those who burn the forest and part to other mysterious fires. What's certain is that the woods will all be gone, turned to clouds of smoke and plains of ash. The soldier in charge of the patrol wheeled his horse at Vaca Manuela and knocked her down. The workers stepped in to defend their mistress. Machetes, mausers, horses, men in the light of the fire. The workers gripped the left sleeves of their shirts with their teeth as they were hit by the rifle bullets, and ripped them to stop up the blood with the rags. By now they too had managed to unhorse two of the riders with their machetes, but there were about fourteen of them, at a quick count. The maizefields which had still not caught fire thundered just from the heat of the immense bonfire before catching, and once they had caught they went on echoing the hammering of the mausers. Machetes went flying from hand to hand, shining red from the coloring that spattered over the horses of the wounded riders and began to form pools of blood on the ground. People are like tamales wrapped in clothes. The red drips out of them. The dry bagasse of the fire which went rolling on with its face like an inflamed eye in the rushing of the wind, began to dry their mouths. But they went on fighting. The dead like fallen maize-leaf scarecrows. The wounded trampled underfoot by the horses. The workers went on fighting the soldiers without noticing that the fire had been encircling them on a slightly elevated piece of ground. The ranch house of the hacienda, the stables, the granaries, the dovecotes, everything was in flames. The animals fled away in terror toward the open country. The fire had devoured the posts of the fences surrounding the house. Barbed wire with the red barbs melting, some of it stuck to the fenceposts, some now free of the staples. How many men were left? How many horses? The struggle between the authorities and the peons had suddenly changed. There were no longer authorities or peons. The mausers were without ammunition, the machetes blunt, and men fought men for horses, to escape from burning to death. With the butt ends of guns, with bent machetes, but most of all with teeth and nails, arms that curved like lariats around the bodies and necks of their adversaries, knees bent to strike with the patella, to cripple. Little by little, all those savage men in the midst of a sea of fire were succumbing, some for good, some writhing in the pain of their wounds, their burns, others overcome by exhaustion, with a cold fury in their eyes, watching the riderless horses trying to reach safety, forcing their way through the curtain of smoke, animals of smoke with golden manes, also failing to reach the safety of the shore. Two thin burned legs inside a petticoat of ash, a head with no ears and a small lock of hair, also of ash, and a few curled fingernails, was all that could be lifted from the ground where Vaca Manuela Machojón had fallen.

THE DEER OF THE SEVENTH FIRE

VI

"I take it he hasn't passed by?"

"No. And all this time I've been waiting here. How is our Nana?"

"Sick, just as you last saw her. Worse, maybe. The hiccups won't leave her in peace, and her flesh is turning cold."

The shadows which had spoken these words melted one after the other into the darkness of the canebrake. It was summer, and the river was running slow.

"And what did the curer say?"

"He said we must wait until tomorrow."

"What for?"

"For one of us to take the drink that'll find out who bewitched our Nana, and then see what's to be done. The hiccups ain't an illness, but a mischief someone's done her with some cricket. That's what he said."

"You'll be the one to drink it."

"Depends. Be better if Calistro drank it. He's the eldest. Very likely that's what the curer will order."

"Very likely. And if we find out who did our Nana harm with that bewitching cricket . . ."

"Best say nothing!"

"I know what you're thinking. I was thinking the same thing. One of them no-good maizegrowers."

49

The voices of the lookouts in the canebrake could scarcely be heard. As they talked they kept up their watch for the Deer of the Seventh Fire. At times the wind breathed softly, slenderly, in some guachipilin tree, and the waters of the river would cheep at the edges of the pools, like little chicks. The song of the frogs swung back and forth between the banks. Hot, bluish shadow. Dark, beaten clouds. Nightjars, half birds, half rabbits, flew giddily. They could be heard falling to the ground and dragging themselves along with the sound of maize leaves. These night birds, which bar the way of travelers on the roads, have wings, but when they fall to the ground and drag themselves along their wings turn into rabbit ears. Instead of wings these birds have rabbit ears. The maize-leaf ears of yellow rabbits.

"Be good if the curer came back today, then we'd know at once who slipped the cricket in our Nana's belly."

"That would be really fine."

"If you want, I'll go for the curer, and you can go tell the others, so we'll be there when he arrives."

"Suppose the deer goes by?"

"Let the devil stop him!"

The shadows moved away from one another as they left the darkness of the canefield. One went along by the river. In the sand it left the imprint of bare feet. The other climbed up into the hills more swiftly than a hare. The water ran slowly, and smelled of sweet pineapples.

"We must make up a fire of living trees so the night will have a tail of fresh fire, the tail of a yellow rabbit, before Calistro takes the drink to find out who it was put the cricket through Señora Yaca's navel and into her belly."

So said the curer, passing his long-nailed fingers like flutes of fluted stone along his earthy lips the color of black mud. The five brothers went out to look for green firewood. They could be heard struggling with the trees. The branches resisted, but the night was the night, the men's hands were men's hands, and the five brothers returned from the woods with their arms full of branches that showed signs of breaking and tearing.

50

They lit the bonfire of living wood prescribed by the curer, whose lips of black mud slowly formed these words: "Here the night. Here the fire. Here are we, reflections of chickens with wasp's blood, with the blood of coral snakes, the fire that brings the maizefields, that brings dreams, that brings good and evil humors . . ."

And repeating these and other words, speaking as though he were killing lice with his teeth, he went back into the rancho for a gourd to give Calistro the drink, which he brought out in a little gourd cup the color of a green goiter.

"Light another fire in the rancho, by the sick woman," he commanded as he returned with the gourd, a half calabash shiny on the outside and wrinkled on the inside.

They did as he said. Each brother stole a burning brand from the bonfire of living trees burning outside in the open.

Only Calistro did not move. In the half darkness, beside the sick woman, he looked just like a motionless lizard. Two wrinkles in his narrow brow, three hairs in his moustache, magnificent long white sharp teeth, and a great many pockmarks in his face. The sick woman kept curling up and stretching out in her rags and all on the sweaty, greasy petate, in time with the elastic of the hiccups working on her insides, in her entrails, her soul bulging out of her aged, deep-set eyes, pleading mutely for relief. Breathing in the smoke from burning rags had done no good, nor had the salt they gave her, like a calf with indigestion, nor making her lay her tongue on a brick soaked in vinegar water, nor all of them biting her little fingers, till they hurt, Uperto, Gaudencio, Felipe, all her sons.

The curer emptied the divining water into the gourd and gave it to Calistro. The brothers followed the scene in silence, one next the other, up against the wall of the rancho.

When he'd finished the drink—it went down his gullet like castor oil—Calistro wiped his mouth with his hand and fingers, looked fearfully at his brothers, and backed up against the bamboo wall. He wept without knowing why. The fire in the open was going out. Shadows and flickers of light. The curer ran to the door, stretched out his arms to the night, his fingers

51

like flutes of fluted stone, and returned to pass his open hands over the eyes of the sick woman to brighten her gaze with the light of the stars. He said nothing, but through the gestures of that man acquainted with mysteries passed storms of dry sand, tidal waves of weeping that makes everything salty, because tears are salty, because man is made salty by weeping from the moment he is born, and tarred flights of nocturnal birds, long-clawed and carnivorous.

Calistro's laughter interrupted the comings and goings of the curer. It sizzled between his teeth and he spat it out like fire that was burning him inside. He soon stopped roaring with laughter and went moaning and groaning to search for the darkest corner to vomit, eyes staring, bulging, terrible. The brothers ran after their brother, who had fallen to the ground after his spasm with open eyes the color of cinder water.

"Calistro, who was it did our Nana harm?"

"Listen to us, Calistro, tell us who put the cricket in Nanita's belly."

"Speak, tell us . . ."

"Calistro, Calistro . . ."

Meanwhile the sick woman kept doubling up and stretching out, clothes and all, on the petate, skinny, tormented, elastic, her breast boiling, her eyes by this time growing white.

Urged by the curer, Calistro spoke, spoke in his sleep. "My Nanita was done wrong by the Zacatones, and to cure her we must cut the heads off of every one of them."

So saying, he closed his eyes.

The brothers looked at the curer, and without waiting for explanations they ran out of the rancho brandishing their machetes. There were five of them. The curer wedged himself in the door, bathed by the crickets, a thousand small hiccups answering the hiccups of the sick woman inside, and stood counting the shooting stars, the yellow rabbits of the wizards who lived in virgin doeskin, who put on and took off eyelashes of breathing from the eyes of the soul.

The five brothers went along a path of soft grass from the

canefield to a patch of trees that looked a bit ragged. Guard dogs barking. The howling of dogs that see the approach of death. Human cries. In the twinkling of an eye five machetes severed eight heads. The hands of the victims attempted the impossible to escape from death, from the horrible nightmare of the death which dragged them from their beds, in the darkness, already with their heads almost separated from their bodies, this one jawless, that one without ears, another with an eye gouged out, being relieved of everything as they fell into a sleep more complete than when the attack began. The sharpened blades sliced into the heads of the Zacatones like fresh coconuts. The dogs went backing off into the night, toward the silence, scattering, howling.

Canefield again.

"How many do you have?"

"I have a couple."

A hand soaked to the wrist in blood lifted up two heads. The faces disfigured by the machetes did not seem to be those of human beings.

"I got left behind, I only have one."

The skull of a young woman dangled from two pigtails. The one carrying it bumped it on the ground, dragging it through the dust, banging it against the rocks.

"I've got the head of an old man. Must be. It hardly weighs anything at all."

From another blood-red hand hung the head of a child, small and deformed like a custard apple, with its headpiece of stiff cloth embroidered in red thread.

They soon arrived at the rancho, drenched in dew and blood, their faces wild, their bodies trembling. The curer was waiting with his eyes open wide to the things of the sky, the invalid still hiccuping away, Calistro asleep and the eyes of the dogs roaming the air, because even though they were lying down they were awake.

On eight stones, within reach of the fire that still burned in the interior of the room, they placed the heads of the Zacatones. As the flames smelled human blood they fell back, inching away, then crouched for the attack, like golden tigers.

A swift tongue of gold licked round two of the faces, the old man and the child. Beard, moustache, eyelashes, eyebrows, singeing. Singeing of the bloodstained headpiece. On the other side, another flame, a newborn flame, scorched the Zacatón woman's plaits. The day was putting out the bonfire without consuming it. The fire took on a fresh, vegetable color, like a flower emerging from the bud. Of the Zacatones there remained on the stones only eight heads like smoked pots. They were still grinding their white teeth, the size of the maize grains they had eaten.

The curer received an ox for the miracle. The sick woman's hiccups went away, holy remedy, on seeing her sons enter with eight human heads disfigured by wounds from machete blows. The hiccups the Zacatones introduced through her navel in the form of a cricket.

VII

 "I take it he hasn't passed by?"

"No, and all this time I've been waiting here. How is Calistro?"

"Nanita took him to the curer again."

"Calistro gave his senses for the life of our Nana."

"He says, when he's not weeping, that he has nine heads."

"And the curer, did you find out what he said?"

"He left him without treatment, except the Deer of the Seventh Fire must be hunted down."

"Easier said than done."

For more than a month now Calistro has been hanging round the curer's house, and his brothers have been on the lookout for the Deer of the Seventh Fire in the cane thickets.

THE DEER OF THE SEVENTH FIRE

Calistro goes naked, his hair in disorder, his hands twitching. He doesn't eat, he doesn't sleep, he has grown thin, like sugar cane, you can count the knots of his bones. He fights off flies which pursue him everywhere, till he bleeds, and his feet are like tamales crawling with ticks.

"Come, brother, don't wait round no longer for the Deer of the Seventh Fire."

"Wake up, man, can't you see I'm sitting on him!"

"Come on, I say, Calistro has murdered the curer!"

"Are you trying to frighten me, brother?"

"It's the truth."

"How did it happen?"

"He came up from the river dragging the naked body by a foot . . ."

The one sitting on the deer, Gaudencio Tecún, full of his good marksmanship and proud of his shotgun, let himself slide down off the animal until he found himself lying on the ground, pale and speechless like he'd had a fit of vertigo. The brother who brought the news of the curer's death shook him to make him catch breath. Shouted at him. And had he not shouted his name, "Gaudencio Tecún!", at the top of his voice, he would have slipped away from the earth, from his family, from the grief of porcupines that enveloped them.

His brother's cry made him open his eyes, Gaudencio Tecún, and feeling the body of the dead deer close by his arm, he stretched out his fingers to stroke its light red eyelashes, its walnut nose, its lip, its little teeth, its ebony horns, the seven ashes on its crown, its flanks, and a slight plumpness below its testicles.

"Don't tell me you've gone crazy too! Whoever heard of anyone stroking a dead animal. Stop playing the fool, get up and let's get going, I left our Nana in the rancho with the corpse and mad Calistro."

Gaudencio Tecún rubbed the sleep out of his eyes, blinking, to say, with groping words, "It wasn't Calistro who did in the curer."

"What do you know about it?"

"It was me killed the curer . . ."

"I suppose I didn't see Calistro dragging the body along with my own eyes? And I suppose you weren't here keeping watch for the deer? And—"

"I killed the curer. You must have been seeing things."

"I ain't saying you didn't kill the deer; but even though you say I was seeing things, it was Calistro who killed the curer; luckily, everyone saw him, they all know he did it, and nobody blames Calistro, because he's mad."

Gaudencio Tecún straightened up before his brother Uperto—who was shorter than him—shook out his breeches, dirty with earth and forest, and bending his arm to put his left hand over his heart, as he bared his breast on that same side, word for word he said, "The curer and the deer, for your information, were one and the same person. I fired at the deer and did in the curer, because they were one and the same, identical."

"I don't get it. See if you can explain it to me. The curer and the deer," Uperto raised his hand and put his two middle fingers together, "they were like seeing one fat finger made up of two fingers."

"No, not that. They were the same finger. Not two, one. The curer and the deer were like you and your shadow, you and your soul, you and your lifebreath. That's why when Nanita was ill with the cricket the curer said it was necessary to hunt down the deer for her to get well, and now he's repeated it with Calistro, he's said it again."

"Identical, you say they were, Gaudencio."

"Like two drops of water in one swig. The curer moved from one place to another in a sigh . . ."

"He went in the form of a deer . . ."

"That's how he knew about the death of Chief Gaspar Ilóm right away. See, it was useful to him, being both man and deer at the same time, it really was. Sick people never had to wait about. The moment you called him he was there with herbal medicines from miles away. He used to arrive, see the patient, and set off to the coast for the remedy."

56

"Then what was Calistro doing with the body?"

"It's the same thing. Calistro had been hanging round him for days. He must have followed him down to the creek this afternoon and before he could catch him up he must have turned into a deer, and as a deer he must have come running this way only for me to put a bullet in him."

"That's right, except he didn't leave his body here. It turned up in the other place."

"That's what always happens in these cases. Those who are lucky enough to be both people and animals, when they lose their lives they leave their real body where they made the change and their animal body where death overtook them. The curer changed into a deer up ahead of Calistro, and that's where he left his human form when I shot him, because that's where he changed, and he came here to leave his deer form, where I brought him to death."

"That must be it."

"You go on ahead and look at his scar."

"Right. Wait for me along the trail. And be sure to hide the gun."

"Of course. The war goes on."

Gaudencio Tecún brought his eyes flying back—he had been gazing down at the canebrake, which in the clear night was like looking at green water—and listened out for the rancho of his Nana, it was over there and he could hear it over here.

Charass . . . charass . . . charass . . .

He pricked up his ears to work out where the rancho was from the sound of the idle wind sweeping the guarumo tree which breathed outside in the yard. The crickets counted the grass, the grass counted the stars, the stars counted the number of hairs on the madman's head, mad Calistro, who could also be heard, shouting in the distance.

"Through my own stupidity I have another dead man on my conscience," he told himself, spelling the words out slowly (he was alone), "if I'd known I wouldn't have fired. Deer of the Seventh Fire, how swiftly you flew! And," now just thinking, not speaking, "I shall have to go back to wake him up before midnight—a bad job fate brought me—and either he wakes up or I bury him . . ."

He blew his nose. His fingers were left crawling with mucus, and the damp breath of the forest. He spat bitterly as he wiped his fingers under his armpit. And as he stuffed his arm down a hole in the ground, groping for the bottom to leave his gun hidden there, his brother Uperto came upon him, on his way back from looking at the dead man's scar, out of breath, he couldn't get there fast enough.

"What you said was sure enough right, you, Gaudencio," he shouted. "The curer has a bullet hole right behind his left ear, just like the deer, it couldn't be more exact, right behind the left ear. Course, someone who didn't know could miss it among all the marks Calistro made on him as he dragged him up by the foot."

"Are our brothers there?" inquired Gaudencio, in a dark voice.

"Felipe got back as I was leaving," replied Uperto, the sweat rolling down his face after running all that way, from the rancho to where Gaudencio was hiding the gun.

"And what did you do about Calistro?"

"We tied him to the trunk of the guarumo so he couldn't do any more harm. He says someone else killed the curer, but as he's out of his senses, no one takes any notice, not since they saw him dragging up the body."

Gaudencio and Uperto set off toward the rancho. "Hear me, Gaudencio Tecún," shouted Uperto, after a few paces. Gaudencio was striding on ahead. He didn't turn round, but he heard him, "Only us two know about the deer and the curer."

"Us and Calistro."

"But Calistro is mad . . ."

◨◨

THE DEER OF THE SEVENTH FIRE

Only Gaudencio and Uperto Tecún know for sure who did in the curer. Their brothers don't even suspect it. Nor does their Nana. Still less the other women in the family, busily making tortillas out in the kitchen and twittering about what had happened. Such a to-do, all slapping one another, calling one another the way tortilla sellers are called from across the street, with little claps of the hand. Their faces are compliant mud ridged with sweat. Their eyes lined with red ocote hems from the smoke. Some with a baby on their backs. Others full-bellied, expecting one. Plaits rolled in snake coils on their heads. All with their arms flaky with dough and scaly with goat's-water.

"Why, here you all are, then—Oh! Oh! Oh! Aren't you going to invite me in?"

The women turned to look, still patting away at their tortillas. Gaudencio Tecún was looking round the kitchen door.

"I've brought you all a drink, if you'd like one."

They thanked him.

"Does one of you have a spare glass?"

"Love, sweet love!" exclaimed the youngest girl, emptying a glass and holding it out to Gaudencio. "Why don't you say what you're really here for instead of coming to us with all that nonsense of yours."

"You flatter yourself. Let me have the glass so I can pour out the drink, and stop fooling."

"Listen, I'm not hard up, and you're not the only man in the world and all the rest of us women, so there."

"Ain't she sweet!"

"I hear an ass braying!"

"And I hear a she-ass answering!"

"Brute!"

"Watch out, one day I'll come to carry you away with me."

"Some folk really are coarse."

"Some folk are educated, but you, you're straight from the forest."

"Where's this drink, then?" interrupted the grinderwoman. "I've a touch of colic, so I hope it's anisette."

"It is."

"I'll have one, too," said another girl, as the grinderwoman wiped her hands on her apron to take the glass. "It gave me a real shock to see Calistro dragging the curer along like that, just like one of them scarecrows they put in the maizefields."

"What were you doing, my little devil, washing?" Gaudencio Tecún asked the girl, who laughed in his face with jasmine-colored teeth, full fleshy lips, her snub nose, and two dimples in her cheeks, after the words they'd exchanged when he arrived, first one, then the other.

"Devil yourself," she replied, and stopped laughing, without hiding a sigh. "Yes, I was wringing out some clothes when the madman turned up with the body. How green people go when they die. Pour me another drink."

"It's well known," said Gaudencio as he tilted the bottle of anisette over the glass, filling it almost to the top, "animal blood turns vegetable before it turns to earth, and that's why you turn green soon after you die."

Out in the yard which smelled of parsley you could hear the footsteps of the madman. He was stamping about beneath the guarumo, as if he were groping around in the dark with the tree on his back.

"Nana," whispered Uperto, in the room where the curer was laid out, his body on a petate spread out on the floor, covered with a woolen blanket to his shoulders and a hat over his face. "Nana, it's hard to get used to seeing people dead."

"Or mad, my son."

"You can't get it in your head that the person you knew alive is dead now, that he's there yet not there, which is how it is with dead people. You'd think they were just sleeping, that they'd be waking up soon. It's a terrible thing to have to bury them, to leave them all alone there in the graveyard."

"You should have let me die of the hiccups. I'd be good and dead, and my boy would be good and well, with his reason, sane. I can't bear to see Calistro mad. A body that goes out of tune, my son, is no good anymore for this life."

"It's bad luck, Nana, real bad luck."

"A dozen boys you were, seven in the graveyard and five still living. Calistro would still be fit and strong like he used to be and I'd be keeping my other sons company in the grave. When we nanas have children both dead and living, we're happy on either side."

"Ain't as though he's gone without medicines."

"God bless you all for that," she whispered, and after a silence counted in tears like the low notes of a cadence of absences, she hastened to find words to say, "the only hope is the Deer of the Seventh Fire, if it can be caught some day soon, Calistro may come back to his senses."

Uperto Tecún diverted his eyes from the eyes of his Nana and they came to rest on the ocote fire that lit up the dead man, he didn't want her reading his mind on the subject of the deer, that bundle of maize leaves wrapped in rags, with her head white and now almost toothless, his Nana.

A woman arrived just then. She came in without making a sound. They noticed her only when she put down the basket she was carrying on her head, bending at the waist to lay it on the floor.

"How are you, comadre? How are you, Señor Uperto?"

"How do you think, after all that's happened here. And what about you, comadre, how are things in your house?"

"Not so good either. When you've got children you don't know whether you're coming or going, if one's not ill it's the other. I've brought you some taters for the pot."

"Bless you, comadre, you shouldn't have gone to the trouble. And how's my compadre, is he well?"

"Ain't been on his feet for days, comadre. He's got a swollen foot, seems like he just can't get rid of it."

"That happened to Gaudencio some years back, couldn't walk a step, all we can do is trust in God if turpentine and hot ash won't cure it."

"I was told about that, so I tried to give it him last night, but he wouldn't have it. Some people just don't get on with remedies."

"Crude salt mixed with suet and cooked over a low flame is good, too."

"Now that I didn't know, comadre."

"Well, if you try it you must tell me how it works out. Poor compadre, he's always been so healthy."

"I brought you some yucca flowers as well."

"God bless you. They're so good in red chili sauce, iguaxte sauce too. Why don't you sit yourself down for a while."

And the three of them sat down on small blocks of wood and stared at the curer's body, which, between the darkness and the flickering torch pine, no sooner foundered in the dark than it came back afloat in the flashes of light.

"They've tied Calistro to the tree," said the Nana, after a long silence in which all three of them, saying nothing, seemed to be keeping better company with the dead man.

"I heard him as I crossed the yard, comadre. It's a real shame to see the boy without his wits. But my man says, he was saying it only the other day, that people come back to their senses if you use a deer's-eye on them. My man's known cases. He says it would definitely work on Señor Calistro."

"I was talking to Uperto about that when you arrived. That deer's-eye is a stone that passes through their senses, and that's how they're cured. It goes round and round their head, like smoothing out maize leaves, and even under their pillow it does them good."

"And this stone, where does the deer have it?" asked Ruperto Tecún, whom they called Uperto. He had seemed far away, not saying a word, afraid they might guess his intention, to go and see whether the Deer of the Seventh Fire might not have vomited up that precious object.

"The animal spits it out when it's wounded, right, comadre?" said the Nana, who had taken some maize-leaf cigarettes from the pocket of her apron, to offer her visitor a smoke.

"That's what they say. The deer spits it out in its death throes, as though its soul was made into a little stone, and it looks like a sucked coyote."

"Comadre, I didn't know it was like that, I had no idea."

"And that's what goes through their senses until they become lucid," Uperto said. With the eyes of his imagination he saw the deer killed by Gaudencio in the darkness of the forest, far off in the forest. And with the eyes in his head, the body of the curer stretched out right there in front of him. To think that the deer and the curer were one single being was so difficult for him that at times he held his head, fearful that his own common sense might be turned. That dead body had been a deer, and the Deer of the Seventh Fire had been a man. As a deer he had loved does and had had fawns, baby deer. His male nostrils in the algebra of stars, the bluish coats of the does, pelage toasted like the summer, nervous, shy, susceptible only to fugitive loves. And as a man, when he was young, he had loved and pursued females, he'd had little human children full of laughter, whose only defense was their weeping. Which had he loved more, the does or the women?

Other visitors turned up. An old centenarian asking for Yaca, the mother of the Tecún boys, boys and now they were men with children and chores of their own. The madman could be heard pacing about in the yard. He was tramping up and down beneath the guarumo, sinking his footsteps in the earth, as if he were walking with the tree on his back.

Two more Tecunes, Roso and Andrés, were in conversation at the side of the rancho. Both with their hats on, crouching, naked machete in hand.

"Smoke, Ta-Nesh?"

His brother's request made Andrés Tecún stop moving his machete, which he was flicking from side to side, steadily shaving off the blades of grass within his reach, and he took out a bundle of maize-leaf cigarettes, bigger than sticks.

"Will these do you?"

"Of course. Give me a light, will you."

"Pleasure. I'll join you."

Andrés Tecún put the cornhusk cigarette to his mouth, took out his lighter, and the flint sent out a shower of sparks as it struck the steel, until it lit a wick that looked like a long curl of orange peel, and with the glow from the wick he lit the cigarettes.

Andrés Tecún picked up his machete and carried on slicing off the blades of grass just at the very top. The two lighted cigarettes glowed in the dark like the eyes of a forest animal.

"And between ourselves, you, Roso," Andrés spoke without leaving his machete in peace, "Calistro didn't kill the curer. There's a bullet hole behind his ear, and Calistro had no gun."

"I noticed there was blood running from his ear. But, Lord, Ta-Nesh, I hadn't thought of what you're telling me."

"The war goes on, brother. It goes on and will keep on going. And us with no way of defending ourselves. Mark my words, they'll pick us off one by one. They've been one step ahead of us ever since Gaspar Ilóm died. It's a crying shame Colonel Godoy got the better of him."

"Accursed man, don't speak of him. Only by being murdered would he become good again. May God will it."

"He has us where he wants us."

"Right, brother, like oxen we are."

"The war goes on. In Pisigüilito, it's said, there are plenty of folk who don't believe Gaspar journeyed to the other world just because he threw himself into the river. He was like a fish in the water and must have dived in so as to come out further down, where the patrol couldn't reach him. He must be hiding somewhere."

"People always think that by hoping for something they'll make it come true. Pity it ain't so. Gaspar was drowned, not because he couldn't swim—as you say, he swam like a fish— but because instead of people he found only corpses, they'd made mincemeat of everyone in the camp, and that pained him more'n anyone, because he was the leader, and he knew it was up to him to follow them that were already sacrificed. And so as not to give the patrol the satisfaction of killing him he threw himself into the river, not like a man, but like a stone. I tell you, when Gaspar swam, first he was a cloud, then he was a stone, and then the shadow of his shadow in the water."

Roso and Andrés Tecún fell silent. In the silence you could hear the coming and going of their machetes, which were part of the breathing of those men. They went on snipping away at the grass.

"The chief could have beaten that colonel if he hadn't murdered all his men," said Roso by way of conclusion, at the same time as he spat out a strand of tobacco which had stuck to his tongue.

"Of course, of course he could," agreed Andrés, by now moving his machete with an uneasy mind, "and that's how war ought to be, killing in battle and not like they did to him, giving him poison like he was a dog, and like they're doing to us. Take the curer there: ambush, bullet, and no one to even shovel earth over you. The misery of not being armed. Bedding down alive not knowing if you'll wake up in the morning; waking up in the morning not knowing if you'll see the night fall again. And still they sow maize in the cold lands. It's poverty, the worst poverty. Their seeds should have turned to poison."

The whole family felt better, they couldn't have said why, when the madman stopped pacing up and down beneath the guarumo. It was a pain they all of them felt. Calistro stopped for long moments beneath the green ears of the tree, the guarumo ticklish with wind, to sniff at the trunk and babble words with his rigid jaws, his loroco tongue, his furrowed face burrowed by insanity, and his wide open eyes.

"Red moon . . . Red moon . . . I gopher . . . I gopher . . . Fire, fire, fire . . . Darkness of crab's blood . . . Darkness of ground-bees' honey . . . Darkness, darkness, darkness . . ."

65

Plac, clap, plac, the noise Gaudencio Tecún made on the body of the Deer of the Seventh Fire, slapping it with his hand, plac, clap, plac, first here, then there.

Little punches, tickles, pinches.

He despairs of the animal, it won't wake, lazy great beast, and goes for water. He brings it from the river in the crown of his hat and with his mouth sprinkles it over its head, its eyes, its hoofs.

"Maybe this'll bring you round!"

As the trees lean back against one another the birds flee, and Gaudencio takes their flying as a sign the moon is about to appear.

Sure enough, that golden potato peel soon emerges.

He despairs of the deer, sprinkled water fails to wake it, and starts to hit it on the forehead, the belly, the neck.

Nocturnal birds fly diagonally, crows and goatsuckers, leaving in the atmosphere the swift slashing hisses of machetes swung hard.

Perhaps that's why men flinch in the night, even when there's no one around and they're asleep, because of those doubts in the whispering air!

The water sprinkled, the animal beaten, Gaudencio wraps his feet, his arms, his head with purple cane leaf, and clothed thus in sugar cane he dances round the deer making wild gestures to frighten it.

"Run for it," says he as he dances, "run for it, little deer, run far away. Cheat death of its dues. Trick it!"

"Run for it," he says as he dances. "Run for it, little deer, run far away on the Night of the Seventh Fire. I remember a long time ago . . . It was before I was born, before my mother and father were born, before my grandmother and grandfather were born, but I remember all that happened to the firefly wizards when I wash my face in rainwater. Run right away, little deer with the three fireflies on your forehead. Take heart. Not for nothing am I called darkness of blood, not for nothing are you called darkness of ground-bees' honey, your horns are sweet, my bitter little buck."

THE DEER OF THE SEVENTH FIRE

He drags a length of sugar cane behind him as a tail, rides it. Dressed thus in sugar-cane leaves, Gaudencio Tecún dances till weariness prostrates him alongside the dead stag.

"Run for it, little deer, run far away, midnight is approaching, the fire is coming, the last fire, don't pretend you can't hear me, or that you're dead, your house is near here, your cave is near here, your forest is near here, run for it, my bitter little buck."

As he finishes his entreaties he brings out a yellow wax candle, and lights it with great difficulty, because first he sets a leaf alight with the spark from his flint-and-steel lighter. And with the lighted candle in his hand, he kneels and prays.

"Farewell, little deer, here you left me in the deep pool after I swang you in the hammock of death, just to teach you how it is they take your life away! I came close to your breast and I heard the ravines, and I stooped to smell your breath, and your nose was like frozen moss. Why do you smell of orange blossoms, if you are not an orange tree? In your eyes the winter sees with firefly eyes. Where did you leave your tent of virgin does?"

A shadow returns through the canebrake, step by step. It is Gaudencio Tecún. The Deer of the Seventh Fire is left deep in the earth, he buried him good and deep. He could hear the dogs barking, the cries of the madman, and as he came nearer, climbing up from the river that ran through the cane thickets, the voices of the women praying for the dead man's soul.

"God free him from his trials and take him to eternal rest . . . God free him from his trials and take him to eternal rest . . ."

The Deer of the Seventh Fire lay buried deep in the earth, but its blood of red citrus juice bathed the moon.

A lake of black syrup, syrup from a black cane, envelops Gaudencio, who has put his hand down into the hole in which he left his gun hidden, down to the armpit, who has brought it out content because the gun is there, and who, before advancing along the flat approach to the rancho, where the wake is still in progress, after making the sign of the cross with his hand and kissing it three times, has said out loud, looking at the red moon:

"I, Gaudencio Tecún, guarantee the soul of the curer, and I swear by my lady mother, who is alive, and my father, who is dead, to deliver it to his body in the place where they bury him, and if when I hand it over he should come back to life, to take him on as a peon and treat him well. I, Gaudencio Tecún . . ."

And he walked toward the rancho, thinking: man who carves the will of God in living rock, man who faces up to the bloodied moon.

"You, Gaudencio, the deer's not there anymore."

Gaudencio recognized the voice of Uperto, his brother.

"You've been where it was, haven't you?"

"Yes, I surely have."

"And you didn't find it?"

"No, I surely didn't."

"But did you see it when it took off . . .?"

"Did you see it, Gaudencio?"

"I'm not sure whether I saw it or dreamed it . . ."

"It came back to life, then. And now the curer will come back to life. What a shock our Nana's gonna get when she sees the man start to sit up, and what a shock he'll get when he hears them all praying over him."

"Things that don't come as a shock in this life aren't worth much. Me, I sure got a shock at midnight, I can tell you. A strange light, like when it rains stars, lit up the sky. The deer opened its eyes, I went to see whether I ought to bury it, seeing it wasn't just an animal, but an animal that was a person. Like I say, it opened its eyes, gave off golden smoke, and stampeded away reflected in the river, the color of a dream."

"The sand, you mean."

"Yes, sand is the color of dreams."

"No wonder I didn't find it where you killed it. I went just in case it had spat out that stone our Nana says is so good for bringing madmen back to their senses."

"Did you find anything?"

"Not a thing at first. But I kept on looking, and found it, and I have it here. Stone from a deer's eye, I can't wait to take it to our Nana so she can smoothe out Calistro's senses and brain, maybe then he'll be cured of his attack."

"That was lucky, Uperto Tecún, because the deer's-eye stone is carried only by those deer who are not only deer."

"This Deer of the Seventh Fire had it because he was a person, and as it's good for other ills I tell myself when I'm alone that the curer was right when Nanita was sick and he said she could only be cured of the cricket by the deer being hunted, and it wasn't for lack of looking that we didn't find it, whole days and nights I spent in the canefield watching out for him to come, gun at the ready, and the death was yours, Gaudencio, because you brought him down with a bullet, and you brought down the curer, too. But you're not to blame, because you didn't know, if you'd known that the deer and the curer were one and the same person, you never would have fired."

A weight was lifted from the whole Tecún family when the madman stopped pacing up and down beneath the guarumo tree. It was a pain they all of them felt, sixteen families with the name of Tecún, who lived in the Cattle Pass, the madness of Calistro, who would stop at times beneath the tree's big green ears, sniff at its trunk, and babble words they didn't understand: "Red moon . . . Red moon . . . I gopher . . . I gopher . . . Fire, fire, fire . . . Darkness of blood . . . Darkness of ground-bees' honey . . ."

His Nana stroked his temples and crown with the deer's-eye stone. Calistro's head was of average size, but because he was mad it looked enormous. Big and heavy, with two hanging locks, it rested on the black skirt smelling of stews and sauces, of his Nana, and he gave himself over, just like a child, to the humming he once heard when they used to take out his lice, swinging the eye to and fro, until he got his wits together again. The madman's vision is like a mirror broken inside him and in the pieces he sees what he saw whole before. Calistro explained all this very well. What no one could explain was the death of the curer. An incomplete dream, because next to him he said he saw, without being able to describe his face, the man who really did kill him, that man who was a shadow, a person, a dream. Physically Calistro felt he had had him very close, squeezed against him like a twin brother in the maternal womb, and had been part of that person, without actually being him, when he did the curer in.

They all stood staring at Calistro. Perhaps he wasn't better after all. Only Gaudencio and Ruperto Tecún knew that he was cured all right. The cure. The seed from a deer's eye does not fail.

COLONEL CHALO GODOY

VIII

 Long-maned, green as a maizefield tomato, stinking of fever, shirt and breeches made out of flour sacking with the markings indistinct around the armpits, beneath the crotch, a straw hat shaped more like a basket, leather leggings and stubby spurs fixed nearer his shins than his scaly heels, Second Lieutenant Secundino Musús spurred his flea-bitten horse along the stretches of good road to come half alongside Colonel Chalo Godoy, Commander of the Mounted Patrol, and sneak a look at his face, sly as he could, because the man was in a foul temper, and heaven help him if he bumped into him and knocked him out of his stride.

No doubt about it, because of the patrol—God only knows how long they'd been waiting for them to catch up, or where they eventually would—the chief was in a real foul temper. Sour as hell he was.

And for that reason he hadn't said a word, he who was so fond of telling stories, in all those hours they'd been climbing that sad stone-littered slope on which the horses, grown old with fatigue, dragged their steps out ever more slowly, and the riders, blinded by the night, began to turn evil-hearted. The second lieutenant would come up alongside him, get a quick look out of the corner of his eye, and seeing the chief's expression of displeasure, he'd keep well back on his old nag.

71

But as he tried it once more his horse broke into a trot, and then a canter, and that did it. As Colonel Godoy felt someone sitting on his tail he turned his head with the eyes of a boiled crab and unleashed a stream of obscenities, while Musús tried to control his horse, sitting up like a flea in the stirrups, buttock-battered by the trot.

"It's you, fuck you! I keep thinking the patrol has caught us up, and it's only you. All because you can't leave your animal friend in peace. And what's the matter with the rest of them, why haven't they caught us up yet? I suppose they're aping about, passing round the food and drink, dismounting every other yard on the pretext of a loose girth, having a piss, looking out for us with their ears to the ground. Why can't they hurry themselves along? Be the kind who say: let's get a move on, 'cause the chief's up ahead. Always supposing they haven't gone stealing cattle. Women and poultry are in danger, too. Everything that can be eaten or fondled had better watch out for men whose only concern is to give vent to their every urge. Philanderers, idlers, scoundrels. I know them. They've taken to hanging behind to see what they can filch, why should they hurry. Only this time they're in for it. Me here with my liver turned to pulp and them following behind at a snail's pace. I'll roast them alive. And this ain't a hill any longer, what is it, for fuck's sake: a greasy pole for mules?"

The second lieutenant stayed very quiet, but to show the chief he could hear all those shouts that kept bounding from his mouth like leaping goats, he moved his Adam's apple up and down, swallowing neither air nor saliva in his, anguish, feeling very small and frightened through the panting of his horse which in place of a neck seemed to have a saw for sawing wood.

Like having hair in your eyes and grease over your skin, as the hills went on growing in the dark nocturnal clarity. The night fell combed and humid from the tumultuous sky of the hilltops. The horses' hoofs echoed like pewter pots as they struck against stones left by earthslides. Flittermice batted their bodies of living rubber among dry leaves and spider's webs, skeletons like shells, the remains of tree trunks hollowed out by ants, silk-cotton trees in clouds of moss vine. Birds of gray air passed their beaks along the teeth of invisible combs, kiruee! kiruee! Others of sky-blue plumage were falling asleep with the day folded beneath their wings, as yet others dripped the collyrium of their trills into the great myopic eyes of the ravines.

"Some slope, fuck it!"

"And the worst is still to come, colonel, sir, though it's true we're almost at the top. I can tell by that ridge of oak trees."

"About time."

"And from the summit, on to the Earthshaker, as they call it."

"We'll give the patrol a chance to catch us up when we get there. I can't stand idlers, and yet idlers is what I always get, one sweet heap of shit."

"The Cattle Pass ain't just a name. There are lots of cattle thieves in that region. Why, only a while back they cut the heads off of all the Zacatones. But these maizegrowers are dull-witted folk, colonel. They see the danger coming, but they don't get out of the way. The maizegrower in the cold lands dies poor or dies murdered. The land is punishing them through the hands of the Indians. Why sow where the harvest is bad? If they're maizegrowers, why don't they go down to the coastlands, where they'll find the table already laid for them, and no need for them to knock down so much fine timber."

"It's not far to the Earthshaker now."

"That's right, it ain't."

"The moon must be about to come up, too."

"That's right, it must."

"To hell with your responses, man—"

"Only following the rulebook, colonel."

"You're asking for a shower of blinder lashes, piece of petate. I'm surprised you can ride yoked to me all this time without getting to know my ways. You don't show respect for your leaders through all that slobbering. Lies and flattery are for women, and that's why academy-trained soldiers become effeminate, through the rulebook. Priests who rely on the catechism, musicians who play from their scores, and academy-trained soldiers, you can keep them. That's something you'll have to learn if you want to be promoted. Religion, music and soldiering are three different things, but they all have something in common, they're all instinctive, if you can do them you can do them, and if you can't there's no learning you."

He urged his stallion forward, shouting, "Stupid horse!" And he added, "Brute of a horse! Like I was saying, the catechism, sheet music, and army regulations were invented for people who don't have the first idea of what they want to be, and who start saying mass, singing or giving orders because they were taught to do it, not because they feel it, and the art of soldiering is the art of arts, the art of killing off your enemies by keeping one step ahead of them, because that's how war is. The art of soldiering is my art, and I can chew 'em all up and spit out the pieces without ever having studied a line."

They rode out on to the summit. The red-hot moon glowed like a live coal. The horses looked like flying kites. Down in the hollows of the valley they divined strips of river, groves of trees in flashes of green parrots, and flattened hilltops.

"Second Lieutenant Musús, eyes right!" shouted the colonel. They emerged from the slope one after the other into a double light of fine cloth. "The moon is in battle dress."

Secundino gaped at the enormous bloodsoaked disk on the horizon, as he answered, "This is the season for setting fires, colonel, sir, and that's why the moon is painted red. Unless it's the hot weather . . ."

"Eyes right, I said, without explanations, you're turning soft again, and a regulation salute, the moon is in military mood!"

The second lieutenant was hurt by this harsh reproof. But as the chief had said that what best suited a soldier was to be tough, as he saluted the moon with his hand by the brim of his hat, he said eagerly, "The smoke from the fires stains everything like you was seeing blood, colonel, sir, and it's as if they were waging war on the moon and there were lots of dead and wounded . . . Like they was making war," he repeated, now without paying much attention to his last words, because his eyes were fixed on a long serpent of trees which appeared to be crawling between the mountains with the sound of thunder. What was called the Earthshaker.

Pleasure swirled through every cavity of Don Chalo Godoy's weather-beaten face. There was nothing he liked more than talking about war.

"Well, I like this time of year," he said, reconciled now with his second lieutenant, "because it brings it all back. To see them burning like that at these hours is just like being in battle. Brushwood sounds like gunfire when it burns and there's smoke rising, and it looks like troops advancing where the fire catches fast, and falling back when a contrary wind blows. I'm telling you all this so you'll know. Guerrilla warfare is like the flames in the clearing fires, you cut it off on one side and it turns up somewhere else. Fighting guerrillas is like playing with fire, and if I was able to defeat Gaspar Ilóm it's because when I was a small boy I learned to jump over firecrackers come the Immaculate Conception and the Day of Saint John. That Gaspar Ilóm was a devil of a man."

"You said it, colonel."

"You could never guess his thought, it was wayward as the flames in the clearing fires. Here, there, everywhere his thought leaped, burning, and it had to be put out, and how was it to be put out if it was the thought of a man at war."

"You said it, colonel."

"And that's no lie. Once I saw him uproot a hog-plum tree, just by standing looking at it, the work of his thought, of his strength, and take hold of it like a broom to sweep all my men away, the soldiers looked like little scraps of garbage, the horses, the supplies . . ."

"You said it, colonel."

"And I'm not certain," said Don Chalo, as his eyes followed the road down to the Earthshaker between stones and leaves toasted dry, "but according to the tales of times gone by, just round here where we're passing, up in these very mountains, one day when that being who shakes the earth just as though he was stirring a chocolate gourd was busy changing the water for his fish-mountains, the hurricane seized the chance to frighten away the hills he was taking to trade down in hell, that wasp's nest of hills you can see from here down to the ocean."

"You can see them, colonel."

"The hills would like to return to the corral of Cabracán. They are wasps. But the wind that blows without rest from the sea will not permit it. And the ravines are the hollows that remained in the honeycomb when they were frightened away. One ravine for every wasp, for every hill."

The stallion and horse on which master and aide were riding kept changing the set of their ears following the shapes taken by the sound in the Earthshaker, that place boxed in by the mountains, that spiral of abysses in which the smack of the wind in the pine trees sounded and resounded like water. The animals would point their ears forward when the noise coming to meet them was deep, rotund, monotone. Backwards, with sudden starts, when it took the form of an eight. And one ear forward and the other back, alternating them, as these regular shapes were broken up, which took only the swish of a sapsucker among the branches, the fizz of a harvest fly, the wing-beats of windblown birds, or the voices of the riders, forms which, riding almost alongside one another, conversed in shouts, as though they were on opposite banks of a hot river.

"To think how often I've been along heeeEEEre—and it scares me every tiiiIIIme!"

"I don't know what fear is liiiIIIke! Explain it to meeeEEE! ExplaaaAAAin it!"

The second lieutenant decided to keep quiet by way of reply, and pretended not to hear; but Don Chalo, who was up ahead of him, reined in the stallion and bellowed at him with his mouth open up to his eyes, and such force of lungs that the sound even poured out of his nose.

"ExplaaaAAAin it to me—to me—to me, why don't you explaaaAAAin!"

COLONEL CHALO GODOY

"It's an uneasy feeling you feel behiiiIIInd you!"

"I thought it was in front of you-ou-ou-ou!"

"Well, it depeeeEEEnds!"

"Depends on whaaaAAAt?"

"On which way you feel the instinct to ruuuUUUn! If you feel it behind you, you run straight aheeeEEEad! If you feel it in front of you, you turn and run the other waaaAAAy!"

"And if you feel it in front of you and behind you, you shiiiIIIt yourself!"

The colonel rounded off his shout with a bellow of laughter. The sonorous bloodclots of his laughter could not be heard, but it was joyful paint that splashed over his face and even the stallion started bucking after a dig with the spurs, as if it too had understood and were laughing. It almost threw him out of the saddle. He nearly snapped off the ornamental stirrups with the downward impact he made with his feet as he felt himself take to the air, that sudden jerk from the bucking horse, straightening up as best he could and carrying on, I'm stopping, no, no, I'm not.

Second Lieutenant Musús was left behind, numbed, green as a maizefield tomato, dressed in white rags, all eyes in the sparse undergrowth, eyes in fear of everything that moved outside his skin: the wide double hurricane, the thick clotting blood of the red moon, the scudding clouds, the damp tremulous stars, and the dark forest which stank of horses.

"I'm a nobody, I ain't important," Musús agreed after riding on a bit, as if he were talking to someone else, "but it's hard to spend your life on horseback, cold, hungry, afeared they'll kill you when you least expect it, and not only that, without a single thing you can call your own, 'cause men who come and go ain't in no position to have even a woman, leastways not a woman of their own bought outright, 'cause a man who comes and goes can have women all right, but for rent only, nor can he have himself children, a home, and one of those guitars that when you strum them seems like you was shaking a tortilla gourd with coins in, and a big silk handkerchief color of sugar syrup slung round the collar of your new jacket and fastened

77

right on your Adam's apple with a ring or a courbaril stone with a hole through it. Maybe deserting's the answer, ain't as though I didn't want to, if they don't let me out, who knows . . . Life ain't no iguana's tail where you chop off one piece and another comes out to face the danger anew. You lose it and it stays lost. Don't sprout again. Ain't on permanent lease."

But even he couldn't hear what he was saying, such was the noise of the hurricane wind as it came down from the summit into the Earthshaker.

In the dwarfish underbrush you could just see the riders from the waist up, like statuettes of souls in torment. The forest flooded in red moonlight, who knows if the fire of Purgatory might not be the red fire of the moon. And when the pull of the wind diminished, you could hear something like the boiling fizz of water produced by the stubborn flight of insects, the tin-pan serenade of toads jumping about the mudbanks and spring water pools down in the hollows, and the shrill shrieks of cicadas, shorter and more implacable when the enemy opened their bellies and started eating them alive in the darkness like water and live coals produced by the livid reflection of the moon suspended between the mountains and the deep blue of the sky.

The chief's form was lost in the vegetation. Then he appeared further along. Appeared and disappeared. Musús didn't take his eyes off him. Wherever that shape went he watched it, followed it. Neither lose him nor move up alongside him, he wasn't going to let him play the devil and hit him with his whip as he felt him come close, working off his anger against the patrol that just didn't seem like it was ever going to catch them up.

Don Chalo moved not a single muscle of his face. His pale blue eyes staring, mildewed green by an evening which was ending up in a moon of blood, the jaw with its huge bone just like a swing gate, his moustache covering the hinges, and memories in his mind. Thus he went. Why go over what's past? But he went over and over and over it. Easy to say there's no use crying over spilt milk. But some of us have spilt far too much to feel easy. When Chief Gaspar Ilóm had been poisoned the Indians had not defended themselves. The darkness of the night, the loss of their leader, the surprise attack and the drunkenness of the celebration had all favored his plans for not killing the Indians, for just frightening them. But the patrol fell upon them like hail on a dry maizefield. They left not a single one alive. No use crying over spilt milk. Though maybe it wasn't such a bad thing they'd killed them all, because the chief threw himself into the river to douse the fire in his intestines which was killing him, and washed away the poison. Unbelievable, he almost drank the river dry! And he appeared the next day, greater than poison, and had the Indians been alive, he'd have placed himself at their head to throw lead and steel again.

Deep thorn thickets in the laps of the trees, massive, bright red beneath a moon the color of hawthorn berries, blistered by the savannah wind which in the wild grasslands lifted up waves that broke over the forms of the riders in undulations of chilca trees, corronchocho bushes and blackberries, amid foam of old-man's-beard and low clouds cushioned on the shadowy peaks of castor-oil palms and the forks of trunks without foliage.

The horses set off at a trot down a path of dry leaves, pelted by the sounds of animals dropping from the trees, striking the ground, ready to attack or slide away with the movement of water through the undergrowth. The blur of a tail, a pinwheel, sparks of green light, hops from branch to branch or squeals from hop to hop, betrayed their lively presence, playful, ticklish, running, jumping, crawling, climbing, falling, flying, fleeing.

Musús cut a long green twig, the first one to hand, to hurry along the flea-bitten horse which paid no heed to word or spur once it became stuck to the ground with the glue of weariness and the thin gum of darkness that was half a dream.

The torrent of hurricane wind was mounting as they neared the Earthshaker. The second lieutenant's ears hummed as though he'd been dosed with quinine. He imagined dreadful things. The tree trunks pecking away at one another among the branches hammocked by the blast of the wind . . . puck . . . puck . . . pushabush . . . stitching in his ears the hateful memory of a line of rifles aimed at the back of a cattle thief who, a moment later, the volley scythed down like underbrush . . . puck . . . puck . . . pushabush . . . You have to be mad to be a cattle thief, or to be a soldier, going round killing people to make them respect authority.

He poked in his ears to dig out from deep inside his hearing the echoing rush of the dragging branches pushabush . . . puck . . . puck . . . and the dry pic blows of the trees as they pick-pecked one another puck . . . puck . . . pushabush . . .

All that remained of the chilca switch was the smell in his hand. It went out like a candle. A liana would be better. And taking care not to prick himself he pulled on a liana which as it stirred the leaves of the tree from which it hung, splashed his back and hat with the water sleeping in the leaves. He pulled on the liana and threatened the horse out loud, because his thoughts emerged in words as his body trembled with the spray of night dew down his back:

"Get on, mare, you'll have to be liana-lashed to make you move!"

The hurricane bent the great trees, the earth creaked with the sob of a huge earthenware jar, cracking, the torn vegetation wept with the sky over the blind mass of frothy thickets, and even the hair on the saddle seemed to stand up on end in fright to prick Secundino from below. With each push of the wind, with each hammocking of the earth—the earth in the Earthshaker shook all the time—Secundino tightened his legs around the horse, although they were already like pitchfork prongs from all the riding he'd done, not only to hold himself firm but to feel the rowing movement of the horse that advanced through the overgrowth breaking above his head into clumps of shadow like houses falling down or mountains collapsing. But for a few moments, just as the danger reached its

80

peak, the hurricane would diminish, the curdling of the hurricane, and its great broken force, the fierce gusting wind. Then, little by little, the branches would unbraid themselves and in the seat of darkness the color of pitch thinned out by the embers of the moon which burned like a ball of fire, everything began falling still, sifted, fragile, floating leaves and branches, underground rumblings, silver-coin necklaces of clear water and mountains of leaves that woke at each disturbance, each gust of wind with the clamor of a swarm of locusts sandpapering the air.

Musús shifted his buttocks on the overheated seat of his disintegrating saddle, without relaxing his legs and without dismounting his eyes from the form of his leader, who disappeared from the stallion whenever he leaned back on his shoulders, still going forward, forward, to gaze serenely upon the immensely high skylights opened between the tops of the pines through which entered, not streams, floods of glossy moon, a moon now without its red rind, moon without gleam of sapodilla stone, moon without blood.

And because the chief leaned backwards on his mount, with his eyes in the clouds and in the aerial shadows of the pine trees torn by leaps of splendorous light, and the aide following his form, tipping back his head from time to time to drink in sips the landscape of little lakes of sky the chief was taking in great gulps, neither one of them, before so attentive to the changes in the trail, missed the brushwood thickets now dissolved in a rain of crickets and replaced by carpets of dry pine needles, rivulets which the shine of the moon turned into navigable rivers of white honey along bare hillsides surrounded by pine groves, cages of trunks in which the enraged wind raged again and the shadows of the branches leaped about like wild beasts intimidated by the lashing of the lianas.

The night like seeing the day. Solitude of a great mirror. Vegetation creeping like smoke along the rocky soil. Squirrels with the leap of chocolate froth in their tails. Moles moving like lava trying to perforate the earth before it grows cold, and

81

lolling this way and that. Gigantic parasites with flowers of porcelain and candy floss. Pine cones like the bodies of tiny motionless birds, sacrificed birds petrified with terror on the ever convulsing branches. And the unceasing lament of the dry leaves dragged along by the wind. Sadness of the cold burnished moon. The maize-blighting moon. The trail became lost in the cages of trunks carpeted by dry pine needles, to reappear further along, now in the grip of hollows riddled with ground-squirrel holes in a trembling of lights cut to shreds by the branches of low trees that fell over the riders with the sound of water stirred by continual slaps. Downhill, after the pine-carpeted flat lands, the vegetation turned heavy, continuous, close-knit, forming long tunnels through which the barely visible road looked like the skin of a snake.

The stallion tossed its head as it felt the splash of large drops of white moon. Round holes like cold white musk roses large and small perforated the sponge and toad penumbra of the tightly woven awning of branches upon branches through which they were traveling. As it felt that sprinkle of limy light the stallion flicked its croup with its short tail, then lifted it up to let out air and dung. The fanfare made the colonel blink. The hands of the second lieutenant looked like squabbling spiders beneath the play of lights and shadows. The colonel wiped his nose. The second lieutenant ground his teeth. The light and shade had awoken the itching of the mange between his fingers.

"Serpent of CastiiilIIle!" shouted the second lieutenant. "Make the sign of the cross if you've got scaaaAAAbies!"

"It's coming to light us uuuUUUp!"

"Sure looks that waaaAAAy!"

"You'll bring it closer still with all your yeeeEEElling!"

"Glimmering beeeEEEast! Beastly beeeEEEast!"

"Pure superstiiilIItion!"

"Maybe so," he said to himself, "maybe so, Secundino Musús; but the plain fact is the Serpent of Castile makes animals squint, gives babies lice, makes women go cross-eyed, makes the deaf even deafer, and folks with scabies, if they don't cross themselves in time, it brings them out in lumps."

The Serpent of Castile went on mirroring its drops of light in a shimmering mass of little black jigger-flea dots whose only reality was the appearance of movement lent by the moon particles scattered between the leaves of that dark tunnel of contorted branches stirred by the wind above the riders, and the road continued snaking low and ever more narrow with room for only one horse between white rocks striped black by the oblique shadows of the trunks of pines which everywhere rose elastic and slender with a quivering tuft at the top.

The riders closed their eyes at the first blow, like a slap with a horse blinder. They closed them instinctively, but they had them open at once, looked around. Ready to throw steel with their machetes and lead with their pistols, and run for it, because brave men also run, they quickly realized it was the trunks of the pine trees projected by the moon in ribbons of shadow which seemed to be lashing their faces with blinders, and they only half flinched to defend themselves from that dazzling lightning flash. The moonbeams that passed between the trunks, among the pine groves, shone on the black coat of the stallion with the flickering shadows of the trees which imprinted themselves in black stripes on the flour-dusted shirt of Second Lieutenant Musús. Air and earth, as the riders advanced, seemed to be folded in dark and luminous pleats, blinking, and the stones and black spinebushes gave grasshopper jumps.

In the light and not in the light, in the darkness and not in the darkness, riders and horses kept going out and lighting up, motionless and in movement. After the blinder lash in their eyes, with the sensation of a clap of empty darkness, something vague yet existent, came a point-blank explosion of light, and after the lash of light, still another blinder lash of darkness.

And the colonel was in no mood for fun and games. He was in a foul humor. Sour as hell he was through the fault of the patrol that seemed like it was never ever going to catch them up.

They hadn't seen the thickets fading as they entered the Earthshaker, because they'd been peering up at the moon, and riding now through that enclosed trellis of moon and shadow, the pine groves in which both stallion and horse looked like zebras striped with silver and the second lieutenant seemed dressed in white cotton cloth like an acrobat or a convict in a black-striped suit, they paid no great attention to the penumbra of soft transparent moss in which veins of brushwood were turning to forest among the trees, thickets falling into the denseness to become impenetrable shadow, as if their vegetable existence had been no more than a step between the light and the profound darkness.

The wind cracked its whip in the depths, while in the still illuminated woods the solemn conacaste trees, the corpulent and fragrant cedars, the ceibas so old they had clouds of cotton in their eyes, the capulin trees, the ebonies, the guayacanes were approaching, coming closer and closer one to another, until together they formed solid walls of bark and nervations, roots out of the ground, old nests, abandoned cotton moss, dust, gusts of wind and stretches of indefinable darkness, though as the light failed completely all that remained of that movement of inert bodies was a faint pall of white, veined smoke, and deeper within, the sound of a storm-blown sea.

Nothing could be seen, but the riders went on advancing like something fluid, non-existent, over rumbling earthslides and beneath downpours of leaves as heavy as amphibious birds. From time to time they were caught by low or fallen branches which felt like watery spiders grazing their faces.

"Maaa-cho! Maaa-cho!"

The colonel's voice drowned Second Lieutenant Musús' whistle, which was less of a whistle than the tip of his respiration, a human chayote vine finding its way by following its breathing. A branch tried to knock his hat off. Musús drowned his whistle and retrieved it, protesting:

"Get out, goddam tree! Fucking about with my hat . . . Get the hell away!"

Bones give off flames by night, in the graveyard. But the brightness that was coming at them now, gropingly, mid a beautiful darkness, seemed more like a star in the sky forgotten there since the beginning of the world. Where was that glow of chaos coming from? They didn't know, they didn't try to find out, and they wouldn't have known had they not seen a tree the size of an oak lit up by millions of tiny luminous dots glittering before their eyes.

Musús came up alongside the chief to tell him, "Look, colonel, sir, the glowworms are mating." But all he said, the babbling apple jiggling up and down like a bobbin in the malarial hide of his throat, all he managed was, "Look, chief!"

The females clinging to the highest branches called their cyclop-eyed lovers, and the worms, slowly waving their lighted lanterns, millions of eyes of light in the immense night breathing with all their hot masculine strength, turned up their diamond beacons and set off, displacing themselves skywards like blood with the bluish glow of pearl, up the trunk, up the branches and twigs, the leaves and the flowers. As the worms grew closer, still heightening their lights with their lustful respiration, the females inflamed their own nubile brilliances still further, coaxing them on with the thousand movements of a star, until after the nuptial encounter the lights began softening, and all that remained of that luminary was an opaque mass, the remains of a milky way, a tree that dreamed it was a morning star.

The moon enlisted them again. They came up over the tapering edge of a crater the size of a town square. The rocks, faintly orange in color, were reflected in the film of moon and water that covered them like the surface of a mirror, dark masses moving from side to side like mysterious spots. But the heart of the Earthshaker into which, at last, they repaired, along a scrap of a trail that looked more like the unraveled bed of a winter stream, held other secrets. The noise of four long

85

leagues of leaves shaken incessantly by the gusting wind, ceased, as though by enchantment, in the interior of that great twinkling bowl, and they could hear the tinkling of stones as they sang beneath the horses' hoofs. Here and there as they passed an iguana fled beneath dry debris of leaves trapped in smoke-colored spider's webs, leaving behind them a grating noise like swimmers on dry land. You could see the sharp-clawed tracks of a forest cat at the turnoff to the trail that pitched them deep into the bed of the Earthshaker.

Mysterious shadows, singing stones, and an atmosphere in which they could speak without shrieking. And there they would have set camp to wait on the men who formed the bulk of the patrol, so they could all ride on to the Cattle Pass together, meantime having some of what they were carrying in their bottle gourds—coffee, chilate, cane liquor—and re-fresh their steaming horses—sweat against dew—if those same horses, which were half dead with fatigue, had not both revived at the same time, and given such a jerk, so suddenly, that they very nearly threw their riders on their faces and left them biting the dust.

A stone's throw away, lying across the road of singing stones which ran through the Earthshaker, was a coffin.

"What the—!" the colonel managed to say, as the stallion turned and bucked in the air, tailed by the flea-bitten horse, which was free of its rein because the second lieutenant wanted both hands to aim his mauser at the coffin, once he'd made it to the ledge which rimmed the floor of the Earthshaker, but the colonel, who was hanging onto his pistol, borne by the undulating respiration of a stallion which was by now just that, a black respiration trying to save itself, shouted at him just in time, don't shoot. The torrent of leaves kicked up by the wind beat against their faces and submerged them at once; but now, one step away from the desolation of the Earthshaker, in which they had felt naked unto death, how comforting were those green surging waves, rumbling, ruminating, deafening, cover-ing them, insulating them, protecting them. Leaves on stems, monkeys shrieking with human faces, the tense leaps of wild beasts, meteors falling with their tendons bleeding light, shooting stars that cheeped in the sky like little chicks lost in the immensity, withered guachipilin trees snapping like supreme suicides, the collapse of a vegetable being which no longer has the will to resist the onrush of the wind. A man who flees from danger and meets a vast crowd of people and mingles with them and continues to go forward with all those thousands and thousands of moving people feels as safe as the colonel and Secundino felt as they left the Earthshaker and emerged into that circulating torrent of wind which shook heaven and earth for many leagues around.

"Idiot, can't you see they're watching over a dead man," was all the second lieutenant heard, and that was why he didn't loose his bullet.

They fled. The wind closed their eyes, opened their mouths, dilated their nostrils, numbed their ears. They literally merged their necks with the necks of their horses, to offer the least resistance, and because contact with living, sweating animals which smelled like sacks of salt afforded them the vague security of companionship in the midst of danger.

They didn't stop until they reached the summit, the very top of that slope whose bottom their weariness and recent memory reminded them was very deep. Colonel Godoy untied the sweat-soaked handkerchief around his neck and wiped his face.

Musús lowered his eyelids so as not to see the owl which had appeared before him. The moon bathed its lettuce wings, ribbed with little veins of banana pith. "A bad omen, a brown owl and a dead man's coffin," his blood cried out to him.

"Colonel," said Musús, without moving his lips, paralyzed in word and jaw.

And Godoy replied, in the same tone, without moving his mouth, "Colonel . . . Oh, yes indeed . . . Colonel . . ."

"The cattle thief's wake—"

"Oh, yes indeed . . . The cattle thief's wake . . ."

"Except now there's no dead man, only a coffin—"

"They're getting careful. You see, in former times one of the slobs would act dead on a petate, and they'd even put four candles round him. But now they've decided it's better just to leave the box there, folks won't carry on along the trail once they've seen a coffin, and the thieves can drive their stolen cattle with the road clear all the way."

"I heard you did in a fellow called Apolinario Chijoloy, colonel, who was always having to play the dead man because he was crippled and couldn't go thieving."

"You heard about that?"

"Yes, they told me the whole story. It was after you got the better of the chief of Ilóm. We really were within a hair's-breadth of death that time, only because you had the nerve to carry out your plans are we alive to tell the tale. I mean, going up into those mountains to take on that chief who was be-witched by yellow rabbits, and chopping up his men while he was washing out his guts in the river. I saw all those Indians falling in little pieces as the patrol moved in. Six years ago that was, and still people are talking of nothing else."

"And this is the seventh year," the colonel cut in. "I keep count of them because according to the Indians, the firefly wizards, who we also made mincemeat of, have me sentenced to death come the seventh. Me snuff it this year? To hell with them!"

"Apolinario Chijoloy was the last man you killed for good."

"I must confess I played a dirty trick on him. I caught him napping by the roadside, under the shadow of some great bushes clinging to the edge of a precipice, down which I slid to escape before his pals could come to take revenge. The poor devil was playing the dead man lying on an old blanket, with three candles round him, one of which had gone out. I fired quickly for fear the other three would go out, too. He only half curled up as the bullet hit him."

"And still the patrol hasn't got here."

"And all we can do is wait. It would be dangerous, fool-hardy, to go back to the road without reinforcements. There's no one with more nerve than these bandits, and they're so crafty, real crafty, danger makes people sharp, sharpens their hearing, their eyesight, makes them almost divine what they should and shouldn't do."

"That's right, they're cunning as mountain lions, ocelots, snakes, sly as the wind in the undergrowth."

Because they were talking they heard horses approaching only when they had the forms on top of them, ready to fall on them. Their speech deserted them. They fled for their horses, which were tethered nearby to freshen their noses in the damp of the forest, with some grass to kill their hunger, and in his panic the colonel tore up the bush he'd tied the stallion to with his halter, and the second lieutenant snapped the noose of his lasso.

It was the patrol. The seventeen men of the mounted patrol, flour-dusted with earth and moon. There's nothing like a mounted man. Who would disagree with that? Mounted for love or for war, there's nothing like a mounted man.

That thought passed through the mind of the Leader of the Expeditionary Force, Colonel Gonzalo Godoy, when, at the head of his men, taking command of his forces, he gave orders for them to deploy themselves in an attacking, outflanking formation.

They moved off at the gallop, eager to test themselves against the bandits. There's nothing like an assembly of bullets to shake off cold and misery. The torrential sound of the Earth-shaker made them throng together, and together they all emerged at the spot where the coffin had been left lying across the road. The moonlight showed up the angles of the tragic, unpainted wooden box, unadorned white pinewood which, as it returned the clarity, was ringed by a shining halo of light.

Part of the patrol had stayed at the entrance to the Earth-shaker under the command of Second Lieutenant Musús, to avoid a surprise attack. They were all eyes and ears. Musús' saliva dried up on him. He tried to loose one of his barking commands, sergeant-major-like, and all he sent out was a little parched air. From high above the second lieutenant and his men watched what was happening in the Earthshaker, as in a bull ring. The colonel got down from his horse and went up to the coffin, followed by the troopers, all with gun in hand, pointing, ready to fire. With the barrel of his pistol the colonel knocked on the lid, imperiously. Nothing. It was empty. Just as he had said it would be. Empty. A new ploy by the bandits to steal cattle, which did not require any of their number to act the hero by acting the dead man, and risk ending up really dead through acting so smart. Again Don Chalo struck the coffin with his pistol barrel, imperiously, and now with more confidence. Nothing. Empty. He banged again, and again no one answered.

By order of the colonel, who sometimes gave commands with his eyes and his head, two soldiers stepped forward to open the lid. Only the chief stayed in his place, the rest retreated and very nearly ran for it. Inside the coffin was a man dressed in white, with his straw hat covering his face. A stream of cold sweat ran down the colonel's back. Who was that man?

The orange-colored stones reflected riders and horses, only the shadows spilled like ink from black inkwells seemed not to stay on the surface, but to penetrate the stone.

The colonel pushed the hat from the man's face with his pistol, and as the occupant of the coffin received the moonlight full in his face he leaped up in fright and jumped out of his lugubrious canoe. The colonel returned to where he had been standing, having retreated a step, in case it was a spirit from the other world, maybe they were bringing the dead back to life now. Wasting no time, whilst he threatened with his pistol that person whom he still didn't know, not even if he was human, a threat he extended into a fanlike gesture telling his men to approach, he asked him, "Are you of this world or the other one?"

"Carrier, señor," replied the filleted voice of a man who had just been woken up feeling faint with hunger.

Perceiving that he wasn't dealing with a dead man, the

colonel felt much more at ease, and sure now of what he was about, he inquired, "What are you carrying?"

"This coffin, I went into town to fetch it."

"Tell the truth or I'll blow your brains out."

"I'm a carrier, like I said. Just like I said. I went to town to bring the coffin to bury a curer who died yesterday, up the trail a way, in the Cattle Pass."

The troopers had been moving closer. The Indian, with his hat in his hand, his white breeches above the knee, his white shirt with short sleeves, seemed made of bronzed stone.

"I buy the coffin and I set off fast as I can go. By the time I get here I'm feeling tired, so as I've got the coffin with me I get inside to feel safer. There's a lot of peccary, black widows, all kinds of harmful animals round here."

"That coffin and you are the sign that someone round here is stealing other folks' cattle."

"That may be, but the coffin's the sign, then, not me. The bandits don't like us Indians, they say we're a race of yeller dogs."

"Then that's why they forced you to get in there, you know what they say, don't you, you lose an Indian you ain't lost nothing. That's the start of it, so now spit out the rest of what you know about the bandits who must be prowling somewhere round here, or you'll be going back in that coffin."

The barrel of Colonel Godoy's revolver was hard in the Indian's ribs, painted against his shirt licked by the moon and the cold, it made him step back, almost knocked him down, toward the pinewood coffin.

"Talk, you understand Spanish all right."

"I ain't staying in no coffin that's meant for no curer. You kill me if you want, and bury me right here, but not in the curer's coffin, because then it'll go bad for me in the other life. And if you're gonna shoot me, have the coffin sent to the Cattle Pass."

"And who are you going to deliver it to? The corpse?" joked the colonel, sure the Indian was merely a wile of the bandits, for everyone knew they were in the area. At times like this his jokes had often helped him get at the truth. "And the dead man will embrace you and say, 'God bless you, you've brought me my last change of clothes,' and if he's poor that'll likely be the last outfit he'll ever have made to measure, because I'm sure they must have given you his measurements . . ."

"Yes, señor, and I'm to deliver the casket to the people at the wake."

"Casket, you call it! You might call it that if it was perfectly finished, varnished on the outside and lined on the inside. But that thing you're carrying is just an ordinary pine box. And who is at this wake?"

"Women?"

"And men?"

"More women than men."

"So he died, what of, they kill him?"

"He died of old age."

"Well, before we put a bullet in you, we'll find out if you're telling the truth. My second-in-command, Second Lieutenant Musús, will take five men, tie you up, and go with you. If it's not true, if you've lied to me, they'll have orders to put you in the coffin, close it, stand it up against a tree, and shoot you, all boxed up, all ready to throw you into the hole."

The carrier picked up the coffin like a man born again, lifted it onto his back, and trotted off, running rather than walking, to get away from that man whose pale blue eyes shone like crystals of fire. The patrol rode after him along the jagged line of crags which ringed that volcanic bowl, and from there, on Godoy's orders, Second Lieutenant Musús set off with five of the soldiers, the meanest ones, toward the Cattle Pass. The carrier, tied somewhat pointlessly by the arms, and using a tumpline to carry the coffin, went first. Soon they were lost in the murmuring of the leaves.

IX

The mother of the Tecunes, their Nana, seemed to carry many years and many labors on her shoulders. Years grimy with yellow maize chilate, years whitened by white atole mixed with sweetcorn grains, fingernails of fresh green maize kernels, years soaked in the red horror of puliques, years blackened by wood smoke, years running with sweat, and her aching neck, aching hair, aching forehead growing wrinkled and baggy beneath the weight of baskets carried on her head. The weight, there on top, up above her.

Years and labors weigh down on the heads of old folk, sunk in their shoulders, sagging forward, with a half bending at the knees as though they were forever about to fall to the ground before the objects of their worship.

Old Yaca, mother of the Tecunes, their Nana, who went about with her hand the color of burnt wood held over her stomach ever since a bewitched cricket gave her that mortal hiccup, clicked her little snake's eyes against the damp shadow of the air, pushing a lighted ocote torch forward with her other hand, to see who it was arriving in the middle of the night. She saw nothing. She moved to the door with a mastication of words. She had heard men arriving on horseback. So the boys, her sons and grandsons, weren't around anymore.

Soon she was surrounded by men with guns. As they closed in on the rancho they led their horses by the rein. Barefoot, all dressed differently, but all with soldier's straps and belts on.

"Excuse us, ma'am," said the one in charge, none other than Musús, "can you tell us where the curer lives, we have a sick man along with us who's been taken real bad, and will surely die if he don't get to see the curer."

93

MEN OF MAIZE

"He can see him, all right," replied the old woman, growling a little, and she turned the light from the ocote torch toward the interior of the rancho, where the body of the curer could indeed be seen laid out on the dirt floor strewn with woodland flowers and cypress leaves to hide the smell.

Musús, who aped Colonel Godoy in every possible detail, with the monkeylike servility of a minion, advanced toward the body of the curer and gave him a prod in the navel with the end of his pistol. Only the cloth shirt gave way, and you could see the skin of his swollen belly.

"What do you say he died of?" asked Musús, afraid that this one too might rise from the ground, as the Indian rose from his coffin.

"Of old age," affirmed the old woman. "Old age is the worst of ills, it kills you for sure."

"You're real sick yourself, then . . . ."

"Yes, I sure am," the old woman consented again, moving a little way inside, though holding back the ocote torch, for fear the soldiers might decide to examine the body of the curer whom Calistro, as he dragged the corpse home over the stones, left looking like the image of Christ. Mad Calistro. Mad no longer. He came back to his senses thanks to the deer's-eye stone. It was doubly lucky. Lucky because he returned to his senses just by having his forehead and crown smoothed with that deer's-eye stone; and lucky because he was able to leave with his brothers before the patrol arrived. Just as well they decided not to drink chocolate mixed with blood.

All this the Nana of the Tecunes was thinking, without neglecting her visitors, and with the ocote torch turned always to the door, to avoid trouble, otherwise they might see that the dead man wasn't just dead, but murdered. They'd tie them all up and take them away, without waiting for explanations.

"Well, men, there you have it," stammered Second Lieutenant Musús in the direction of his men, scratching his head, which showed up like a big coyote topped with hair, it really got up his nose that the carrier should escape from being shot

94

like the chief had ordered. Put him in the coffin, close it, stand it up on end, and—fire!

The Indian dragged in the coffin as the patrol rode out of the Cattle Pass to meet up with Colonel Godoy in the Earthshaker. After Musús, who found time as he took his leave to be the colonel in word and manner by declaring that the coffin was the curer's "last stinking-place," the soldiers jumped on their horses one by one and moved quickly away, they scarcely had time to take some maize-leaf cigarettes offered them by the Nana, which they clapped to their mouths unlighted, all except Benito Ramos, who had a pact with the devil to the effect that when a cigarette arrived in his mouth, it lit up by itself. The strangest man. He had swallowed one of the devil's hairs. That was part of the agreement. And he had turned dry, dry skin the color of ash, black eyes the color of coal. It was thought the devil had told him he would know every time his woman was untrue. But he never knew, because she was deceiving him with the devil. A beautiful woman, imagine fair skin, long hair, eyes the black color of frijoles fried in plenty of fat. She was a woman to have for breakfast, that one. For her eyes.

The riders immersed themselves in the language of the leaves, galloping one after the other. The road fell steeply. Lucky. That way they'd soon be back in the heart of the Earthshaker, to sleep a while. In the darkness, treacherous long-spined bushes, the ones the wind can't move, like the skeletons of unburied trees, scratched at them, all except Benito Ramos, who could see by night with his eyes of coal. He was riding at the back. Was he riding at the back or not? He always stayed in the rearguard. He was the tail of the mounted patrol. And wickeder than Judas.

The sky was cramming full of stars. The woods stretched out like a black stain. Thus they saw it at their feet, as the road went winding down falling between precipices from the Cattle Pass to the Earthshaker. Snorts from the horses, early morning catarrh, the distant howling of coyotes in lunar syrup, squirrels gnawing with laughter as they chewed on cheerful thoughts,

the long-drawn calls of nocturnal birds landing in trees mid the
punishing murmur of the undergrowth.

They were in the forest now. The moon had fallen with its
slow decaying light in a convex sky weepy with night dew. The
human presence of the riders settled into a lack of movement
which made them absent men of moss, heavy of skin, the color
of rotten eggs. The hangover you get from weariness and lack
of sleep. The hangover you get from too much riding. Trembling staircases of trees down which the sky descends branch
by branch, fresh with stars, to rivulets of little broken mirrors
which looked like liquid light between the hills. Thus they
went, with an anguish of cockroaches, meaner than ringworm,
leaving the horses to sink with their heads pushed well forward, rumps well up, in a descent which became ever steeper,
so much so they had to lean backwards, literally lying down in
the saddle, until the saddlehorns touched their hats. A smell of
ocote turpentine in that wasplike vibration, that atmosphere
agitated by the whispering sea of vegetation in the Earthshaker. Suffocation of sulphur fumes in which disease seemed
to float, flayings of castrated animals, eyes of toads. They were
nauseated by everything. By the descent, by fatigue, by lack of
sleep, by the penetrating turpentine, and by the whiplashing
of the fierce wind which passed through, at times alone and at
times armed with razor leaves.

The first clue was a faint smell of burning brushwood,
scarcely perceptible, but enough to quicken the foreboding
which Benito Ramos had passed on to them before they turned
back. He didn't say it all because he was a man of few words,
or maybe because he didn't want to aggrieve them. But that's
the thing about having a pact with Satan. Knowing about
things before they happen.

"When you look down at the Earthshaker, lads," Ramos had
told them in the Cattle Pass, "you'll see it's a funnel, a gigantic
funnel of rocks like glazed earthenware. The hurricane is real
fierce, but there it falls still. More than likely it doesn't penetrate at all, it doesn't go down, it doesn't want to make widows

of the clouds, the leaves, all the female things the hurricane impregnates. And after riding the rapids with leafy trees deafening you, you even feel frightened yourself, when you reach the edge of that funnel, where nothing moves at all, not even the blades of grass. Peace in the midst of the storm. Calm in the midst of the tempest. Tranquility in the midst of the wildest commotion. Like you'd gone deaf from a blow on the head. The Earthshaker, you've already been down to the bottom of it, is a cave in the shape of a funnel, not beneath the ground, but beneath the sky. The darkness down there is not black, as it is in the underground caves, it is blue. And now you listen, without asking me questions, because you know I say what I have to say and no more. Down in the bottom of the funnel is Colonel Godoy with his men. He's smoking his cigar. He feels like eating purslane soup. He asks if there's any about. Someone says it might be dangerous. Better stick to what's in the rations. Only has to be heated up. On no account, says the colonel, will I permit any lighting of fires, we'll eat the rations cold and take some purslane up to make soup in the Cattle Pass tomorrow. Now there's nothing wrong in wanting to eat purslane. Only that he should have felt like eating in that place, where there almost certainly isn't any to be found, and that he should have been afraid to light a fire, to let his men light a fire to heat the coffee, the dried beef and crumbling tortillas from their saddlebags, so that they would have to be eaten cold. Purslane is the food of dead men. It is a soft green flame of the earth which penetrates with a consuming clarity the flesh of those who are heading underground to sleep the eternal sleep. When a man is in danger, like the colonel sentenced to die come the seventh fire, wanting to eat purslane is a bad sign. And while this is going on between the soldiers and the colonel, their horses shake their ears and flick their tails and clash their hoofs together, as though they were moving away in their sleep. Animals run away from places of danger in the dreams they seem to have in their heads; but since their instinct doesn't rise to thought they stay where they are. While this goes on at the bottom of the funnel—the colonel, his men, the rations, the waiting horses—three fences are forming around them, around the funnel, three dead man's crowns, three circles, three cartwheels without axles or spokes. The first, counting from the inside outwards, from the bottom up, is formed by the eyes of owls. Hundreds of thousands of owl's eyes staring, frozen, round. The second circle is formed by the faces of wizards without bodies. Hundreds of thousands of faces hanging in the air, like the moon in the sky, without bodies, without anything to hold them up. The third circle, furthest away and not the least vengeful, looks like a boiling cauldron, and is formed by endless rounds of yuccas, daggers bloodstained by a great fire. The owl's eyes stare fixedly at the colonel, nailing him down, as many as there are of them, pore by pore, like a cowhide, on a thick board dripping foul resin. The wizards of the second circle stare at the colonel as though he were a doll made of entrails, a nonsense, gold teeth, pistols, and testicles. Faces without bodies gazing out of tents of virgin doeskin. Their bodies are made up of fireflies, which is why in winter they are everywhere, turning their existence off and on. One, two, three, four, five, six years they have meted out to the colonel, and the seventh, inside the Earthshaker, will be a fire of golden owls which the owls will hurl from the depths of their pupils. Little by little, after the frost will come the blight, and after the blight the fire of those golden owls will burn everything with icy cold. The first thing the men accompanying Colonel Godoy will feel is an aching in their earlobes. They will finger their ears. They will rub them. In their confusion, and their anxiety to be rid of the irritation, they put their right hand to their left ear, and their left hand to their right ear, until they are left like that with their hands crossed, rubbing their ears, poking them, almost pulling them off because of the tingling of the cold, until they snap just as though they were made of glass. They'll see blood spurting from either side of one another's heads, without paying much heed to this vision, because they'll be tearing off their own eyelids, also crystallized, until their eyes are left naked, open, burned by a fire of golden owls. And then, after casting off their eyelids like bits of umbilical cord with hair on, they will tear off their lips and bare their teeth like grains of maize on cobs of red bone. Only the colonel, nailed down pore by pore on a board by the eyes of the owls which will keep on staring fixedly at him, only he will remain intact, with his ears, his eyelids, his lips. Not even the ash of his cigar will fall. Hands of darkness brandishing daggers will force him to suicide. But it will be only his shadow, a skin of shadow among the yuccas. The bullet will burst in his temples, he will fall to the ground, but other dark hands will lift his body, they will mount him on his horse, and will begin to shrink him horse and all until he is the size of a piece of sugar candy. The close-knit throng of yuccas will wave their daggers, daggers stained red with fire right up to their hilts."

Second Lieutenant Musús rode off to reconnoitre. The smell of burning forest was so strong that he halted for a moment. One of his men cried, "Can you smeeeEEEll it? Someone must have dropped a cigareeeEEEtte!"

Near and far the sound of hands and hats as men slapped their clothes to brush away the sparks, those who were burning. And in a turbulent sea of sweet air, the buzzing voices: It wasn't me . . . Nothing to do with me . . . It wasn't us . . . The smell's coming from up ahead . . . I had a fag end in my mouth, but it wasn't lit . . . How could you start a fire with a lousy cigarette in this soaking wet darkness . . . Unless the water caught fire . . . Look at us, we're dripping with dew . . . And . . . And I ain't getting down to have a shit after all . . . And . . . You don't have to see the sparks, just catch that stink . . .

"A stink is what he's leaving there," someone joked, as they heard a horse stopping and a man dismounting, then grunting.

The stink, however, was by now fire in the air, clearing fires, burning forest.

And the buzzing among the horsemen: Wonder what's going on down there . . . Too bad if the chief decided to sleep with his cigar behind his ear and set fire to himself . . . But . . . It's raining in the Earthshaker . . . God forbid there's a fire beneath the water, the water will catch and everything will burn . . . No . . . It's the air . . . It's the leaves . . . It's the air . . . It's the leaves . . . The leaves . . . The air . . .

It became clear to them all at once. At the gallop. They looked at one another. They were there. They were there together, sweating, panting, as if they all had fever. Light of living glass. Their eyes and the eyes of the horses. They scattered. They seemed to go up the hill downwards, so swiftly did they climb, like human debris in the midst of the smoke. The yuccas, bloodstained daggers. The smoke. Flames like lashing reins. Desert. Musús' last order may have been that. Break ranks!

Benito Ramos stayed back among the yuccas. The flames didn't touch him. Not for nothing did he have a pact with the devil. He let his horse escape after throwing away the bit. Swooning of bats which fell asphyxiated. Deer passing like pea-shooter pellets. Black wasps smelling of hot cane liquor fleeing from honeycombs the color of excrement sown in the earth, half honeycomb, half ant's-nest.

In other nearby hills blurred forms in the overgrowth savored the fire as it rose on all sides from the Earthshaker. Flames in the form of bloodstained hands were painted on the walls of the air. Hands dripping the blood of chickens sacrificed in maizefield masses. The behatted forms, smokers of small cigars as chili-hot as stinging nettles, dressed in coarse black frieze, sitting without resting their buttocks on the ground, on feet folded over like tortillas, were those of Calistro, Eusebio, Ruperto, Tomás and Roso Tecún. They smoked steadily and spoke softly, slowly, without emphasis.

"Usebio," said Calistro, "talked to the Deer of the Seventh Fire. From beneath the earth the deer called on him, and asked to be unburied. And Usebio unburied him. The deer spoke to him with the voice of a person, just like us, with words he

100

spoke to him. 'Usebio,' he says the deer said, 'trep, trep, trep,' and he made his left hoof spin like a corkscrew, to show he was trepanning something under the earth—"

"That ain't exactly what he said," intervened Eusebio Tecún, "but what is certainly certain and true is that soon after I got him out of the hole where he was buried, he sat himself on a rock like a chair. In the seat and on the back, as the deer sat down, brown flowers speckled with white sprang up, and little worms began wriggling, some with tiny horns and green eyes, others red, and others black. All those eyes sparkled, the eyes of worms which began falling still until they formed between the deer and the seat and back of his chair a thick-haired plush cover. Once seated, he crossed his legs just like a town mayor and, smiling at me, every time he smiled the moon entered his mouth and lit up his teeth of unshone copal, smiling at me, he blinked just as though a golden fly had settled on his left eyelid, and he said, 'For your information, Usebio, this is the seventh fire, on which I was to die and come back to life, for I have seven lives, as a cat has nine. I was one of the firefly wizards who were with Gaspar Ilóm when the patrol caught up with him. There I lost my first life, I lost five more after, and now this seventh one, by your hand, by your ambush, by your patience and your eye for waiting for me to pass along by the creek through the canefield. It was good. I am not sorry that you killed me. I came back to life only to get rid of a man who had also arrived at his seventh fire.' "

"And this is it!" chorused Calistro, Tomás, Uperto and Rosendo, as the women called him. The men called him Roso and the women Rosendo.

"That's right," Eusebio was careful to say, and he added, the fire still trepanning away in the Earthshaker, "without saying more, the deer scratched his ear, the left one, and set off running downhill. Soon after, the fire could be seen."

"And you caught him on the left side, and brought him down . . ."

"Not so much mouth, boy, and more eyes, because they

101

might get by us, it's some time since I left them back at the rancho questioning our Nana about the curer's death," Roso Tecún muttered harshly.

A hail of shotgun slugs was the reply. The muskets sneezed almost all at the same time. Pon, pon, pon, pon, and they stayed silent, gazing at the result, among the mortal daggers of the yuccas and the hands of the flames, hands from the maize-field masses.

Many of the men were shot in the saddle as they rode up from the Earthshaker, trying to save their skins, mistaking those shadowy forms for Musús' men, who had stampeded away before they reached the spot where the Tecunes were posted. If they had to die, it was better to help fulfill the vengeance along paths of red earth shaded by lofty pine trees.

MARÍA TECÚN

X

 From his liana tongue, from his teeth of coyote's milk, from the roots of his weeping the rumbling earthslides of his cries were riven:

> *"María TecúúúÚÚÚn! . . .*
> *María TecúúúÚÚÚn! . . ."*

The voice went tumbling down the ravines:

> *"María TecúúúÚÚÚn! . . .*
> *María TecúúúÚÚÚn! . . ."*

The crouching mountains resounding with echoes:

> *"María TecúúúÚÚÚn! . . .*
> *María TecúúúÚÚÚn! . . ."*

But the echo also went tumbling down the ravines:

> *"María TecúúúÚÚÚn! . . .*
> *María TecúúúÚÚÚn! . . ."*

"Go to hell!" said a freckled woman with reddish hair in long fleeing plaits, rather tall, and skinny. No one could have said whether these words came from her breast or her huipile. They came from her breast where her huipile had come away at the seam. Been torn, rather. And with one child in the rise of her belly, another in her arms, the small waving hands of those who could just walk hanging onto her flying petticoats,

103

and the raised ones steering the oxcart, she ran away from that man who was useless, but useless, incapable of chopping wood, pasturing animals, cutting combs from hives, or gelding cats. They took everything they had. They didn't have much, but what they had they took. They didn't want to leave a single thing behind. Why should they leave anything behind, when the best thing that man could do was lay himself down and die.

"María TecúúúÚÚÚn! . . . María TecúúúÚÚÚn! . . ." shouted Goyo Yic, without breathing, weary of inquiring with his hands, his nose, his ears, in things and in the air, which way his woman and children had gone. Little streams of weeping, like brown sugar water, ran through the dust of the roads on his cheeks.

And he went on shouting, in a tantrum, a man who had remained a child, calling her with his hair in the wind, lost, without eyes and now almost without touch. The fugitives led him on with shouts and feigned laughter, as though they were going to Pisigüilito, and then fled in the opposite direction fast as their feet would carry them. Soon, before their eyes, in the highest part of the sierra, they would have the coast sprawling below them with its respiration smothered by the roaring of the Pacific Ocean. Down there was where they were headed, along a heap of stones that in summer was a road and in winter a river. The water goes down from the mountains to the sea, good and clean, good and healthy, fine and good, like the happy crowds of people who go down from the cold lands to work on the coast. A laughing of clouds among the pinewoods, which have turned into birds because of all the birds of every color they have crowning them and flying over them. But water and people become sluggish in the sloth of the coast-lands. Water and people end up stinking with cold fever among the tendons of the mangrove swamps, reflections and slime.

Goyo Yic stood cocking his ear, without breathing, because he was drowning in air and he had to breathe quickly some-times and sometimes he had to stop breathing altogether. What a shock to find them gone, though he could still hear them, and he could hear a splintering of nerves in his wrists. Leaves? Birds? Flying water? An earth tremor making everything shudder?

They were knocking down trees. And the smallest tree they knocked down around there, three men couldn't lift it, so his children had told him.

"*María TecúúúÚÚÚn!* . . .
          María TecúúúÚÚÚn! . . ."

He went back to the house still calling them. His throat was hoarse from so much shouting. He ironed out his thin legs with his bony hands. What could the time be? Goyo Yic was famous for being able to work out the time, and in the cold of the forest beneath his old man's feet, swollen like tamales from chigoes, he could tell it was getting late. At midday the cloud forest burns. In the morning it soaks. And it grows chill, like the fur of a dead animal, at night.

"Don't be cruel, María TecúúúÚÚÚn! Don't hide, it's you I'm talking to, María TecúúúÚÚÚn! What are you up to, children, what are you doooOOOing? ChiiiIIIldren! My chiiiIIIldren! You'll pay for this, fuck you. I'm tired of calling you, María, María Tecún, MaríííÍÍÍa Tecún! Answer me, chiiiIIIldren! ChildreeeEEEn! My chiiiIIIldren . . . My chiiiIII . . ."

His shouts turned to steady weeping. And after sniveling for a while, and falling quiet for another long while, he took up his shouting again.

"You're like stones that can't heeeEEEar! You ain't got my permission to goooOOO! María Tecún, if you've run off with someone new, give me back my little chiiiIIIldren. The children are miiiIIIne, they belong to meeeEEE!"

He slapped himself on the face, pulled his own hair, tore at his own clothes, and with no more breath to shout, he kept on, just talking, "You didn't even leave me my clean clothes. You can go stuff yourself after what you've done to me, you no-good slut, harlot, curse you. But you're gonna pay for it. The headless bodies of the Zacatones are my witness. It was me picked you up from beneath that cot. It's thanks to me you ain't dead. You'd have died a baby. It's thanks to me the ants didn't eat you, like some leftover. You were bleating for your Nana's teat. Your hot little hands found it, at least I reckon so, 'cause you went quiet. But only to cry all the harder, tears and yet more tears: your Nana was a mountain of frozen hair. And you screamed still more when you crawled up from her breast; innocent as you were, you wanted to do what you used to do when she was sleeping, wake her up with your demands; I expect you were looking for her nose, her cheeks, her eyes, her forehead, her ears, and you didn't find anything because the Tecunes had carried her head away. Indian sow, slattern, to treat me this way when I picked you up and revived you by blowing on you like a fire when all that's left of it is a spark. I took you from death like a rigid baby iguana."

The lament buzzed away like a tumblebug, in Goyo Yic's flat, boneless nose with a few smallpox marks.

"The old nag, that's what you call me, isn't it, María Tecún? Well, the old nag bore you from the house of the Zacatones all twisted up with colic, and fetched herbs from the forest to make you vomit up the serum you sucked from your headless mother. And then the old nag—that is what you call me behind my back, isn't it, María Tecún?—the old nag nursed you with a pig's bladder tied round his chest, you wouldn't take a bottle or a cup, like a woman's tit filled with goat's milk and limewater, which you sucked through a little hole I made with a cactus spine, till you fell asleep."

The ravines breathed in, and that made Goyo Yic realize he was perilously close. He was walking, sniveling, stumbling, toward his house, from which he had run shouting a good while before.

106

"And at the old nag's side you grew up, and through your hands and eyes the old nag worked in the fields, you spot-faced Indian. Maize, beans, pumpkins, greens, chayotes. The old nag fattened pigs. The old nag went begging in fairs to dress you in fancy beads. We bought needles and thread to darn the clothes. I bought animals. And through the hand you left in my hand, like a bony little coin, like one more piece of alms, as we slept, the old nag dreamed that he could see, but he couldn't see anything, though he could see you, materialized through your body.

"Didn't you have me in your hands, María Tecún? Well, why didn't you push me down the ravine? You could have given me a shove as I went by a precipice. It would have been easy. And in the blindness of death, and my love for you, I could have followed and found you."

His sons had been in the henhouse since the early hours. They were up much earlier than usual. Maybe they hadn't even gone to bed. Why go to bed, if you've got to get right up again? The daylight found them with the oxen yoked up, ready to go, and all the things they were to carry in the cart stacked out on the verandah and in the yard: the grinding stone, the comales, the pots, an empty barrel, a cot frame strung with strips of rawhide, some petates, packsaddles, nets, martingales, palm-leaf rainshields, a bit of old mortar in a can of phosphorus folded in on all sides, quick-lime in a sack, roof tiles, sheets of zinc, the ocote, the hearthstones, and the images of the saints.

The cart squeaked over the stones of the corral gate, as if its ungreased axles knew they were taking off for some other place.

Goyo Yic found full evidence of their flight in the kitchen. First with his foot half raised to use the big toe, then with his hands, he looked for the three hearthstones on all fours. Those shapeless rocks, like stone goiters, symbols of family life because they are the goiters of our grandmother earth, faithful to the fire, the comale and the coffeepot, scorched and scaly with soot, and covered in ash, were not in their place. And through the scantily furnished roof where they'd taken the zinc sheeting, the sky entered. The weight of the sky on his blind man's shoulders made him feel that something big was missing above the kitchen. The sky weighs down like water in earthen jars. His shoulders knew that weight. He took refuge in his house, in roofed places, beneath roadside trees, so he wouldn't snap beneath the weight of the sky, air, clouds, stars, birds known only by their calls, after supporting it all day begging out in the open. His children had unroofed the kitchen and part of the house. The clarity of the moon, to him it was heat, seeped into rooms with no tiles, no furniture, and no people.

If Goyo Yic had been able to look about him: chili shrubs torn up by the roots, trampled on; the chayote vine lying on the ground with its leaves wrinkled; and the corner where they kept the box with all those half pesos he had garnered by dint of spending day after day with outstretched hand at the foot of an old amate in the bend of the road to Pisigüilito, empty. His back wore down the rough-barked trunk of the amate against which he leaned to ask for alms, when he didn't do it right at the roadside, in danger of being run down by mule-trains or herds of cattle. In summer he was clothed in dust, but when the first rains fell the winter washed him, refreshed and rejuvenated him, until his flesh felt the damp that brings rheumatism. The rheumatism went on long journeys around his body, long winter journeys warping his bones, knotting his tendons, and he ended up almost rigid from carrying so much water. He wore down the rough bark of the amate, begging, and he used the coins he collected to give to those he thought were his—his, his, his—a roof, bread, clothing, and to buy them what was indispensable for their work, tools and oxen.

Goyo Yic felt the air of the night like rain. The frozen air of the night in the mountains is almost like rain. The trees escaped through the voyaging noise their branches produced in the wind, as if they too were fugitives. Goyo Yic slumped down in the dew-soaked grass, aching, put his hat over his face, and went to sleep.

The fireflies played at little candles in the darkness. If only

Goyo Yic could have seen one of those small greenish lights, the color of hope, which lit up his pockmarked face, quite dry and expressionless, like cowdung.

A guardabarranca carried off a forest in a trill. A mockingbird's trill returned it to its place. The guardabarranca with the aid of some trogons took it further, quickly. The mockingbird, reinforced by woodpeckers, restored it in a flash. Guardabarrancas and mockingbirds, water trogons and woodpeckers, hangnests and troupials, fetched and carried forests and stretches of forest, as the dawn came.

The burning heat of the sun woke up the blind man. Great stones, thornbushes, eyelashes of dry forest passed by in the distance, but he felt them in his fingers. He felt them through his fingertips, which touched everything that surrounded him from afar. The echo of the flock of grackles in the silk-cotton tree down in Pisigüilito kept flapping around the valley below. Trees do not breathe the same way when they are planted close to ravines. He found the path on his right. The sound of lizards in the brush. The promise of fresh grass in the smell of the water in the irrigation dam as he came out on the high road. The old amate and Goyo Yic together again, only now he was a Goyo Yic without his woman and his children, together again after a day without seeing one another, for the amate saw him with the flower hidden in its fruit, and the blind man saw with eyes to which the flower of the amate was visible.

The first almspiece that day was a hot little worm which dropped from the end of some bird. Yic put his hand to his nose and loosed a shower of insults as he smelled it was bird-shit. A bad day, perhaps. He wiped the palm of his hand on the grass and stretched it out again, moving away from the amate step by step, to be nearer the road.

A muletrain's bell set Goyo Yic's teeth on edge, ringing like a crooked hoe. By the gait of the beasts and the mood of the muleteers he could tell whether they were on their way out or coming back. If they were heavily laden they were headed for town or for one of the villages round about, and if they were unladen they were on their way home. If they were bent beneath the weight of the loads, horses and mules would sink their hoofs in the earth, and the muleteers would get through to them with blinder lashes, insults and screeches; and if they were riding back empty, the movement of the hoofs was quick and rhythmic, and the muleteers would give free rein to idle talk, with horselaughs and cheerful bantering. You can tell whether a muleteer is coming or going, on the road, silent on the way out and jaunty on the way back.

Processions of oxcarts filed before Goyo Yic's flat nose. Tooluk, tooluk, the flapping of the wheels, the slow-treading hoofs of the stubborn beasts, and the ringing shouts of the carters, echoing "Ox! Piebald ox! Ox, ox!" and not only did they make the echoes ring, they disturbed the clouds, enormous white oxen, so the blind man had been told, to explain to him what the clouds were like.

"Whoa! Whoa! Clumsy ox! Whoa, forward, damn you!" The sticks sounded like snapping guitar strings on the docile backs of the oxen, or like taps on an empty skull when they struck them on the crown to make them back up, so the cart could move backwards.

Tortilla sellers with their babies in shawls on their backs and a basket carried on a roundlet upon their heads, and those who had no child, with their shawl around the basket in the form of a curtain which fell on either side of their ears to shield them from the force of the sun, a gaily colored shift, petticoats and underskirts tucked up into their skirts, and very clean bare feet which scarcely touched the ground as they went running by. Goyo Yic could tell them by their quick, continuous pat-pat-pattering gait, as though they were making tortillas of earth, and because they would catch their breath with the gasp of a woman milling maize as she changes the rhythm of her hand on the grindstone.

110

On the way back from Pisigüilito they no longer ran, they came back step by step and stopped to talk, as though they were waiting out the evening. Goyo Yic would listen to them, giving no sign of life, afraid they would fly away like birds. To hear them speak was better than charity now, in his solitude, when to hear a voice in his house he had to talk himself, and it's not the same at all when you talk to yourself, it's a human voice, but it's the human voice of a madman.

"You seem in a hurry, Teresa."

"Sell anything?"

"A bit, how about you? What are you selling?"

"The same."

"What was your price?"

"Ten tortillas a peso. Didn't you sell any?"

"I didn't get any maize ready last night. I took cooked chayote. Señora Ildefonsa did, too. What's that you're eating?"

"Mango."

"What about your friends, then?"

"How can I offer you some if I only bought the one, and anyway, it ain't so good. Have you heard, Señor Goyo has been left alone, all by himself."

"I did hear something. His woman ran away with the kids."

"Is that all they know?"

"They've gone down to the coast, that's the way they were headed."

"I wonder why she did it?"

"She got fed up with him. I expect it was because he kept her pregnant all the time."

"He must be jealous."

"Blind men always are."

"Yes, 'cause when you see something you ain't jealous, you can see it."

"But she didn't run off with no man."

"No, she just took the children. She'll find someone else, though, 'cause Goyo's eyes will stop him going after her."

"Yes, he's good and blind. I liked the woman, I don't mind telling you. Quiet, hard-working, and goodhearted. You could see she was long-suffering. The name María suited her, because of her fair skin. María Tecún. Fair-skinned and redheaded."

The blind man blinked, blinked, blinked, standing stockstill, bathed in cold sweat, his head sunk in his shoulders, his ears flapping. And to make his presence known he lifted his voice:

"Alms for the love of God, for a poor blind man. Alms, charitable souls, for the Mother of God, the Holy Apostles, Holy Confessors, Holy Martyrs," and hearing the soft steps along the road getting longer, with the sound of starched petticoats, he took hold of his hands and pinched them until it hurt, muttering between his teeth, "Bitches, they do it on purpose, talking like that when they see me, about María Tecún, talking and talking and talking, saying things a man can't make out . . . Curse them . . . Brazen slatterns, scum . . ."

XI

The road wasn't wide enough for the pilgrimage of the Second Friday. As rivers rise, so the people rose, and as rivers overflow their banks the pilgrims overflowed to reach Pisigüilito across stubblefields, fences of stone upon stone, flatlands of chilacayote and guava trees. The blind man wearied of hearing so many people passing and passing all day and all night and of repeating unto nausea his prayers for alms. People. People. People from the highlands smelling of wool, crags, and black poplars. People from the coast stinking of salt and sea sweat. People from the east, made of hillside earth, giving off an odor of tobacco, dry cheese, yucca paste and corn starch, and people from the north smelling of drizzle, mockingbird cages, and boiled water. Some had journeyed from the fractured lands of the peaks laid waste by maizegrowers and washed by winter; others from lofty tablelands with fertile fields like chicken breasts; and others from the stony stretch of the land by the sea, horizonless, torrid, steaming with heat, blinded fields to be sown and resown thanks to the floods of rain that pour down on them. But as the "Hymn to the Precious Blood of Christ" began, local differences were at an end, and those from the cold lands, the temperate lands and the hot lands, those in sandals and those in boots, dwarfs and giants, poor men and people with saddlebags and purses bursting with silver, they all sang in unison:

> *Down your glorious side*
> *flowed the rubies divine,*
> *and in the silent sky*
> *they hung like drops of wine.*

Goyo Yic abandoned the amate tree as soon as the pilgrimage of the Second Friday was over, a festival he made good use of to collect money. In a handkerchief a yard across he tied several knots for the coins: more half pesos than pesos, more quarters than halves, and the odd note. His knees rubbed hard by kneeling, a cramping of bones and muscles in his arm from keeping it outstretched, his tongue sleeping after mumbling incoherent prayers in concubinage with oaths against stray dogs, a mask of dust over his bony face, thus he was and thus he went. He didn't wait for the first rains to wash him down. He abandoned the amate, which was his pulpit and his tribune, before the first drops of water round and heavy as silver coins came to prune the pilgrimage of the Second Friday.

> *Down your glorious side*
> *flowed the rubies divine,*
> *and in the silent sky*
> *they hung like drops of wine.*

113

The flat spoons of Goyo Yic's old man's fingernails could not untie the double knot round the fifth little money goiter in his handkerchief and, cursing and grunting, he had to put his teeth to it. He almost tore the discolored cloth of the handkerchief, which was so dirty it was more like a kitchen rag, and from his mouth, as the knot gave, the last coins leaped just as though he'd spat them into the volcano of nickel he had in the bottom of his hat, between his legs, sitting with his back to the road facing a rock. He spent a long while counting and recounting. Quarters the size of the nails on his little fingers, half pesos like the nails on his middle fingers, and big peso coins the size of his thumbnails. He worked things out. No need to go mad paying Señor Chigüichón Culebro. He set a bit aside here, a bit there, and once that was done he tied the handkerchief in knots again, and went on his way, guiding himself by the directions people gave him, to find the house. Rocks, floodwaters, trees, roots, ranchos with people, twists and turns, until he went across an old stone bridge.

Señor Chigüichón Culebro's house was no distance at all from the bridge. He stumbled across it, for the surface was uneven, by a matasano grove. The enveloping smell of the matasano trees told Goyo Yic he was there. He sniffed like a dog, to be sure it really was the place, and because he liked to fill himself with the smell of those deliciously perfumed fruits. As he finished crossing the bridge he bumped straight into the house he was looking for.

"Because you see only the amate flower you want to be cured to see all the other flowers, too. How dark is your ingratitude, vengeance and blindness from birth are alike, black as bitter molasses! You who have been granted the endless years of eternity by the amate where you stand to beg, support and shade, you want me to make your sight better to stop you seeing the flower of the amate, the flower hidden within the fruit, the flower only blind men see."

"Well, it ain't exactly for that reason," Goyo Yic cut in, making a ridiculous movement with his head to get his bearings and find the exact place where the herbalist was, where he was speaking hoarsely, so hoarsely no human ear ever heard anyone speak so hoarse, "that ain't exactly it, and besides, no one could ever get by without being a little bit ungrateful, and there are many ungrateful people, very ungrateful, very, very ungrateful, Señor Chigüichón, and they still get their own way."

"I always told you I'd cure your blindness if it was the right kind, but you never wanted it, because you were scared: you preferred to go round with two bags of worms instead of eyes, worms that ooze cheese water. We'll have to see if there's still time to cure your trouble, because even sickness has its time, my son, and we can't always do the things we want to do."

"I want you to tell me how much it'll cost, so I'll know if the pesos I collected at the pilgrimage of the Second Friday will be enough. I've brought them with me for you, see . . . But I don't know if they'll go far enough."

"You mustn't think you can be cured just like having a tooth pulled, people like you who see only the flower of the amate, Goyo Yic. First we have to know where the moon is, that round cemetery where the ashes of the Holy Mother and Father lie buried. We have to know whether the air in the beehives is like a cat among the eucalyptuses, or whether it is fretful; if the former, favorable, if not, no, because beehive air turns the atmosphere to honey and for this cure we need air that isn't sticky. And I shall have to see again what kind of blindness you have, because there are many kinds: blindness from birth, blindness from a black spine prick, from worms that wound without your ever realizing it, because they get in the blood and wound you treacherously. The easiest to cure is white blindness. You can remove it from the eyes just like the yarn from a spool. That's what it is, a thread that got tangled up all at once from a sudden chilling of the eyeball, or little by little, over the years. And to cure it you have to keep unwinding the person's eyeball until you leave it like a spool with no thread. It hurts terrible, it's like putting chili on an open wound."

"No matter how much it hurts, I'll thank you to do it for me if I can be cured, because it's sad to see only the flower of the amate when you have feelings and you're hurt worse even than you've described."

Señor Chigüichón Culebro bent over to count the blind man's money on a grindstone on the edge of the verandah, a utensil he used to sharpen his carpentry tools. It was his custom to count his cash on the grindstone. To sharpen it up, he said, half smiling and half serious, so it will cut through the pockets of misers and scratch the hands of swindlers.

Goyo Yic, whose clothes were in threads as though he were dressed in old banana leaves, with his straw hat broken at the crown through which his hair stuck out like a weed, looking for the herbalist with a movement of his milky eyelids, said, "Forgive me making out I'm brave, saying I don't care how much it hurts, but it's the truth: I'd let myself be roasted alive to get my eyes, and be cured."

"Night dew blindness can also be cured," the herbalist went on explaining; after counting out the nickel coins he felt the blind man's eyes to get hold of the exact spot where the evil was, kneading the baggy skin of Yic's eyelids with his fingers. "You can cure white blindness, or night dew blindness, or gust of wind . . ."

Goyo Yic relaxed, content to be in those hands at last, as if rather than hurting him as they squeezed his eyes so hard, they were tickling and caressing him, listening to the chewing sound the herbalist left all around him, chomp chomp with his teeth, as he rolled a lump of pig's-ball copal, soft and very white, from cheek to cheek. Between the eyes of Goyo Yic and the copal thunderbolt he was chewing, Señor Chigüichón Culebro seemed to be establishing a kind of salivous relationship.

"Sooner or later," he went on explaining, "the white blindness strikes women who are ironing and suddenly have to go outside, it clouds their eyes as the air strikes them, be better if it struck that dripping moss they hang out, for down there they have no eyes, or if they went out before they felt the need

116

so bad, because they wouldn't have to rush out at the last moment, without covering their eyes. And for what you have, Goyo Yic, there is nothing so good as a scraping with a razor, or the milk from that forest of bluish leaves and stems, yellow flowers made of butterfly wings, and little spring fruits which are the food of doves."

"I'll lodge here if I may," said the blind man, smarting from the examination given him by the herbalist, putting his fingertips to his eyes, as if to say to them: I'm here, don't be afraid, this gentleman is going to cure you, make you better, make you clean again.

"Yes, you can stay here, and if you want a bite to eat, just ask in the kitchen."

"God bless you, I thank you for the favor."

And there Goyo Yic stayed, among dogs and the mastication of the herbalist, which in the silence of the night seemed to fill the whole house. Never, as he listened to the crickets outside and the rats running inside, never had Goyo Yic been so intent on the noise of copal resin being chewed, rhythmically, just like a clock. There are sun clocks, sand clocks, and pendulum clocks. The herbalist was a copal clock. Each squeezing of the copal brought him closer to the moment when he would be cured. At times Goyo Yic would move his own mouth, but it was his thoughts that he was chewing: she was no good, no good, no good, María Tecún, María Tecún was no good, no good, no good . . . If she was here, why would I be exposing myself to having my eyes cut with a razor. He took fright. It's no joke to be scraped with a razor. He sat up. The chewing of his heart rose to his ears: no *good*, no *good*, no *good*. He was on a heap of straw with the smell of harvesting hands, summer sun, hoofs of untied horses. He could hear someone sawing and planing wood close by, he didn't know where, above his head, over his shoulder, on his hands, on his face, on his knees, on his feet. Maybe Señor Chigüichón Culebro was making a coffin to bury him in. He must have realized he had more money than he'd said. He took hold of the handkerchief full of little coin goiters, just like a strip of intestine. He didn't care about death. He was afraid of being buried alive, carrying within his heart, like the fruit of the amate, the hidden flower of an ungrateful woman, the black flower of a perjuress. In his desperation Yic imagined that when he opened his eyes, after he was cured, María Tecún would be before him. She was what he wanted to see, first and always. The light, things, people, nothing else was important. Her, that no-good woman, the one he found among the headless Zacatones, the one he brought up and later made pregnant. The copal chewing of Chigüichón continued, and when it wasn't the chewing it was the sawing, and when it wasn't the sawing it was the planing. Her Zacatón body collapsed abruptly in his wandering dream, because she was not María Tecún, that no-good, but María Zacatón. He named her with the name Tecún because it was the Tecunes who cut off the heads of all the Zacatones. He lay somewhere between waking and sleeping in the canes of a cot trembling with the song of birds which were not birds, but beguiling words. He smiled in his sleep. Him afraid of a coffin. On the edge of ravines, along lonely paths, from the mountaintops he had called on death since she ran away from home, with his children, María Tecún.

The herbalist woke him before dawn, and in a very quiet voice, perceptible to his blind man's ear alone, he informed him that he had prepared the carpet of sawdust and shavings they needed to suck the freshness from the morning star. And he helped him up, and led him by the arm.

"We," he went on telling him in a very quiet voice, "are in the land of sawdust and shavings, and my body will be your stick. We must kill the pimento berry, step on it, disembowel it. I do not hear your footsteps, nor do the steps of your stick make any sound. We spit and we do not hear the saliva fall to the ground, as though we were spitting over the edge of a ravine. Where are we going? Or, or, or . . . where are we walking with our feet thus unsupported, in a ravine?"

The blind man heard the sky palpitate like some feathered

118

creature, and a strange itching troubled his groin and nipples, as if his sweat were eating away his courage as acid corrodes metal.

"We must go," the herbalist's deep voice pushed the blind man along step by step, "in search of a razor to clean Goyo Yic's vision, the plant that gives green islands to cover his eyes with two green islands after the cleansing, the swallowwort drops to refresh his eyelids, and the polypody, the contrayerva, and the prickly poppy, in case of need. And we bend"—the herbalist pressed the blind man's spine to make him lean forward—"until our heads touch the good earth, and we cannot see what the land of sawdust and shavings is like, because we cannot see, and our foreheads become rough and grimy like an animal's crown. And our hands frolic like dogs," the herbalist continued in his hoarse, majestic voice, tickling the blind man, "playful, rolling in contentment, for now, with black watermelon teeth, the darkness is coming out of her house."

More steps, and a long pause in which the ballock of copal thundered several times more, a vegetable paste in which his teeth were nailed as far as the gums, to free themselves at once, then be nailed again, and quickly freed, more quickly, more quickly yet, in an imprisoning and liberation of the jaws which resembles a jump. Someone who has the knack gives the impression, not of chewing, but of jumping, of jumping along.

"We have been deceived! Where is the moon? Only flies buzz in this the house of Madam Watermelon of the black teeth. Flies that bite, flies that fly, flies that talk and say: the laboring fingers of these two men dig with their shovels, their nails, into the cloud of sawdust and shavings that play, tremble, scatter beneath the breath which flies from their nostrils as from a double-barreled shotgun."

The herbalist took Goyo Yic's undernourished body in his arms. Goyo Yic quivered like a blind arrow in the bow of a great destiny. He lifted him from the ground and dropped him so he would fall abandoned to his own weight, and began to wrestle with him, shouting hoarsely:

119

"We are enemies, blind immensities at war like men who kill one another among towers and fortresses, we have lost the gleam of the bird that stole the light and left us in the darkness waiting for the armies of sleep and dream which will return defeated from the cities. The Moor has given us his scimitar with bees-honey, the Christian his sword with Credo honey, and the Turk has cut off his own ears to sail in them and arrive by unknown seas to die in Constantinople."

And still struggling with the blind man, who was protesting, not altogether sure that this was a make-believe fight, he added, yet more hoarsely:

"Goh, goh, goh! The rain is born old and weeps like a newborn child. She is an old girl. The moon is born blind and weeps to see us, but cannot see us. She is the size of a fingernail when she is born, a nail with which she gradually peels the skin of darkness from her eyes, as the nail of the razor will cut the eyes of Goyo Yic."

Once the ceremony was over, Culebro lay the blind man down on a carpenter's bench to tie him with the symbolic lianas. The brown liana which will prevent the patient's wounds from festering, because it grows around the tobacco plant; the mottled liana to stop the cords snapping under the efforts he will make when he starts to choke with pain; the moist liana, of green vegetable gossamer, to keep his tongue from going down his throat; and the liana of his mother's umbilical cord. After the symbolic lianas, which weren't really meant to hold him down at all, came the toughest part for the blind man. The thongs tying him to the bench began to hurt. While talking of symbolic lianas the herbalist had been passing thongs around his chest, arms and legs, which he was now pulling tight so that Yic couldn't move, he had to remain motionless while his eyes were scraped with the razor.

The herbalist began the operation with half a dozen of those sharp green vegetal scalpels at the ready, cutting, scraping, blowing on his patient's eyes to help him bear the pain. Like a tied, defenseless animal, the blind man let out cavernous roars in which were mingled not only cries of pain but also shouts of "no good," which had almost become María Tecún's second name.

He wet himself with the pain. The razor came down again. Deep strokes of the blade sinking down into the flesh to cut at consciousness, leaving the human mass shuddering endlessly. His jaw began to twitch and his breathing grew heavy.

Culebro scraped harder. The blind man loosed a sound like the screeching of a cat burning over a slow fire, rigid from head to toe, his arms and legs like poles for tying nets beneath the tight, trembling thongs. His nose bled. He could smell it. As he did so, the blood went back up his nose and all but choked him. He nearly sneezed but couldn't. The nervous itch of a cough and he couldn't cough. He used his saliva to water down the blood a little.

After the third scraping with the razor the herbalist softened his stern voice and said, "The film is beginning to move when I blow, just like skimming the cream off milk, so we'll go straight on and take it off by twirling it round a spine. If you can bear it just a little longer, the worst will be over."

With astounding surgical skill the herbalist began to wind the little white membranes which covered Yic's eyes around the spine. His fingers seemed bigger and coarser performing such a delicate operation: unstitching the film from a blind man's eyes. As soon as he had finished removing the milky membranes from the left eye, he covered it with a green leaf and set about removing the membrane from the right eye. With a deft movement he took the green leaf off the left eye and sprinkled drops of spurge juice in both of them, after which he covered up the two poor scraped eyes with the same thick green leaves and skillfully bandaged his face and head with long supple strips of fresh bark until, when it was finished, he looked like a large bundle the size of a cheese.

As the thongs were loosened, the blind man let out a deep sigh. He was unconscious. Chigüichón lifted him with special care, to move him to the darkest room in the house, where he

121

left him lying in a folding cot, with no pillow, and lots of bedclothes, two ponchos, three ponchos, so he wouldn't catch cold. Tomorrow he would give him a verdigris bath. And if he caught a fever . . .

Yic slowly recovered consciousness, with the nausea produced by the acute pain, and a fever. The herbalist, three days after the razor scraping, gave him a purgative of loofah, and placed a good number of floripondio flowers beneath his head to help him sleep—sleep is the great remedy—with some infusions of red guarumo, to keep his heart active. Some Jerusalem thorn did him good. It cleared the blood he had swallowed from his stomach. Still to come was a purgative of fireflower, after seven days. And then little doses of passionflower water, refreshing and sleep-inducing.

"No good, no good, no good!" was all that Goyo Yic could manage to say. He no longer said it, it was just a bagasse of thought, a "gd" buzzing on his lips, and between his teeth, which ached to the very roots when the itching in the living flesh of his eyes began to come on strong. He clawed at the petate with his fingernails in the moments of greatest desperation.

On the ninth day he got up. Culebro made him. He took the bandages off his head now, but he had to stay indoors. In such cases the light is more dangerous than a knife. Four days and nights he stayed in the dark, until the thirteenth day, when Chigüichón took him out on the verandah, in the late afternoon. In the peaceful sun that was falling, timorous, sad, long as a whip, he gazed at things with their damp shine of surfaces he didn't know, and which seemed so funny to him.

"You have to know where the brittle stage is with your eyes, it's like boiling sugar," Chigüichón warned.

The blind man looked at Chigüichón, who made the same sonorous impression on him as the water of the Waterspout, when he went there with María Tecún. That was what the herbalist was like. He looked at him, but the association with water making its mortal leap among the rocks was something he couldn't get out of his head. He was not a man. He was the sound of water. For him he was not visible. He was sonorous. He would remain a being represented by a loud noise.

The herbalist left him alone. He had to get into the habit of using his eyes, instead of going about with his eyes open, then looking at things, yet not daring to move without first stretching out his hand, as if still guided by touch. The noise of the rapids he could hear falling between the crags, dragging everything down in the rising flood, had just merged, in inundating transparence, with something finer than the milled water he had in the two little gourds of his eyes, a film of water that vibrated without sound, present even when he covered his ears. Two sprays of tears drowned his vision. He wept with his breast bursting with gratitude. He stretched out a hand to touch a stool, steady it with his touch, and sit down. When he was blind, he had never attained the maternity of touching things, as he had now, now that he was seeing them, because he had known their exact position in relation to his body. When he was blind he used to chase pigs through stinging nettles and barbed-wire fences, and he never burned himself on the nettles or tore his clothes on the wire. A little thrush landed on the edge of the verandah, in front of him, as he sat himself silently down on the stool, who knows what for, he had nothing to do, except get well again. The little bird—it looked more like a fallen leaf—came, stopped, gave three hops, and flew away. Minimal. Nervous. An electrified coffee bean. His eyes flew away, too, eyes which, now they had emerged from their shells, would always be running away from him. He sighed in profound appreciation of the life communicated to him by those little windows opened in his face. Flesh, bone, and landscape. He gazed at the trees. For him the trees were hard at the bottom and soft at the top. And so they were. The hard part, the trunk, which before he had touched and now he saw, corresponded to black, brown, dark, whatever you call it, and established, in some elemental fashion, that inexplicable relationship between the opaque shade of the tree trunk and

123

the hardness of it as he grazed his hand across it. The soft part up above, the branches, the leaves, corresponded exactly to the green, light green, dark green, bluish green, that he now saw. The soft upper part used to be sound, not a surface he could touch, and now it was a green vision in the air, just as far away from his touch, but imprisoned now not in sound, but in form and color.

His first walk from the herbalist's house was down to the bridge. He closed and opened his eyes seeing the water full of little mouse squeaks among great stones that stuck out like hands winding skeins, the violent liquid skeins which bounced from side to side sending up waves of foaming saliva in as much abundance as the herbalist chewing on his thunderbolt of copal. All that water went journeying away beneath the walled bridge, bulwarks which looked like oxen straining not to be carried along. Oxen with the yoke of the bridge on top of them. You couldn't see the water going, but it went, comparable only with time, which passes without us noticing: as we always have time, we don't realize we are always short of it, was how Culebro explained it to him.

The herbalist returned with a handful of fuchsias in his giant hand. The contrast between that great boxing glove and those delicate flowers like vegetal earrings, some with red calyxes and double white corollas, others with purple corollas, or blue corollas and pink calyxes. The herbalist looked them over like a jeweler or a goldsmith. He shook his head. The fuchsias made him think about the mystery of life, the creator of beauty. Why were they conceived, those holy flowers the Virgin Mary used as pendants? The maize grows for man to eat, hay so the horses can feed, grass for the beasts of the field, fruits to delight the birds; but fuchsias are merely exquisitely colored ornaments, living pieces of porcelain in which the wisest of artists has blended the simplest of colors. He would come to the end of his days, chewing a ballock of white copal, without making it out. If a man does something it's so people will praise him, but nature produces those flowers in places where no one will see them. A man who had created those porcelain miniatures with all the secrets of low relief coloring and let them wither away, without ever taking them out of his studio, would be called a madman, an egotist, and he too would feel, his talents going thus unappreciated, that his efforts had been cut short, in vain. Those flowers blooming in vain caused anguish in Chigüichón Culebro.

The herbalist left Goyo Yic on the bridge watching the river flow, butterflies flutter, the odd hare jump, followed by another, and a stag flash by swift as a meteor. He gazed lethargically, wandering, without thinking, along the road that would take him back home, when he stumbled, not on anything material, but you could see he had stumbled against something by the gesture he made as he took hold of the parapet, like when he was blind, and by the ash that swept over his face. With great big strides, stumbling back across the bridge, against stones and bushes, against the trunks of the matasanos, against everything in his way, he went back to the herbalist's house.

"Either he's gone blind again or he's gone mad," pronounced Culebro, standing up on the verandah which overlooked the road, waiting for him to get there. At least that was where he was headed. Both things were possible. Some illnesses are more dangerous during convalescence. Reckless people never get well. And Yic was one. Through pleading with him and threatening him, he had managed to keep him there a few days after the cure which, in truth, had been miraculous. To go, go, go, but where, he didn't know. After a razor scraping you have to take it easy, because a flash of light, or an evil air, can bring back the blindness, and then there is no cure will cure it. And the danger of madness as a result of the operation was very real. To avoid it he had treated him with "verdegrease," or hellebore.

Goyo Yic didn't make it to the verandah, he fell and slid like a lifeless body down the earth slope which led up from the road to the steps. A maizefield scarecrow with glass eyes, open,

125

clear, shining. Culebro ran down, wondering "what's got into him," and arrived just in time, before Yic, half crazed, could dig his nails into his eyes, into his newborn pupils, still fresh with the smell of dew and early morning light.

His fingers were like scorpion claws entangled in his locks, as Chigüichón took hold of his wrists. He ground his teeth and closed his lips of tough dried beef. His eyes were no use to him. He didn't know María Tecún, who was his amate flower, he had seen her only as a blind man, inside the fruit of his love, as he called his children, a flower invisible to the eyes of one who sees from outside and not from within, flower and fruit in his closed eyes, in his loving darkness which was hearing, blood, sweat, saliva, a quivering of the spine, a choking for breath which turns to hair, something like the nipple of a lemon in the half light, a baby which leaps into life on the end of a firework-maker's smoking agave fuse, and the gourds of the breasts already filled with milk, and the weeping with the first attack of wind, and the fever from evil eye, and the chili rubbed around the granular nipples to wean it from the breast, and crude animals made of feathers to frighten someone who should now be eating tortillas and drinking black bean soup, black as life itself. And he did not depart from that well of darkness filled with weeping until the water dried out inside him, and he felt thirsty.

The herbalist persuaded him it would be easy to find her, because he knew her by ear.

"You know her better than anyone else you may hear . . ."

"Maybe you're right," Goyo Yic replied, not really convinced.

"Better than anyone else, you'll come across her somewhere. She's the one who ain't going to know you, even if you swear it's you, with your eyes cured."

"God bless you for that . . ."

And as Goyo Yic moved off from the herbalist's house, not only Señor Chigüichón Culebro, with his ballock of copal between his teeth, shining white copal and shining white teeth,

126

but also the river beneath the bridge, his forgotten homeland, for as he crossed it he forgot it, the gusting, changeable wind, the muletrains, the oxen, the cartwheels, the echoing voices of horsemen riding through the dense overgrowth, everything seemed to be repeating in his ear: better than anyone else, better than anyone else, better than anyone else . . .

XII

Each woman stopped beneath the portico to lift her shawl over hair strummed by the wind from the mountains, each man paused briefly to spit out the butt of a maize-leaf cigarette and take off a hat like a cold tortilla. They were frozen, like hailstones. The church, inside, was a mass of flames. The confraternities, men and women, the oldest of them with bands round their heads, held small bundles of candles between fingers streaming sweat and hot wax. Other candles, a hundred, two hundred, were burning on the floor, fixed directly to the ground, on islands of cypress branches and choreque petals. Other candles of various sizes, from highborn ones with silver paper decorations and votive offerings pinned to them, down to the smallest tapers, waxes of more value, in candleholders which looked like tinplate flowerpots. And the candles at the altar adorned with pine branches, pacaya leaves. In the center of all this veneration stood a wooden cross painted green and spotted with red to represent the precious blood, and a white altar cloth draped hammock-style over the arms of the cross, also spotted with blood. The people, the color of hog-plum bark, motionless in front of those rigid timbers, seemed to root their supplications in the holy sign of suffering with a whispering of leached ashes.

"And this I ask of you, Holy Cross"—and the man who

127

prayed in this way raised up his hands and made the sign of the cross with both—"and this, and this, Holy Cross, and this: either you separate them peaceable, I don't like my son-in-law, or I'll separate them the other way. If they turn up at my house together, my daughter will become a widow!"

"For his own evil ends he took out a title to the plot that was mine, handed down by my father, so I ask you, Holy Cross, to get him out of my way, make him die a natural death, or I'll get rid of him myself for sure. See how good it would be, my little Cross, if you got rid of that swindler for me!"

"The shaking of the earth tremor blinded the waterholes all round these parts, and there ain't no more springs anywhere, it's better down there where there's less snakes, less curses, less sickness. If you send me down there this year, I'll come back next year on the pilgrimage, I swear to God I will, for your sake, Holy Cross of May, and if I don't carry out my promise you can punish me: I'll accept the punishment, but send me down there, do!"

"Better if the boy could die, Holy Cross of May, 'cause there's no cure for him, like a blind chicken, like paste gone black, who knows what he's got in his body, there's no life left in him, he's done for, ain't no medicine can help him."

They looked up at the cross covered in river water, in volcanic lava, in chicken's blood, hen's feathers, maize silk, seeing it as something domestic, functional, solitary along the roads, valiant in the face of the storm, the devil and his thunderbolts, the hurricane, the plague and death, and they went on praying with the low murmur and even the acrid smell of leaching ashes, until their tongues were like loofahs, their knees deadened from so much kneeling, their hands dripping the white smallpox from the candles they held in bundles, their eyes like liana grapes.

The clatter of shoes as they entered the church, the weeping of babes in arms carried pickaback in white sheets by their Indian mothers, an interminable chiming of bells and firing of rockets, and once again, the Holy Cross carried in procession from the church to the confraternity, as if by lame people, such was its erratic motion as it swayed between lines of confreres and women, women, confreres and children, who then followed behind in a buzzing swarm.

Between the moving cross and the immovable church, in a space of sky and field that seemed to be measuring the ringing, lay fields plowed ready for maize planting, live fences of blossoming yuccas, tufts of long moss woven by spiders of turpentine, ranchos like curled worms, a few houses with tiled roofs and white walls, and around the pump of the dark-painted square, the stunned color of the air beneath the silk-cotton tree, fair stalls spread out beneath cypress fronds, petate awnings held up by three poles, or colored sheets knotted to four bamboo canes and blown up by the wind like balloons.

Goyo Yic went into the church at Santa Cruz de las Cruces with the weeping of his open eyes on display. He could not kneel down. He staggered forward and fell headlong. The few worshippers who had remained in the church seeing to the candles started to laugh.

"What color is weeping?" he shouted, stretched out on the ground, and in the same shout, with the very ache of his weeping, he replied, "It is the color of white rum!"

A leader of a confraternity, in a blue frieze jacket with six rows of buttons on the sleeves, and two assistants dressed in cloak, shirt and breeches, took him out of the church, dragging him by the arms to the portico, where he lay like some sort of rubbish, gradually covered over with flies.

The voices of women arriving at the church or crossing nearby, chattering away, made him shake himself, complain, stretch out an arm, pull in a leg. He was searching for María Tecún, but in the recesses of his consciousness he searched for her no longer. He had lost her. To get women to speak, he knew María Tecún only by ear, he had become a peddler. Roads, towns, fairs . . .

"Mirrors, my girls, pretty little mirrors! Combs! Soaps! Florida water for florid young ladies! Almanacs, fine yarn, ribbons, pearl earrings! Lovely bracelets, handkerchiefs, pencils, writing paper for lovers, pins, needles, and look at these little bottles of perfume: heliotrope, Japanese, or rose water! Here, take it, I'm not overcharging you, young lady, you asked for the expensive kind! Crucifixes made of pilgrim's plaster! . . ."

They all talked, made offers, inquiries, sorting through the trinkets, until they bought something. Others placed orders. If he came back that way and could remember, would he bring some prettier shawlpins, buttons and spangles, silks and round sewing boxes. Some ordered the "Secretary of Lovers," and—did they dare—love potions, which don't allow neglect to ever come, and postcards with words of love and evocative names: Carmen . . . María . . . Luisa . . . Margarita . . .

He coaxed the older women, who just stood looking—his merchandise held precious little interest for them—with novenas, rosaries, basins of holy water, lockets, little black mantillas, ointments for rheumatism, tonic pills for lack of energy, naphthalene balls for the old age of things, camphor oil, ether pills, balsams against catarrh, miracle drops for toothache, whalebone stays for corsets . . .

"She was no good, María Tecún," he would say, as he tramped the roads, carrying all that rubbish in a big peddler's tray which he loaded on his back whenever he traveled, and carried just above his waist, in front of him, making use of a sweaty canvas strap with leather binding when he started work.

Returning at night to his lodging, during his wanderings through towns and fairs, stopping in every town where there was a fair, he gazed at his shadow by the light of the moon: a long stringy body, like a beanpod, and a tray in front level with the top of his stomach, it was like seeing the shadow of a she-opossum. The moonlight turned him from a man into an animal, an opossum, a female opossum, with a pouch in front of him to carry the babies in.

He let himself be bathed, one of those moonlit nights when everything looks just as it does by day, in the tree milk that

130

flows down from the machete cuts in the bark of the moon, that light of copal the wizards cook in receptacles of dream and oblivion. White copal, which is the mysterious white brother to rubber, the black brother, the darkness that jumps. And the man-possum jumped, white with moon, and his black rubber shadow jumped.

"You who are the patron saint of peddlers, O Possum, can lead me by the most winding of paths or by the straightest, to the place where María Tecún and my children are. For you know that a man carries his children in a pouch as the possum does, and he can't know their faces, nor hear their laughter, nor learn the speech they speak with new voices, until they've been in the nine by thirty days of the woman, until the mother throws them out, pushes them out of herself, and they emerge, among roots of cold humors and hot skins, just like possums, hairy, blackish and squealing. O Possum, help Goyo Yic the peddler, so that as soon as possible he may come upon the Tecún woman, her voice, her tongue vibrating in the air like a rattlesnake!"

Goyo Yic, in his world of thirsting water and bones to which the skin adheres painfully, changed position. The force of the sun was making him sweat, and mixed in with the sweat were the sobs of a drunkard who has failed to forget his misfortunes. The church was locked. The women's voices were no longer to be heard. But he lay sprawled in the portico loosing words without thread and waving his arms. In the fairs, everyone would stop alongside his stand, a sheet stretched out over four bamboo poles supported like a roof, not only to look through his eyecatching trinkets, but to see the little possum which hid its pointed head from the onlookers, women and children, mostly women. What kind of animal is it, they would ask the peddler, dissolving, almost all of them, in affectations and nervous gestures, with their big black eyes opened still wider to look at the possum, and the naked laugh of surprise, stretching out their hands without daring to touch it, through fear and disgust, for it looked rather like a large rat.

The peddler was pleased to have them all talking at once, that way he could listen to lots of female voices with no need to offer his wares as anything other than a bait to loosen their tongues, one day one of them, better than any other, would be María Tecún, every day was more promising than the last. He told them:

"It's a possum. I found it abandoned by the roadside, and took it along with me. It's brought me good luck and so I've kept it. Come rain or shine, it stays by me."

"What's its name?"

"Poppa-possum."

Then some of them would pluck up courage and touch its ears, calling, "Poppa-Possum! . . . Poppa-Possum!"

The possum would back away, fearful, glutinous, bristling. And the women would shiver and turn to the trinkets instead.

From fair to fair, among poncho-wearing traders in harnesses and saddles from the cold lands, Indians dressed in white, maize-leaf dolls who dealt in pans, chocolate mills, stirrers and fire fanners, and other Indians the color of pitch, dealers in achiote, garlic, onions, and seeds, and others, slight, malarial, sellers of sugar buns, grapefruit, candied orange peel, molasses with anise, and coconut candy, among these and all the others who turn up at fairs, Goyo Yic was known, rather than by his own name, by the nickname of Poppa-Possum.

"That's how I am, I don't get angry, least of all with pretty women: me Poppa-Possum, and you pretty-mamma," and what with fine words and sweet caresses, the woman agreed to go with him, just a little way. Muddy earth, the odd bush, and a small lake, where the clouds came down to drink. He had her pressed fast beneath his body until the early morning, he scarcely detached himself from her, between her and him there was room maybe for a machete blade. He who since María Tecún ran away had kept her there inside him, as if his pores had sealed over, him with another woman. There was little joy in it, and all there was left of him was his skin crushed between María Tecún, who was inside, and the woman he had outside.

The one he was with. And more than his other senses, his sense of smell. María Tecún's fine hair with its odor of dampened ocote embers, a deep lustrous red, and her breasts, like soft squashes, which covered her whole bosom, and her squirming groin. He smelt María Tecún in his insides and he felt the other woman outside him, beneath his body, in the middle of a night that was clear, star-filled, infinite. He closed his eyes and pressed down on her breasts to caress her, then pull himself up, and run. The woman made a sound of splintering teeth, grinding them, and of bones straining in their joints, stretching out, curling up, crushing her face with tears which interlocked the sorrow of sinfulness to her placid smile of contentment. One step this way and another that, through darkness that was shadows or earth piled up behind the awnings, canopies and canvas tents of the fair. The sky moved. It was extraordinary to see it going like a clock. Marimbas, guitars, accordions, and the throaty shouts of people singing the words of "The Rebels," "The One Who Sang to Saint Peter," "The Mermaid," "Dying for Her Kiss," "A Sting in the Tail," "Portrait of a Woman," or "The Tricolor Flag." He passed between the gaming stalls, lotteries, hoopla stands, wheels of fortune, between groups of people who moved as though they were magnetized, until he reached his tent, where the false treasures of his peddler's tray were secure under lock and key. He tossed a nickel coin to the fellow who had looked after it for him, and went straight in to look for the possum, to stroke it. Out of remorse. His hand felt inside the empty bag. A cold electric shock burned up his arm from his fingertips, for this time they had failed to find that little animal's close-cropped spine. He picked up the bag and crushed it in his hand. The possum had run away. He dropped the empty bag into his tray, and stood stock-still. The flower of the amate, transformed into the possum, had just left its fruit empty, escaping like María Tecún so that the man who was no longer blind would not see her, he who could now see other women. A woman who is truly loved cannot be seen, she is the flower of the amate seen only by the blind, the flower of blind men, men blinded by love, blinded by faith, blinded by life. He tore off his hat. There was a mystery. He lit a match to see the possum's tracks. They were clearly marked, though not very deep, light, on the very surface. He rubbed them out with his left hand and rubbed the dust on his fingers and palm over his face, over his tongue, which smelled of a woman who wasn't his own, and closed his eyes, searching in vain for the one whom now he would never find, either in reality or in that coffinlike darkness, the size of his body, closed in on him by his eyelids.

"You, Poppa-Possum, what are you going to give me for satisfying your need?"

Goyo Yic heard the woman's voice in the silence, that sense of uninhabitedness that fairs give as they fall still, and without more ado he picked up the tray, went to where the woman's outline showed against the white sheeting around his stall, and dumped it on top of her, the great glass-topped wooden box with all his wares in. The woman's dark silhouette which had looked like a black coffee stain behind the thin sheet, slid noiselessly away, as the bottles smashed to pieces, followed by the mirrors, necklaces, earrings, bracelets, cheap flasks of perfume, rosaries, thimbles, pins, needles, soaps, combs, unrolled ribbons, hairpins, handkerchiefs, crucifixes . . .

Run. Sure. He too was a possum. And he wandered the forest so long as a fugitive that he went black. Worse, being alone in the forest was driving him mad, and he kept getting caught up with María Tecún who, even though she was no good, deserved to be chatted to like that when there was no one else around. If he came across some little tree wearing a shawl of blossoms, he would stretch out his trembling hand. You are mad, he warned himself, and went on his way, deep in the forest, only to see his beloved tormentor once more in a spray of graceful water, he put his cheek to it to be tickled by the foam, so like the laughter of . . . she was no good. His spirits wilted through not seeing people, not seeing dogs: after all, dogs have something human about them. He ate whatever he could chew and swallow. Thick roots that tasted like raw potatoes, fruits the birds had pecked, so that he knew they weren't poisonous, fleshy leaves, and some little saplings the squirrels ate.

From a long way off that man who had been blind almost all his life could smell there was a town nearby. He could never have explained how it was things became materialized in the air, from a distance: what his eyes couldn't reach was there in his nose. And so he went down, field upon field, desperate to see people and eat hot food, to Santa Cruz de las Cruces, attaching himself to a train of wagons as it wound its way, lurching, down to the town. He found himself caught between the last cart and a group of men in masks. It was the great parade of the Fair of the Cross of Crosses. Dressed in festive red, green, yellow, black and purple, they were playing instruments, cracking whips, and dancing.

Goyo Yic, who was now little more than a skeleton with eyes, hair and teeth, followed the pirouettes and commentaries of the masked dancers with the rapture of a child. The ones with colored feathers on their heads were the kings, their hair and beards silver, their eyes with golden lids, and thick silvery lips. There were others wearing crowns and others with hats that looked more like baskets of rice-paper flowers. And in the midst of all these people, dancing, jumping, lashing at the spectators, came the bull-ring monkey, the monkey-in-the-hole, his eyes in red wheels and his mouth red with white teeth, with horns and a long tail.

Goyo Yic, Poppa-Possum, left the cart he had climbed on to be carried along, and mingled in the tumult and dust of those people whom the town of Santa Cruz de las Cruces welcomed as heralds of the greatest festival of the year. The parade entered the town between the stakes of a corral gate, followed by a crowd of children of all ages, the oldest with agave slings or other instruments of torture, down to the little snivelers, the bigger girls with heads decked in ribbons, like cows at a show, and the care-afflicted old ladies with hair the years had turned the color of thorns, and wrinkles of dried earth.

In the confraternity's large clean-swept courtyard smelling

of damp earth, water and earth mixed into the smell of the afternoon, beneath hog-plum trees heavy with fruits green as leaves, some just beginning to turn yellow, and avocado trees sad and somnolent to look at, they set up tables with glasses already filled: orgeat, with its soft smell of chufas, cinnamon water that seemed to soften and refine metal tumblers until they made one think of dark little horses, cool spice drinks shaken with aniseed, ginger, and sapodilla seeds, bittersweet, piquant. And in front of all these jugs of orgeat, cinnamon water and spice waters, rolls filled with black frijoles and grated cheese, others with pickles and lettuce, sardines, and enchiladas beneath storms of flies brushed parsimoniously away by the woman selling all that, a gaunt-faced, hollow-eyed mulatto woman.

At other tables—the confraternity was a religious market beneath the merry flight of grackles—stood other cooling drinks: chia made with little black salvia seeds which settled at the bottom of the glasses, and which the vendor stirred as she served it, a young woman who resembled María Tecún, little seeds that went revolving towards your throat, like some astronomical proof of the creation of the planets; rose water the color of poinsettias, sweet, honeyed; and pumpkin squash, a drink with a gulf-weed beard, and pips, small black pips.

At the back of all this rose the great bower of the altar, high at the front, low behind, like an enormous halo round a saint, dressed front and back all in pine needles, cypress and chilca fronds, pacaya leaves, festoons of angel's-hair with flowers like birds, and ripening fruits. The Holy Cross, patron of the confraternity, stood on a platform with a red curtain petticoat. In front of it, in candlesticks or on the brick floor—theirs was the only confraternity whose altar had a brick floor—yellow candles decorated with purple rice paper and scraps of gold stuck on with cotton wax, candles of all sizes, down to the humblest of tallows, dwarflike, but no less brilliant. Outside this celestial ring of candles, this bonfire of tiny seraph's tongues and little snakes of smoke, the altar itself, consisting of a long table

136

covered with a starched tablecloth. On this altar pilgrims and members of the brotherhood placed flowers, fruits, chickens, forest animals, doves, sweet corn, beanpods, and other gifts. At the center of this altar there was an alms dish, which was repeated on a table placed to the right, between long-necked, fat-bellied flagons of liquor, with yellow nances, lemon peel, cherries and fruits of other flavors forming a crystalline world in which the liquors seemed to sleep like transparent lizards, with the fixed laugh of dead men.

The marimba was waiting for six o'clock to strike. Goyo Yic, who was staring sorrowfully about him, with big possum eyes, offered to blow on the fire prepared for the firing of bombs and rockets at the foot of a very tall avocado tree with long spreading roots. The embers flexed their skin of fire as Goyo Yic fanned them with his hat. The fire reminded him of María Tecún. The heat of the fire in the hearthstones. If he waved his hat quickly over the flames, each brand became a live rattlesnake, if he idled with it the burning logs became dressed in scales of ash, scales lighter than air, for as he fanned diligently once more they flew up and away, leaving the bloody limbs of amputated trees in the corncob embering of the fire.

"She was no good, María Tecún . . ."

He had stopped fanning the fire and his thoughts were interrupted by the arrival of the men whose job it was to set the rockets and flying bombs. Hatless, their feet washed, with new clothes, colored shirts, glazed cotton handkerchiefs round their necks, and the insignia of the confraternity, which consisted, depending on their duties as overseers or assistants, of crosses of various sizes on rosettes of white or purple ribbon.

The hour was announced by a presentiment of birds that flew from neighboring trees when the team of men come to fire the rockets appeared just after the procession, ready to begin, a whinnying like small, maddened horses, the moment the vespertide bells rang out.

The bells chimed out at once. The sound rose up into the immense, soft, and admonishing silence of the evening, which poured pink depths and flaming red clouds over the mountain-tops.

And as the bells rang, the dark hands of the fireworkers released one, then another, another, another and still more rockets cleaving the purity of the air with the whine of a congested nose, then exploding high in the sky, others over the houses, and others, those which didn't take off successfully, between the fences and the ground. Meanwhile the flying bombs were set by lads still learning the ropes. When the projectile fell in the mortar with the end of the fuse left outside like a rat's tail, others, more experienced, put the brand to it and . . . boom . . . boom . . . boom . . . violent terraqueous explosions, followed by booming detonations high up in a vast sky now full of stars.

The night submerged Santa Cruz de las Cruces in its deep lake waters, to the height of the surrounding hills, with their necklace of bonfires. Goyo Yic, cold as a possum, kept on fanning and fanning at the fire with his poor old straw hat, for something to do, because the fireworks were over, and the firebrands had done their job.

All that remained of the six o'clock clamor was the lovelorn marimba beaten black and blue like trees when they beat them to knock down the fruit, like troublesome animals when they beat them just to teach them not to cause trouble and not to be lazy, like women when they beat them to keep them from running away, like men when the authorities beat them to knock out the manhood they have inside them. He no longer had any manhood inside him. He had become a possum, a she-possum which carried its children with it in the pouch of its soul. María Tecún had finished him. For good. Her and the herbalist who took out his own eyes and gave him possum's eyes.

Festival of Santa Cruz de las Cruces! For the sign of your fires that call on the water the troupials carry in their scrutinizing eyes. For the sake of the peasant who on your day becomes an exile from the earth and climbs up your mastlike arms, your bloodied sails, to call on God. For those who before your huts, in your streets, with litter, dry twigs and green branches light their fires to dream they have a red star at their feet. Lines of stout-bodied candles lash one another with tongues of fire before you, the mourner of life, formed of two destinies that crossed, that of God and that of man, among mortal enemies, denials, tempests, and a mother's rending cry. Holy Cross of Crosses, may the water come, may the kites come soon to trace their great winged crosses of shadow through the sky. Joy to him, Holy Cross of Crosses, who worships you, on your day, at your hour, in your moment! The deer, up there where they cannot be seen, but there they are, point their ears toward your festival of hunters who bring you the first catch. The trees know their richest fruits are to adorn this date on which the agony of the world has its birthday, and they push forth their sweetest sap with little knots of wooden will so it may be honey squeezed within the bark, and wasps with black stings which bring fever when they bite, turn into the miracle-working rings of bishops. Holy Cross of Crosses, married in a requiem mass to Jesus, you celebrate the risk taken by the man who tears himself away from the evil life and embraces you, body to body, not knowing whether he is embracing you or struggling against you, to be left thereafter just a skeleton's coat and hat, to frighten off the pigeons in the maizefields!

Night like a tamale wrapped in the green leaves of the mountains which formed the sacred bundle around the town of Santa Cruz de las Cruces. In front of the Holy Cross, in the altar branchery, the confreres danced to the marimba, all feeling as though their hearts had taken some dreadful shock. And to bring their hearts back into beat, they moved over to the table where the drinks stood and poured the contents of the flasks into small glasses, giving alms in exchange for liquor. Glugluglug the drink down the gullet, and the chinkchink of nickel, a nickel coin in the alms dish, and a bow to the Holy Cross.

Midnight. In the courtyard and around you could hear the

stamping of horses sleeping beneath the sky, see cooking fires blazing, ocote torches waving over stands selling drinks, bread, and hot chocolate, and groups of people, friends and relations, strolling quietly around, barefoot, their laughter so old it was scarred on their faces, the faces of bandaged ghosts.

Goyo Yic, after having some coffee, lent a woman a hand so she could put down a basket of greens and alfalfa, turkeys and chickens, she was carrying on her head. She stood looking at him in gratitude, the roasted pips of her eyes in a face pale with panting, her hair all awry from the roundlet, and between gasps, she let out a God-bless-you, in such a low voice that Yic could scarcely hear the sound. He helped her drag the basket off toward the hills. Yic's hand touched hers. His body began to tremble. But another God bless you broke the spell. No. It wasn't María Tecún. But how like her voice. He rubbed his back against a post, as the woman disappeared into the night. He heard her stop for a pee. But what use was that in recognizing his woman, if they all pee alike. The glow of the fires turned his head to gold, his lean coppery face orphaned from the motion of his body. In the darkness, air swathed in cobwebs, the cowherds smoked. Sneezes of flint on steel and the glow of maize-leaf cigarettes or loose-rolled cigars. Goyo Yic smoked with them and got drunk with them. They offered him a swig and he knocked back the whole bottle. Almost. Left just a drop.

"What are you trying so hard to forget, you, that you drink rum like that?" asked a cowherd with a face like an old sandal.

"Only that sadness turns you into some sort of possum," was his answer, but the liquor was already working through his blood, in his eyes, his movements and gestures.

"This one won't be on his feet again tonight," said another cowherd.

"You bet he won't," said another.

But Goyo Yic did stand up again, and he went walking and dancing all night, he couldn't have said where, until the next morning when he fell headlong inside the church, and was dragged out to lie beneath the portico.

Being parched made him stand up. The sun was now low in the sky. He had been lying in the portico all day, sometimes hearing women talking as they passed, sometimes unaware of anything. He stood up as best he could. His legs trembled. Straight to the pump in the square to drink water which stank of birdcage droppings. You have to suffer to bring yourself round.

"Right, then," a countryman taller than he came up to talk to him, "we'll set off today, the deal's all fixed, we put down half each, and we go halves on all sales; but we've got to be away early to give ourselves plenty of time."

Goyo Yic looked for his handkerchief, with its little goiters full of coins, but he didn't have it anymore. And moreover . . .

"You can stop searching, I looked after it for you, and here it is. Let's go, then. But we'll take some coffee for the road, if you like."

The man started walking and behind him, like a cripple, went Goyo Yic, just like a possum after some unknown fellow.

The coffee settled his stomach. Then he noticed, right then, that this new friend was carrying a demijohn on his back. At midday they went down to drink water, along a little footpath, to a stream. When they got back to the highway, his friend said, "Now you carry it . . ."

Goyo Yic heaved the demijohn onto his back and set off again. Not till then, carrying the empty demijohn, did he remember the deal, the agreement he'd made with his companion. He was curious to learn his name, and he asked him.

"Domingo Revolorio. So you don't remember all we said. How you hugged me and said yes, yes, yes, that I'd put down half the dough and you'd put half, that we'd buy the liquor and come back to Santa Cruz de las Cruces to sell it. The business is a profitable one, if we keep our word not to give anyone a free drink, whoever it is, even our best friend, even a relative of yours, or mine. Nothing given away. If they want it, they pay for it. Cash in hand, liquor in glass. Not even you or I can drink without paying for it. If you want to have yourself a swig, you pay me for it; if I want one, I pay you, and no matter that we're in business together."

It was late and Domingo Revolorio, in accordance with the agreement to share all expenses, work and income, took the demijohn until they reached a township where, ancient wisdom, they distilled excellent cane liquor in receptacles of adobe.

A gourd of boiling water and chili powder was all they had had to eat. So the first thing, therefore, on arrival, was to eat. Tortillas, cheese, frijoles, coffee. And a couple of drinks. They went in through a stable to a tavern which smelled of sancocho. They followed the smell. Domingo Revolorio came to an arrangement with the woman who owned it, and they ate and slept there, after taking a walk round the town. Only when he heard some women talking did Goyo Yic remember that he was looking for María Tecún. He hadn't been thinking about her so much lately. He thought about her all right, but not like before. This was not because he was resigned, but because . . . he just didn't. Soul of the possum! Eyes of the possum! He was a coward. Man is cowardly. Now, when he thought about her as he heard other women talking, it no longer made his heart miss a beat, and he amused himself imagining her with some rich man, with lots of power, lots of pull . . . Why should he go looking for her, he who, though he had recovered his eyes, had a possum slipped into his soul? The years, the grief that doesn't hang you with a noose but hangs you just the same, all those nights he'd slept out in the open in bad weather on his peddling tours, searching through all the towns and villages along the coast, and the red liver blotches over his face from drinking so much liquor, to try and sweeten the bitter taste of his absent woman, little by little it diminished him, until he was turned into someone who was no one. He did things because he had to do them, not like before, with the pleasure of doing them to some purpose, and it was still worse when he lost all hope of finding his woman and children. There are woes that shelter a man. Goyo Yic's was a rough weather woe. He pulled in his legs, curled up, and slept until the following day, before the cocks crowed.

"You were up early, compadre," Domingo Revolorio greeted him and asked him for the pesos he was to put into their liquor business.

He called him compadre. They called each other compadre. That's how they started out and they just kept it up. Though it wasn't clear which of the two was the father and which the godfather, and whether or not the baby was the demijohn.

"There's no more to come if that ain't enough, compadre Mingo," said Poppa-Possum, scratching his eyebrows. "Count up, for heaven's sake, we must make time so the full heat of the sun won't catch us on the road, I've already given you all the cash I had."

"And it's exactly right, compadre Goyo. Take it. It should cost eighty-six pesos, by my reckoning, a flagon of twenty bottles; we should have brought a bigger one."

In the inn the muleteers were sorting out their loads, some were watering their animals and others harnessing them up. On the packsaddles they would place the load, flour in white sacks and sugar in foreign canvas bags.

Goyo Yic carrying the money, and compadre Mingo following behind, saying, among other things, "We go half and half. Soon as the flagon's full we'll start carrying it, first you, then me, and out of what we earn, half each, everything sliced down the middle: the coins to buy it, the work of carrying it, and the earnings. May God smile on us."

"Of course, of course, of course," repeated Goyo Yic in the openings his compadre Mingo left him to give his own opinion. "And the best thing is our agreement—not to give away a single drink, not even us, not even among ourselves, the joint owners, can we dispose of a single drink, without paying cash in advance."

"That's the only way this business will work out good. I once had two cases of liquor, and I drank the lot from one case; the

143

second one my friends drank. Two cases was all I had, and it taught me a lesson."

"I should think it would, compadre Mingo. The really grand thing is that we'll be arriving at Santa Cruz just when they're short of liquor. It'll be a profitable deal, cash only, no free drinks or credit."

"We're gonna make over twelve hundred pesos on the eighty-six the flagon'll cost us."

"Sure to."

"And you'll have enough for more love affairs. You like loving, compadre Goyo, and to love with dough is better than loving without it. Love can't live with poverty, whatever folks may say. Love is luxury, and poverty—what luxury is there in that? A poor man's love is suffering, a rich man's is pleasure."

"And how could you tell, compadre, that I was in love?"

"The way you stop and listen to every woman's voice. Even if she's nothing to do with you, you stop and listen."

"I've already told you I'm looking for a woman I know only by ear. I've never seen her. I've only heard her speak, and maybe that's the way I'll identify her. It may be I'll find her some day, because hope doesn't die in a man's heart, even if they kill it."

"And if you don't find her, compadre Goyo, better forget her, or swap her for a better one. Because if you bump into her and she's sweet on someone new, it'll kill you."

"Don't even say it, compadre. If she's just with someone else, I won't mind; but if she's taken the wrong path and is setting the children the wrong example, then heaven help her. You couldn't spell out all I feel in my body: sometimes the tickle of wanting to hear news of them or wanting to peer right across everything that's hiding them from me, to see how they are; sometimes a suffocating feeling that won't go away until I start walking, as if by walking, by moving along, I was shortening the distance between me and them. But it's been so long that now I don't feel anything. Before, compadre, I searched to find her: now I search so as not to find her."

144

Mingo Revolorio, low in body, with black feathered hair, close-knit eyebrows which met in the middle, and fairish skin, looked younger than he was. If he laughed he seemed to be playing a musical instrument, if he was quiet he disappeared. And when he started to talk he always made the gesture of rolling up his sleeves.

Several times he made as though to roll up the sleeves of his jacket, but he said nothing, barely forming the odd number between his lips, counting the bottles of liquor which were filling the demijohn one by one, whilst his compadre, Goyo Yic, paid over the price of the liquor and bought an excise permit to be able to move freely along the roads. He paid eighty pesos for the lot.

"Compadre Mingo," he ran to tell him, "it worked out better than we thought, we've six pesos over. They only charged eighty pesos, including the permit. There's six pesos over."

"Good, compadre, very good, that means we don't have to go back with nothing in our pockets. It's always good to have a few pesos for the road."

"Six, there are."

"You hold on to them, compadre; later, when we get there, we'll count up, after all we put forty-three pesos each, but as there are six over, we only put forty, and so we each get three back."

"I'll give you your three now, if you like."

"No, compadre, keep it all together. We've bought some real good liquor, the best there is, cacao-flavored, and it's got the color of fine brandy, which will make it that much easier to sell, 'cause they say it really does you good, as well as making you feel good. We could have bought sheep's-head, which is even more like a food, almost a tonic, but it was sure to cost us a few pesos more, and we'd have been out of pocket."

Mingo Revolorio put the demijohn in a net and lifted it onto his back, to hit the worst of the road as soon as possible. The day's first streaks of dye looked like a fruit market—oranges, lemons, watermelons, pitahayas, pomegranates, limes, grapefruits, cherries, hawberries, nances, cucumbers, soursops, sapodillas—fruits that gradually ceased being fruits over the violet-colored mountains, and turned to flowers of every form and hue—carnations, geraniums, roses, dahlias, camellias, orchids, hydrangeas—flowers which condensed their colors once the sun appeared until they formed the chlorophyll green of the mountain ridges and changed themselves into leaves.

"You'll not deny it's cold, compadre," exclaimed Goyo Yic, as he passed between two walls of rock, climbing, descending, jumping, hunching himself in to fit on the road, which was called the Split Peak.

"Yes, compadre, it's cold; but walking gets rid of it."

Goyo Yic looked at the demijohn on his compadre's back with the thirst the hot cold of malaria puts in your eyes, and repeated, "Real cold, compadre, icy cold . . ."

"Keep moving, you'll soon warm up, and don't let it get you down, the sun's about to come out."

"Look, compadre Mingo, maybe a drink would do us good, because although it never does you harm, now it would do us a whole lot of good, it would me, anyway."

"It might do your belly good, compadre; but we can't afford it, so we'd best push on. We didn't make our agreement for the fun of it, we gave our word we wouldn't give anyone, not even ourselves, a drink out of this flagon without due payment."

"You mean you feel like one too."

"Course I do, but I can't have one because, apart from our promise, compadre, we must remember it's our own interests that are at stake if we start having free drinks. One drink for you, then one for me, and we'll finish the flagon and arrive at Santa Cruz with nothing. What I put in was all I had, and you put in all your capital, too, if you start swigging without paying me for it, and I do the same, we'll end up in the gutter."

The road, shaded by corpulent trees, great tall ones with

overlapping branches stretching down like layers of green tamale soup, passing between pools of water sprung from rocks which glistened with sand and water as the sun came out, increased in Goyo Yic, Poppa-Possum, the desire for a drink, no doubt because that rumbling moisture and that warmth on the back of his neck as the sun appeared, reminded him of María Tecún when she used to return to the rancho after bathing in the river. Long-suffering woman. He closed his eyes to shut himself off, if only for a moment, from the visible world, and savor the happiness he had known as a blind man.

"Compadre!"—he couldn't stand it any longer—"compadre Mingo, I'll buy a drink off you." He carried in his pockets, all he did carry, the six pesos he'd had over after paying for the demijohn, the twenty bottles, and the permit.

"You pay for it, and there's no problem."

"I'll pay in advance, so you won't mistrust me."

"I can't allow you to call me mistrustful, compadre, not of you, my partner in this business. It's just that I can't give you the drink for nothing. We'd be breaking our agreement."

And so saying, Revolorio stopped, his bushy black eyebrows together against his white skin, his voice sort of choking, stifled, on account of his load.

He stopped and took hold of the demijohn, leaning back against the rocks which lined the roadside until it rested against the edge. He put it down, helped by his compadre, who could hardly wait to get his hands round a drink, and after rubbing his hands, which he had rested on the rock, he poured his compadre six pesos worth of liquor in a black-bottomed gourd.

Goyo Yic, Poppa-Possum, paid his compadre Mingo the six pesos and drained the gourd with great gulps, smacking his lips as he finished and giving a taster's approval, like a bird opening and closing its beak after a drink of water. Then he took hold of the demijohn and lifted it on his back. Compadre Revolorio had already carried it, and now it was his turn.

Foot after foot, Poppa-Possum climbed for half a league, panting a bit, crunching the sand of the road beneath his sandals, with the weight of his precious cargo added to his own. Domingo Revolorio had fallen well behind, looking tired. Suddenly he increased his pace, to catch Goyo Yic up, as if he had felt some urgent need.

"Compadre," he said, with his hand on his chest, he was so fair you couldn't see how pale he'd become, "I'm running out of steam, I can't breathe—"

"Were you wanting a drink, compadre?"

"I'm dying!"

"A drink?"

"Give me a few slaps on the back, and give me a drink."

Goyo Yic, Poppa-Possum, slapped him on the back.

"And the drink, compadre," demanded Revolorio.

"Can you pay for it, compadre?"

"Yes, compadre, the six pesos."

"Now you're talking, because I can't give it you for nothing even if you are dying."

The gourd full of cacao-flavored liquor in Revolorio's hands and the six pesos in Poppa-Possum's hands. Revolorio tasted it. He wet his gums, a suggestion of sugar, without being sweet, and rose-petal softness, with the prick of a thorn.

Midday. Sweat ran down the face of Goyo Yic, who was still carrying the sweet precious beautiful liquor on his back, seeing as Mingo Revolorio was a bit poorly. A muletrain came past them: one, two, three, twenty mules loaded with boxes of maize flour, crates of pewter pots packed in straw, and casks of wine. The two compadres flattened themselves against the rock face as the mules trotted past, kicking up clouds of dust, watched by muleteers on foot and followed by the traders who had hired them.

"Stop now, compadre Goyo," said Revolorio, brushing the dirt from his face, he blinked to see clearly, half spitting so as not to swallow earth, "it's my turn to carry the flagon for a bit now, you've done more'n your share already."

"If it won't hurt you, compadre, if it won't strain you . . ."

Poppa-Possum was not at all convinced that his friend was sick.

148

He'd just pretended to be sick to have a drink. Funny his heart should only start to bother him on the way back. Why didn't he feel it on the way there?

"A deal's a deal, and it's my turn to carry it now."

Mingo Revolorio, with stubby arms he moved like a doll, took the load off him, both laughing and pushing and shoving.

"Right, compadre, but tell me if it's too much for you, and wait a moment, don't rush, before you put the flagon on your back I'll have another drink."

"You buying it?"

"With these six pesos. Every sale is cash down, compadre, else we'll be ruined."

Revolorio took the six pesos and filled the gourd with liquor right up to the brim. The liquid shone pale golden beneath the radiant sun. Poppa-Possum downed it in one gulp.

A shower of leaves fell on top of them. Must be eagles or hawks squabbling up in some tree. What was certainly true was that in the drowsiness of the siesta, beneath the torrential sun, scarcely a shadow, they could hear high above them a flutter-bickering of squalling wings that beat against one another, bouncing the branches, from which leaves and flowers were falling. Goyo Yic picked up some yellow flowers to decorate the sweet precious beautiful object on compadre Mingo's back.

"You must feel like a drink, compadre, to be decorating it like that," Revolorio stopped to say, with a laugh on his lips and his cheeks red where the sun had caught them, because a hat's no use at midday, it doesn't cover you.

"No, compadre, I've nothing to pay for it with."

"If you like, I'll lend you these six pesos."

"Well, if you really don't mind. When we make our first sales you can take it out and pay yourself back. You're a practical man, compadre—after all, we're gonna have a nice profit at our disposal."

Revolorio gave the six pesos to Poppa-Possum, Goyo Yic, and filled up the gourd with the black bottom. When it filled up with liquor it looked like a lidless eye, naked, staring at everything. Poppa-Possum savored the liquor, pure cacao, and by way of payment he gave the six pesos back to Revolorio.

"I owe you six pesos, compadre Mingo, and you look in a bad way, give me the flagon, for I can't wait to get there."

They continued, more at a run than a walk, Goyo Yic with the demijohn on his back and Revolorio as his mate.

"I wonder if you'd mind dismounting for a moment, compadre, and selling me a drink. My heart's giving out, it's beating uneven."

"No, compadre, I don't mind, it's good for both of us: you benefit by having a drink when you feel bad, and we both come out winners, because it's a cash sale. The bad thing would be if you and I just drank away for free."

The gourd was filled, bubbling beneath the thirsty eyes of the two compadres. Poppa-Possum took the six pesos from Revolorio, put them away, and lifted the demijohn on his back to march on.

After they'd been going a while, Poppa-Possum said, "If the business is a success, as we expect it to be, and as it's just got to be, you can see that even we, even you, sick, have had to pay for the steps we've taken, because when you felt bad this morning I could easily have let you have a drink, a free measure. But it wasn't out of stinginess or coldheartedness that I didn't, compadre, but because this way we're building the foundations for carrying out what we said. As I was saying, if the business is a success, we'll take the pesos and go and see a herbalist I know, Señor Chigüichón Culebro, the same one who cured my eyes, so he can do something about this heart trouble of yours. Otherwise you're gonna drop dead when you least expect it."

"I've already been doctored. What they say I've got, and it feels like it, is foam on the heart."

"Holy Jesus, what's that?"

"When you've been a drinker all your days, like I have, you're left with liquor froth in your blood, and when that froth reaches your heart it kills you. Your heart can't stand up to liquor froth."

150

"But there must be a cure . . ."

"Another drink."

"All right, compadre, if it's your medicine and you can pay cash."

"Here are the six pesos."

Goyo Yic received that sum and filled the gourd with liquor, rich liquid cacao.

"We're near Susnávar now," Revolorio told him, "which means we'll soon be arriving in Santa Cruz. We'll get a look at it just along the way at the crest of the hill. These Susnávar folk lived in the time of the King, and right about here the sons-of-bitches left some buried treasure. Pure gold bars and precious stones. It's been searched for. Some years back some white men came, white as white and tall as tall they were, with some black men, real black they were, and real big too, and they had a fine time messing about with their mattocks and their picks and shovels and their dynamite. They started to blow the top right off that mountain over there. There where I'm pointing. That mountain. But they didn't find anything."

"Yet there must be a lot there . . ."

"Then they all died off of what you and me'll die of, compadre. The only mine they found was a liquor still, and there they stayed. When they first arrived the white men ate separate from the blacks, and the blacks had to serve them. But later when they all got drunk, the white men served the blacks and they all called one another brother. Though liquor brings its troubles, compadre, it has its good points, too: divisions which make men say you're better than the other man 'cause he's black, or that one's rich and this one's poor, they all come to an end, everyone's equal where liquor's concerned, men are just men."

"Compadre Mingo, you're after another six pesos' worth."

"Well said, trouble is I ain't got no money. I'll be near to ruin if I ask you for credit, because you don't give credit, do you, compadre?"

"Don't you worry about that, compadre. Earlier today you took my word as payment, and now it's time for me to return

151

the favor. Here are the six pesos, I'll subtract them from our earnings."

"After all, when we get there and sell our cane juice, we're gonna have a whole stack of notes."

The gourd was filled and Mingo Revolorio drank. When he'd finished he paid over the six pesos his compadre had lent him to pay for the drink.

"And if I want one and I've got the dough, compadre?" said Goyo Yic, whose desire was awakened by the gusto with which Revolorio emptied the gourd.

"Simple," replied Mingo, with his gesture of rolling up his sleeves, "you just give me the flagon, I serve you, and you pay me."

"Right, then . . ."

Revolorio poured. Poppa-Possum paid, and drank in gentle swigs. It wasn't rotgut. It was a real smooth drink.

"Thank the Lord in His Mercy, there's still some left," he said, sipping down that liquor distilled in mud pots, secretly infused with the flavor of cacao, nothing outrageous, on the contrary, very gentle, very gentle indeed, but very much there.

"And now, compadre," Yic went on, "if you want another one, give me the flagon, and I'll tip the drink in the gourd for you, and you pay me. That way there's no catch. Serving and paying."

"I don't have to be asked, compadre—and I'm not trying to cheat you!"

Goyo Yic took the demijohn with the greatest care—if he'd had more hands he'd have used more hands to take it—and served Revolorio. He'd have used more hands to take it, hold it steady, and serve it, serve it horizontally. It was emptying very quickly.

Mingo Revolorio put his face to the gourd, with his lower lip protruding and the eyes of a thirsty horse. It was a job to swill it down your gullet without spilling a drop. Though not a drop would he have spilled, but his compadre spoke to him, interrupting him.

"No, compadre, before you drink you've got to pay me. We're real compadres, but business is business!"

Revolorio sneezed, coughed, blinked, waved his hands: "I nearly choked 'cause of you, compadre, the rum's got down into my lungs! My compadre is very suspicious, here are your six spots; but still, that's how I like folk to be in business, no fooling around."

"It ain't suspicion, it's a rule we got to follow so's not to be cheated of what's due us. Some folks knock back a drink and then can't pay for it. You lose your drink, 'cause you can't suck it back out of his belly, and you lose your friend, if friend he is, or make an enemy, if he's a stranger. Have me arrested, they say, when the drink's safely inside them. And what's the use of having them arrested? It's a pleasure to see the way you're licking your lips, compadre Mingo. Suppose I was wanting another one myself?"

"Give me the flagon and I'll sell you one."

In a changing of hands, Poppa-Possum took the gourd and Revolorio the demijohn, he had to tip it up still further to pour the drink.

"Tip it in, compadre Minguito, I'll pay you right away."

"Now, compadre, you know I ain't mistrustful. You can have your drink and I'll charge you for it after, though maybe I ain't being wise. If you gotta get old you may as well get smart, my old grandmother used to say. 'Cause what a shame it'd be if you didn't pay me, it would have to come out of the earnings we're hoping to make, about twelve hundred pesos it'll be, give or take a little, and I'll be left short."

Poppa-Possum drank, the skin of his face on fire, his eyes shining, his hair electrified as the liquor passed down his throat, more than liquor it was a shivering feeling inside him, a bristling which went down to the tips of his toes, which were still swollen the way they were when he was blind and used to beg beneath the amate tree in Pisigüilito. Poppa-Possum drank, feeling as though he were standing on a pile of hair, paid the six pesos one by one, and grabbed the demi-

153

john off Revolorio, lemme, gimme, with quarrelsome gestures.

"Hand me this sweet precious beautiful bottle, compadre, and I'll serve you another measure!"

"For courage?"

"No, for the road, and even if it's the condemned man's last swig, it's a drink. Of course, you'll have to pay for it!"

"And I will, compadre, I will, here's your cash."

"Six pesos' worth of cane juice for my old compadre Mingo Revolorio." The liquor slopped into the gourd. "That little head of froth shows it's good stuff."

"I can see myself now, compadre, coining it in in town, selling booze all over the place, you earn more selling by the cup than by the bottle, and cash down, of course, as we're doing here."

"Cash fucking down, compadre Goyo, and as you're such a rich man now, have a last drink, because we're nearly there."

"The last but one, at least, because I ain't dying."

"Last but one, then."

"Yes, give me six-plus-four's worth."

"What's the four?"

"On credit . . ."

"Free drinks died, and credit's dead."

"Just six pesos' worth, then. No holding back or spilling any, compadre Mingo, 'cause the earth's a drinker, too, only it don't get tipsy, and when it does there's an earthquake. Nice name you've got, compadre. Domingo means Sunday. And you're merry, just like Sundays are. I expect you were born on a Sunday, and that's why they called you Domingo."

To pour the drink the demijohn had to be held upside down. Revolorio poured it without seeing the gourd too clearly, that tiny half a calabash which wasn't where Goyo had meant to put it, either, under the mouth of the demijohn, because it waved backwards and forwards, all over the place.

"Look . . . look out . . . look what you're doing!" exclaimed Goyo Yic, with something between a word and a smile which turned out to be dribble between his teeth.

He spat, spat and wiped the whole of his mouth with the whole of his hand, as if he were trying to tear his lips off, and he almost tore them off along with his teeth and his face. He even wiped his ears.

"It's bad business to spill it," Revolorio nagged. "Hold the gourd steady."

"Perhaps you'd better pour it straight down my throat, compadre Mingo. Take proper aim, here where the gourd is, not on the ground. Why, I'm gonna think you're doing it on purpose out of spite, to get back at me . . . why . . . why . . . why . . . w-w-we . . . w-w-w-"

"We made it, compadre . . ."

A liquid mane the color of ebony fell into the gourd, until it spilled over.

"You're spilling blood, compadre, that's liquid profit!"

"We'll put it down to expenses; suck your fingers, my hand slipped and I couldn't stop myself."

Revolorio straightened the demijohn up with some difficulty whilst Poppa-Possum drank, sucked his fingers, and licked the outside of the gourd. Then he passed it to him so he could serve him another measure.

"Gonna have another go, compadre Mingo?"

"Ask me—"

"Anything you say—"

"First the six pesos," Revolorio interrupted, "take them, 'cause I know how rotten mistrustful you are."

"That's the way you've got to be in this life, if you don't want to end up in a jam."

"If you gotta get old you may as well get smart, as my old grandmother, Pascuala Revolorio, used to say."

"You sure do have happy names in your family, compadre: Domingo, Sunday; Pascuala, Christmas—"

"My mother's name was Dolores . . ."

"A fine name for a mother! Mentioning your mother is worth another drink, I'll treat you to one. There!"

"But I'd like to buy you one, too, compadre, take back the six pesos."

The demijohn, ever more exhausted, passed back and forth between the two compadres, but the six pesos—it was cash down or nothing—also kept changing hands.

"Another drink, that's six pesos—"

"Here are the six pesos, give me another—"

"My turn now, six pesos—"

"I haven't had mine yet, I've paid you for it—"

"Then that means you must have six, and I must have six—"

The compadres looked at one another, and couldn't believe it. That is to say, compadre Yic looked at compadre Mingo, not believing it was he, Yic, who was looking, nor that it was compadre Mingo he was looking at. If their heads had been clearer, they might have explained it, because the same thing was happening to Mingo Revolorio: he looked at his compadre Yic, he felt him, and he asked himself, listening to him speak, if he was really there, next to him, when he looked so far away, so very far away, mixed in with the bare sandy mountains in which Santa Cruz de las Cruces lay, mountains covered by scorched vegetation which looked like a great cauldron lying in the red-hot ashes of an afternoon beginning to pour dye on the rigid specters of white rocks at the entrance to the town, among eucalyptus trees and neighborhood voices.

One here the other there, they only found one another when they collided, thus went the compadres, their hats pulled down round their ears like haloes, their hair fringing their faces, weeping willows which laughed alone, liquor dealers, only there wasn't much left in the demijohn, judging by how light it was and the noise the liquid made inside, as it staggered around on compadre Revolorio's shoulders.

Goyo Yic, Poppa-Possum, pulled his hat forward, clapped right down over his eyes—it reached almost to the end of his nose, he did it to make himself blind—but it didn't stop him partnering his compadre in a wavering waltz. As he entered his old domains, hearing and touch, he found María Tecún. How are you, she said, and he replied, very well, and you. What are you doing, she asked him, and he replied, selling liquor, through a friend of mine who became my compadre. I'm in business. Will you make much money, she asked him. Yes, he said, a few pesos.

Revolorio pulled on his jacket and threw him backwards to the ground, then approached him again, the demijohn tottering on his back, and took off his hat.

"Don't go crazy, compadre, talking to your wife. She's not a ghost."

"Let me be, compadre, I'm having a word with her, and I haven't asked her about the children."

"It's bad luck to talk like that to living people when they're not present in the flesh, because they will lose their flesh, and their bones will just turn to nothing, nobody."

"It's as if she was standing here beside me. But since you've spoilt my dream, sell me another tot, now I can make you out, here you are, that's you there, and this is me, the one who wants the drink."

"You weren't asleep, compadre Goyo, so how can you say I spoilt your dream? Don't talk to me about dreams. You were talking like a sleepwalker, the liquor sent you sleepwalking."

Revolorio fell flat on his face, and the demijohn rolled on the ground, whilst Poppa-Possum, who had also fallen over, clawed at the ground himself, but he couldn't stand up.

"A curse on poxy liquor," Poppa-Possum complained, "it's got our business all knotted up . . . biz . . . niss . . . what biz . . . biz . . . bizniss are we going to do like this? We'd have made ourselves rich, right, compadre Revolorio? But the fact is . . . the fact is . . . that's how it goes . . . that's ex-ex-exactly how it goes . . . what goes? The liquor goes . . . that's how the liquor goes . . . it's gone . . . all gone . . . but our takings ain't gone, our earnings, 'cause we only sold cash down . . . at six pesos a time we've collected a lot, and my compadre Mingo's got it all there in his pocket . . . we'll start counting soon as he brings it out, we'll settle up and he'll give me my share, on account of I'm his partner . . . No, business wasn't bad, it was

157

good, the only bad part, what would've been bad, really bad, worse'n bad, bad as bad can be . . . is if we'd knocked back the flagon until we saw the Lord Himself . . . 'cause then we could say goodbye to business, and for good!"

Revolorio was snoring.

"W-w-where . . . where's the cash, compadre?" Poppa-Possum went on. "All our trade was cash down, and we must have far more than what we put in, the ei-ei-eighty you and me put in. Let's say there's two hundred! That means we made about . . . about . . . about how much did we make on the blasted liquor? Say there's even more: threehundredfourhundred . . . five or six hundred profit we'd have made if we'd sold it in town."

The municipal brigade fell on them for disturbing the peace, but when they found the demijohn, they had to call two constables from the excise department.

Nine Indians dressed in white made up the municipal brigade, all with machetes, battered straw hats with wide brims and breeches secured at the waist with sashes colored red, purple and blue. Their swarthy hands and feet seemed alien to their white-clad bodies, as they moved to get the two drunks on their feet, and when they spoke their teeth shone like machete blades.

The excise officers, two chubby men, sniffed at the smell of cacao in the demijohn. The smell was all there was. They sighed, licked their lips, rubbed their hands over their bodies, if only they could taste it.

Poppa-Possum Goyo Yic said, "Let's keep things friendly, shall we, lads, and if you insist on dragging a fellow up, would you mind not ill-treating him," as his head jerked back and forth, and from side to side, and forward again, until the bristles on his chin raked his chest, and then backwards, till the skin on his neck went taut, his ears were bathed in blood, and the veins stood out on his forehead.

They dragged him along by the arms, with his trailing feet marking the ground, and carried Revolorio and the demijohn, and their two hats, like the white shadows of their black heads.

The next day they took them out to make statements, hand-cuffed, guarded, escorted, threatened. There's no bad in prison, everything's worse. But the worst of all ills, in prison, is to have a hangover. Thirsty, trembling, terrified, they were slow to answer the questions put to them by the man acting as judge, because at the time they didn't really catch on to what they heard, not till later, and they replied with words which they found hard to put together. They'd lost the permit. Through taking out the money for all the drinks they'd had on the road, and putting it away again, and again, they'd lost it, and now they were lost. Wretched piece of paper, square-shaped, white. Its value lay in what it said, and in the stamps of the Department of Taxes and the Deposit of Liquors, and in the signatures. They smoked paper-rolled cigarettes which gave off the smell of paper turned to smoke, like the permit. Without the permit they were smugglers; with it, respectable men. With the permit they were free; without it, prisoners, and prisoners guilty of something that was worse than despatching a fellow man to another life. For murder you get out on bail, but not for smuggling, and moreover there was the condition that they had to settle up with the fiscal authorities to the extent of their fraud, multiplied by who knows how much.

In prison there's no bad, everything's worse. Worse belly-ache, worse misery, worse sadness—the worst of the worst. Jailers and judges seem like people without reason, deranged. Compliance with rules and regulations which have nothing to do with reality turns them into madmen, at least they seem so to those who are not under the strange influence of the law.

Little was clarified by their statements as to who sold them that bottled curse, the cane brandy. They weren't explicit. You're not being explicit, the judge kept saying. The com-padres didn't understand. A deafening sound rang in their ears, within the four walls of the tribunal, and their hunger confused them, because all they'd had in their bellies that last day were the two chilates. And how could they be explicit, each one thought in his own head, when they found out what explicit meant, if the people who sold them the twenty bottles of amber liquor smelling of chocolate were still half asleep, because it was in the early morning, all muffled up, wrapped in their ponchos, like women who've just had babies. Nor could it be established whether the liquor the criminals were carrying was legally produced or from some clandestine still, which would make the offense even more serious, because they didn't leave so much as a drop, the demijohn was found empty. Then there were all the contradictions they fell into when they tried to explain that the liquor had been sold for cash, but peso by peso, even though all they had on them was six pesos. Six pesos when, reckoning it up, they ought to have had a thousand at the least. If there were twenty bottles in the demijohn and you get ten average-size gourdfuls from each bottle, and they'd sold each gourd for six pesos, they ought to have at least twelve hundred pesos. The money had just slipped away from them, and now they could let their hopeful hands and nervous fingers frolic much as they pleased in their pockets, their only hope was for the notes and coins to be fashioned anew, there where they had been and from where they had disappeared, as if by magic.

There was no mystery as far as the authorities were concerned. They had spent it—the compadres knew that wasn't so; or they had lost it—the compadres hesitated before they replied—and if they agreed to having mislaid it, it was to save themselves from the crime of smuggling and defrauding the Exchequer, if you added the question of the permit to the money, a plea the tribunal rejected out of hand, maintaining that they never had a permit: either they were robbed as they lay wallowing on the edge of the town—the compadres didn't like that word "wallowing" one little bit; or one of them had hidden the money so the other wouldn't get his share.

In the reproachful hours in which they were led out to face the tribunal, they looked one another's faces over slyly, washing each other with their eyes: first, the exterior, and then, staring intently, trying to penetrate into what was being concealed behind it.

They were suspicious of one another, without enough honesty to say so, because they didn't have enough of anything anymore. Prison puts an end to everything, but what it pulls up by the roots is the sufficiency there is deep down inside a man to face life the good way, the free way.

"Where can that money have gone, compadre?" Goyo Yic scratched away, with the air of a cock looking for a fight.

"That's what I ask myself, compadre," replied Revolorio, bringing his bushy eyebrows together like colliding worms; and rolling up his sleeves, he added, "Because we lost quite a bit, if you work it out."

"The judge did work it out, compadre . . ."

"The loss is hard enough, but the worst thing is we can't explain whether we dropped it along the way, or if it spilled out in the same place as the crock, and only the Lord knows how much liquor there was in it, or whether we were robbed, or—ah well, what's to be done?"

And between the "or" and the "ah well" would fit the phrase "unless you pocketed it, compadre, so as not to give me my share, and enjoy it all by yourself."

They said it. Poppa-Possum Goyo Yic couldn't hold it in, and admitted his evil thoughts to Revolorio, who confessed that in his mind too the doubts had been rising like yeast, perhaps his compadre . . . But no, it couldn't be. In each transaction they had both of them put away what they received, and they would both have to be hiding half their earnings, in which case they would have come out even.

Robbery. Fairs attract evil-doers, and the Fair of Santa Cruz de las Cruces was famous for its miracles, its dry lightning, and its bloody deeds, apart from robberies and other crimes. One month out of the twelve had to be the wild one, and this was it, the one marked with the cross of the Savior of the world, in which the heat went away and the rains came with bad weather good for the crops, low gray skies, and dealings with the law.

Everything about the compadres had been written down on a great many sheets of paper, and was still being written down on a great many more, naming them every little while by their Christian names and surnames, followed by the word "criminal." It was hard to get used to being called criminal, and they were never ready to answer when they were called it: answer, criminal; stand to attention, criminal; criminal, withdraw. Other prisoners waited with their guards, with much yawning and rumbling of bellies, or played tipaches with pieces of black wax like little tortillas.

In view of the lack of security at the prison, the Santa Cruz authorities decided to move the balance of prisoners taken at the fair to an old castle dating from the time of the Spaniards, situated on an island off the Atlantic coast and used as a prison, and among them the two criminals Goyo Yic and Domingo Revolorio, convicted of smuggling and defrauding the Exchequer.

With their arms tied, a bundle of clothing wrapped in a petate on their backs, a sheet and a poncho, a dangling coffeepot, a bottle full of water and a gourd, as well as a jar of bitter-almond oil, the compadres set out from Santa Cruz de las Cruces, guarded by an escort with a captain in charge.

Goyo Yic closed his eyes. For an instant he returned to the world of María Tecún, the flower hidden within the fruit, the woman he carried in his soul. Pale, eyebrows together, Revolorio followed him, trying out the false laugh of a criminal called Domingo, struggling not to roll up his sleeves, he didn't want the chief to think he was trying to work himself free, and commending himself to Our Lord of Good Hope, with the most highly prized prayer of the "Twelve Emmanuels."

That Saturday.

COYOTE-POSTMAN

XIII

The wife of Señor Nicho the postman ran away, while he, on foot, made his way across mountains, villages and plains, trotting to arrive more quickly than the rivers, more quickly than the birds, more quickly than the clouds, at the distant township, with the mail from the capital.

Poor Señor Nicho Aquino, what will he do when he gets there and finds her gone?

He will tear his hair, he will call her, not Chagüita, as he called her before they were married, nor Isabra, as he called her after, but what every woman who runs off is called, "tecuna."

He will call her tecuna, tecuna, his heart chafing him like saddle sores, and he will bite, yes bite his own tail, but bite it alone, all alone in his unlit rancho, his dark solitary shack, whilst the Germans who trade in the town will read two or three times over the letters from their friends and family and the business letters from overseas brought by Señor Nicho, devoted as a dog, from the capital to San Miguel Acatán, a small town built on a shelf of golden stone above abysses where the atmosphere was blue, the color of the sea among pinewoods of dark green shade and fountains of rock, sewing boxes from which streamed threads of water born to line the fields with marigolds, ferns, fire lilies and begonias with heart-shaped leaves.

Poor Señor Nicho Aquino, what will he say when he gets there and finds her gone?

He will be left speechless, trembling, rags, sweat, dust, and

163

on finding his tongue, his speech, a voice to unburden himself, he will call her tecuna, tecuna, tecuna!, while many a mother will sniff back big, swelling, salt tears, needless tears, but tears nonetheless, as they read the letters from their sons away studying in the capital, and the justice of the peace and the local commandant will read letters from their wives, and the garrison officials the letters from some lady friend telling them she's well, even if she's sick, and that she's happy and contented, even if she's sad, and that she's alone and faithful, even if there's someone with her . . .

How many lies that night in San Miguel Acatán after the arrival of the unshod beast, the postman!

How many pious lies emerged from all those envelopes to surround the naked truth that awaited Señor Nicho Aquino!

How many letters in that minuscule town of houses built on mountainsides, one on top of the other like hencoops, whilst Señor Nicho, after shouting his wife's name, will shrivel up like a worm disemboweled by fate as he calls her tecuna, tecuna, tecuna!, until he tires of calling her that, and of wearing out his feet on the solitude of the rancho!

The mail, when it was Señor Nicho, arrived with the evening stars. Open doors and windows watched him go by, with the neighbors behind them, spying, to be sure he really had arrived, and to be able to tell themselves and others: The postman's here . . . Señor Nicho's arrived, did you see! . . . Two bags of mail, yes, two bags he had with him! Those who expected a letter and those who didn't, which of us is not always expecting a letter, all of them waiting, sitting in doorways or leaning out of windows, watching out for the postman, ready to break open the envelope and take out the folded sheets of paper, and read them straight through the first time, and with pauses and comments the second and third times, those who could read or half read, or get someone to read it out to them in the case of the tough-skinned peasants, eyes mossy with sleep, who could only gaze at the letters scrawled across the pages.

Señor Nicho's footsteps rang down the main street. Someone said he was showing off a new outfit, had new sandals on. Must be wanting to make a good impression on his wife, all done up like that, little knowing what was in store for him. The postman's steps rang out across the cobbled square perfumed with jasmine. Then through the galleries of the commandant's department, where a sentry paced up and down. And finally in the postmaster's office, which stank of cigarettes doused in saliva and was lit by a gas lamp above a desk covered in mountains of paper.

Señor Nicho arrived worn out and panting, unable to get his breath. He came running in, so eager to arrive, handed in the mailbags, and when they said everything was in order he went out step by step, dragging his feet. He would wait for his pay as usual, sitting on one of the steps facing the square, which was empty but full of sounds: tumblebugs, crickets, bats. He thought how near he was to his rancho, his woman. When his work took him away from home he imagined that when he got back he would find everything changed, but it never was. Life doesn't change, it's always the same. Only from now on it never would be the same again. A complete change, a sudden turnabout. He worked the crooks of his hands over his knees to ease the fatigue and stretched out his legs to make himself comfortable. His pay. The sixty pesos they gave him for the journey, which he took hat in hand, head bowed.

The postmaster came out onto the steps on his short, fat man's legs, not placing one foot ahead of the other as he walked, but rather swaying from foot to foot, with the motions of a tightrope walker, cigar in mouth, eyes sunk deep into his pork chop cheeks. He was an ill-tempered man, fat as they come but with none of the saving graces of fat people, who are usually good-natured folk, full bellies make contented hearts, and he wouldn't let Señor Nicho hold his hand out very far to take his pay.

"Goddam Indian, hands off, wait till I count it out! That's five, ten, fifteen, twenty, thirty . . ."

165

Before he got to fifty-five, he stopped to warn Señor Nicho that money wasn't for drinking, and that if he got drunk he'd be thrown in jail for fifteen days on bread and water.

"No sir, I'm not a drinking man, you never seen me drunk, not because I don't like it, that's part of being a man, but because it ain't right when you're just wed."

"You just think what you're doing"—the man's voice was like lard in the air—"because you won't settle anything by drinking, just makes things worse, you lose your head and everything goes to the devil."

Señor Nicho stared at him uncomprehendingly. Got hold of the wrong idea, he supposed. The postmaster looked as though he wanted to say something more, but his salivated breath suppurated around the fleshy corners of his mouth.

"What have you got there?"

"Here?"

"Yes, there." The cigar jerked between his lips. He sucked, not so much to smoke as to stop a strand of dribble falling. "Don't you go doing errands for people, because it's against regulations. If you do you'll go to jail. If someone wants something sent somewhere he can bring it along to the office, that's what the service is for, and pay the duty."

"No sir, it's not for someone else, it's for myself. A shawl I bought for my wife, it'll soon be her saint's day. I bought it down in the Chinese quarter. It's finest silk."

Señor Nicho's first impression when he went into his house was that of a man who has landed by mistake in the rancho of a neighbor. This isn't it, he said, I must have been in such a rush I didn't notice . . . In his rancho, every time he returned from the capital with the mail, there were hot yellow-maize tortillas waiting for him in the pancake pan or in the straw basket belonging to his wife's mother, a pot of steaming coffee, beans smelling of coriander, some hard cheese, his bed, sleep, his woman. He ran out, this wasn't his rancho, it was dark and empty. He went running out, not walking, but he didn't get past the door. This rancho was his all right, how could it not be his, how could he have ended up next door when all that was next door was the immense, the endless night. He closed his eyes, in a second he had made sense of the postmaster's words, his warning not to get himself drunk, because drinking doesn't do any good, and he went round touching everything like an idiot, the walls, the hardwood uprights, the cot, the hammock where they had planned to put the little one when it was born, the dead stones of the fireplace.

The dog was trying to tell him something too, something it could express only through little whimpers which might just as well have meant pleasure at his return as grief. It licked his hands. Its hot, dry, rasping tongue translated some untold anguish with fretful urgency, and it pulled on his fingers, on his breeches, taking hold of him with its teeth, without hurting, to lead him outside the house. It led him out, down to the water hole, and as it got nearer its agitation increased, jumping, whining, chasing back and forth, little yelps in the shadows full of stars, of plants bathed in evening dew, of motionless silence. The dog knew where his woman was. But where was she? A distinct impression that she was very close receded when he rejected the now violent and agonized insinuations of the animal, and went back to the rancho, trying to work out what had become of her. Weariness got the better of him, and he lay down and went straight off to sleep, jangled about by the shock and by scorpionlike cramps that woke him up, without waking him.

The rancho didn't seem uninhabited. The wind played with the unbolted door. Opened it, closed it. The houses of tecunas, women who run away from home, are full of mysterious sounds. Sounds and presences. The evil eyes of doubt in those bitter coffee dregs, pupils all watery with black weeping. The clean linen chest, underclothes still fresh from the iron's heat, shakes its handles like metal ears against the hollow wood, blown by the wind that enters from the yard where the clothes line hangs the sky. A shipwrecked mouse in a clay jar of dirty, yellowish water. Black soldier ants surround the provisions.

167

Like rosaries of the Bad Thief they come and go busily among the grain troughs, around the kitchen, in company with the maize-ear gophers, entrenched wholesale in the houses of tecunas, while great birds cackle with glee, and ghostly, invisible dogs—only their footsteps can be heard—sniff out the piss of eternity in the old age of abandoned things, dust and cobwebs, until one fine day, in the midst of all that ruin, all those forgotten things abandoned on the shores of the sleep of death, comes the luxuriant sprouting of the hardwood uprights, a standard-bearer followed by shoots from seeds settled in what once was a straw roof, a window or a door, and on the husk of the rancho life begins to germinate, the earth to flower, because the earth too is a seed that falls from the stars, and no one, not even the old folk, ever again recalls the tragedy of the tecuna, the unseeing woman who wears a dress of black frijoles, like tears of mourning.

Nicho Aquino woke up with the heat of the sun. He changed out of the new clothes he'd arrived in to show his wife —underneath were the old ones, all stiff with sweat and dust —and put on his white cotton shirt and trousers. Tecuna that she was, she'd left him his clothes washed, ironed and all laid out, so his abandonment would hurt all the more, or who knows, perhaps she hadn't been meaning to run off that day, or maybe she planned to wait for him, or maybe someone else forced her, or maybe . . .

Like a white man dressed as an Indian—better an Indian than a half-breed in legal dealings: Indians are bull-headed, Ladinos are chicken—and casting aside suspicions, for there's nothing meaner than jealousy, he arrived at the commandant's office. From all points of view it was as well to notify the authorities. But let them find her dead, let them find her, he said to himself, and then again in time with his footsteps: but let them find her dead, let them find her dead, let them find her dead . . . His hair slicked down with water carried the heavy smell of rue; his nose was flat; his moustache grew in two straggling brushes over the corners of his mouth; he was round-shouldered as a bottle.

The commandant's secretary heard his complaint. An old soldier with a captain's ribbons and the look of those who crucified God. When Señor Nicho had finished—as he spoke he turned his straw hat round and round between his fingers —that veteran flogger of defenseless people, stirring the wrinkles of his sour, puckered face, told him to quit growsing and slobbering and look for another woman, because that's why there are more women than men in the world.

And he added, "She must have gone off with someone else, someone better than you, because women are always on the lookout to better themselves, even if it all comes to nothing in the end."

"Someone must have turned her head . . ."

"Her head? I'd best say no more, because I'm one for saying exactly what I think! Anyhow, we'll send out an order for her arrest, and mind you don't go following her, just remember what they say happened to that blind fellow who fell down a ravine on account of him running after that María Tecún. He heard her speaking, and just as he caught her up he recovered his sight, only to see her turned into stone. He forgot he was on the edge of the precipice, and for your information they're still out looking for him."

"May God repay you," said Señor Nicho with a pained look that emphasized his words.

"God don't repay other folks' debts, so either wipe that slobbering husband's look off your face or get out of here, because a tecuna she well may be, but there ain't no doubt who's the slob . . ."

From the entrance to the commandant's headquarters, where he lit a cornhusk cigar which smelled of figs, a speciality of his woman, who could smooth out the leaves like no one else, roasting the tobacco in the good old way, rolling it and pinching each end with her nails, he went down to the square past the market stalls, past the school among the children, who always came out for lunch at eleven, and sneaked into the Chinaman's store.

"Buy this?" he asked the Chinaman, unwrapping a package, to show him the shawl.

The Chinaman, frozen in silence, among the flies, took out his hand, took hold of the featherlike garment, and slid it over the glass counter. His black hair like an inkstain over his shining skull, his face empty of expression, his body without human bulk. Finally, he replied, "Lobbely?"

"You know more about robbery than I do, you snot-faced Chinaman!"

He picked the shawl up from the counter. He wanted to be rid of it, and not just to get his money back. He had been trembling as he went into the Chinaman's store. He wanted to be rid of it because it represented, in silk the color of blood, a token of love offered to the person who least deserved it. He snatched up the shawl and without wrapping it went straight over to the German's store, which flanked the church, swinging his arms for courage, though he told himself it was to get there more quickly.

"Make way, 'cause here comes the shawl of a beautiful woman!" he shouted to some muleteers he knew, who were unloading bales of merchandise at the door of San Miguel's largest store, and he went straight up to Don Deferic to offer him the shawl.

The Bavarian turned and looked at him with deep blue eyes roofed over by thick straw brows, and he took from his trouser pocket exactly what Nicho was asking for the shawl—he was in the middle of stocktaking—and gave it to him, without accepting the garment.

Nicho thanked him, but insisted he should take the shawl—it would seem such a shame to have to tear it to shreds or throw it in the river—but Don Deferic, for all his pleading, wouldn't hear of it.

When he came out his friends the mule drivers looked the other way. By now they'd heard the rumor about what had happened, and it was better not to talk to him.

They talked when he was out of earshot. Policarpo Mansilla,

the oldest and toughest of them, struggled to the door with an immensely heavy bundle on his back.

"Help me, then, lads!" he said, sweating, and dropped it flat, with a crash. "You're only making out you're carrying. I'm gonna end up ruptured on your account, I feel like my waist's splitting open when I have to strain like that, why don't you help? Chewing the cud, as usual. His wife's run off, and there's an end to it!"

"Lend a hand, you, Pitoso," said another muleteer. "I just stood looking at him, I feel that sorry for him. Fuck all women, I say, and may God protect him from trying to go chasing after her, eh, Policarpo? 'Cause if he does, that no-good tecuna will have him down a ravine."

"You'd believe anything, featherhead! I can see what's going through your mind—his woman, the tecuna, is going to lead him all the way up to the María Tecún Ridge, and when they get to the top, the very top, she'll start cooing like some soft sweet dove, sniveling for forgiveness, let's make up the nest again with feathers and kisses. Nothing but an old wives' tale, because the truth behind what I've just said, and what everyone repeats, is that a man who is made a widower by a tecuna can't adjust to the loss, he sets off to search for her, and as he searches he takes to drinking to keep up his spirits, he drinks so as not to lose hope, or to forget the woman he's looking for even as he looks for her, or he drinks out of anger, and because he doesn't eat he gets sozzled, and sozzled he sees her in his delirium and hears her calling to him, and as he tries to reach her, not looking where he's putting his feet, he goes over the edge . . . Every woman attracts men, like an abyss."

"Our Hilario's in the pulpit again. You're a wonderful sermonizer, my friend. Carry this stuff, damn you, you're a mule driver, not a professor!"

"Heaven forbid, blackie, better a beggar than a teacher. This sack is real heavy, yet it says 'Finest Merchandise' on the side. I'll carry it, but I won't swallow it, as the Indian said."

"What's that?" asked Policarpo Mansilla. "Carry it and talk, you could do both things at the same time if you weren't waving your arms about and making faces. I tell you, Hilario, you'd have made a wonderful clown."

"Well, this Indian was dying, and the holy father, after a thousand difficulties, because he lived far away, brought him the viaticum. The road was so bad the priest lost the host, and when he arrived at the rancho, not finding anything else to give the sick man, he picked up a cockroach and pulled off one of its wings. The Indian was very near the end, gasping, and the holy father, beside the cot, was saying, 'Do you believe this is the body of Our Lord Jesus Christ?' 'Yes, I do,' replies the Indian. 'Do you believe that in this little wafer is his Holy Body?' 'I do,' repeats the Indian. 'And do you believe in life eternal?' 'Yes, yes, I do.' 'Then if you do, open your mouth—' At that moment the Indian pushes the priest's hand away and says, 'I believe it, father, but I ain't swallowing it.' "

The German smiled. His blue eyes, the blue mountains, the blue skies, were in contrast to the mule drivers, dark as their leather trappings, cuirass of tanned leather over their chests, decorated with golden tacks, some with old-style woolen embroidery, long-sleeved jackets with fringes, wide-brimmed hats with guard ribbons, and sweaty leather blinders.

As Nicho left the convent house the priest, Father Valentín, who called him Nichón, because he was good-natured and a bit slow, parted his hands, which he had kept piously folded at his breast, crossed himself, and walked up and down the parlor which served as his study and his office, comfortable to the extent that it had petate matting on the floor, laid over sawdust to cushion it the better, but somewhat desolate due to the height and bareness of its walls.

The consolation of religion is slow to reach those unfortunates who have been abandoned. Devout resignation is not possible for them, the devil recruits them and they come to a bitter end. It's strange, but a man who has seen his wife die resigns himself much more easily, for death assures the sweet repose of that second meeting up in heaven. But a man who knows she has run away, and is made a widower by an absent

172

woman, finds consolation only in losing his senses and losing himself—God's will be done!

He stopped in front of a desk once varnished black, now ashen like his hair, to take out from a locked drawer his nursery of notes, as he called a diary he kept in folio form, and he entered the name of Isaura Terrón de Aquino among the victims of the madness popularly known as "spider's-maze" or "spider-spell."

Earlier he had written, and now reread, "Little is known of 'spider-spell' bites—bites being the popular term—but they cause great suffering in my parish, such is the way of things here, and the same may be said with respect to fabrications about 'naguals,' or animal protectors, who, through the lies and fictions of the devil, these ignorant people believe to be not only their protectors but their other selves, so much so that it is thought they can change their human form for that of the animal which is their 'nagual,' a tale as old as it is foolish. Little is known about, but much suffering is caused by, the stings of these 'spider-spells,' as was noted above, for there are frequent cases of women who are taken with ambulatory madness and escape from their houses, never to be heard of again, thereby swelling the number of 'tecunas,' as they are called, a name which derives from the legend of an unfortunate woman named María Tecún who, it is said, took a pinole powder which had been crawled through by spiders as a result of some mischief done to her, some evil of witchcraft, and set out to wander the roads like a madwoman, followed by her husband, who is depicted as being blind like Cupid. He follows her everywhere and finds her nowhere. Finally, after searching heaven and earth, after a thousand trials, he hears her speak in the most inhospitable place in all Creation. And such is the commotion undergone by his mental faculties that he regains his vision, only to see—unhappy creature—the object of his wanderings turn to stone in the place that henceforth is known as María Tecún Ridge.

"Personally," Father Valentín read swiftly over his burgeoning crop of notes with two small buzzard's eyes, common to all

the Urdáñez family, "personally, on first taking charge of the
parish of San Miguel Acatán, I visited María Tecún Ridge, and
I can testify to what is suffered for various reasons by those who
venture there. The altitude fatigues the heart and the eternal
cold which reigns at midday and at all hours makes one's flesh
and bones ache. Morally, the spirit of the most valiant wilts in
the silence, two syllables of a word which here, as at the Pole,
takes on all its grandeur: silence due to the altitude, 'far from
the madding crowd,' and above all to the fact that in the
constant, swirling mist, no bird ventures, and so saturated is the
vegetation that it seems mute, ghostly, swathed always in a
cloak of frost or migrating rains. Yet this impression of a dead
world due to the silence is accompanied by another no less
dismaying. The low clouds and thick mist blot out the surrounding landscape and then it is that a man feels he is going
blind himself, so much so that when he moves his arms he can
scarcely see his hands, and there are moments when, looking
for his feet, he cannot see them, as though he were already in
a cloud, changed to a winged being. The close proximity of the
abyss completes the picture. If, elsewhere, a man who penetrates deep into the forest goes in fear of wild beasts and senses
their presence even before they become flesh before his terrified gaze, here it is the fangs of the earth which assail him,
the earth transformed into a wild beast, like a female jaguar
whose cubs have been taken from her. The precipices cannot
be seen, for they are covered over with fluffy quilts of white
cloud, but so evident is their threat that the hours seem like
years on a visit to the famous María Tecún Ridge. Inspired by
the Holy Virgin, Our Lady, though without formal authoriza-
tion from my hierarchical superiors, I carried there with me
what was necessary to bless the rock, and I must here record
under oath that as I completed the blessing, and for no appar-
ent reason, our horses kicked out at one another and whinnied,
with their eyes staring from their sockets, as though they had
seen the devil himself.

"And now I shall recount what I have learned from the

174

natives about what they call 'spider-spell madness.' It is an ambulatory frenzy brought on by their spell-weavers, or witch-doctors. To produce it, these traitors to the Catholic faith lay out a straw or reed mat on which they sprinkle red pinole powder, black chia grains, flour or sugar for whiteness, bread and tortilla crumbs, and powdered brown sugar, or any other kind of food or condiment, except salt, because that is used in baptismal ceremonies. Once the powder is sprinkled, from a tortilla gourd or bowl, they take a handful of spiders, great big ones with long legs, and urge them on by blowing on them to make them run like creatures possessed all over the powdered food, food or condiment which, now imprinted with the traces of those frenzied spiders, is given to the victim, who is at once assailed by the desire to escape from her house, to run away from her own ones, to forget and reject her children, such is the power of this accursed potion to invert a woman's natural sentiments.

"But evil rarely walks alone, it is most often accompanied by yet more evil. Men who are deserted by these 'bitten women,' as they are commonly called, though it is more correct to say that they are taken with 'spider's-maze madness,' turn away from goodness, are left like trees that lose the bark which protected them from the elements, and without the compass needle of good love to guide them, they turn to drink or concubinage, those vain refuges of sin which, far from bringing them peace, vex them still further, until they escape in search of the 'tecuna,' ever enticed by the hope of finding her, a hope which is dissolved into tears, since it is the popular belief that when they are finally led on to María Tecún Ridge they see reproduced before their eyes, in that stone which once was a person, the image of the woman who abandoned her home, and who begins to call, all this so that the man, blinded by love, will rush forward to the joyful rendezvous, oblivious of the ravine, or chasm, which in that very moment swallows him whole."

At the end of each note he signed his name—Valentín Ur-

175

dáñez, Presbyter—and he had written a great many more without copying them, rough notes in truly nebulous disorder, on the subject of that malady which may well have been the sickness suffered by Don Quixote, that knight-errant who is riding still because in him Cervantes discovered perpetual motion, as an academic friend of his had put it, scoffing a little at the ingenuousness of this country priest, and recommending as a cure for his tecunas, those women bitten by "spider-spells," and their husbands, let them read the legend of the Minotaur.

He put down his nursery of notes to take up his breviary. Nagualism. Everyone talks about nagualism and no one knows what it is. He has a nagual, they'll say of someone, meaning he has an animal to protect him. This we can understand, because just as we Christians have the Holy Guardian Angel to watch over us, the Indian believes he has a nagual. But what cannot be explained without the aid of the devil is how the Indian can change himself into the animal which protects him, the animal he uses as his nagual. Without going into unnecessary details, they say this Nichón turns into a coyote as he leaves the town to carry the mail up there through the mountains, for the letters seem to fly, so swiftly do they reach their destination. He shook his gray head from side to side. Coyote, coyote . . . if I caught him I'd burn his behind, like Coyote himself.

The postman went into Aleja Cuevas' bar. His despair would not let him be. Wherever he was, he was tormented by wondering why she went away, was it something I did, something I didn't do, something I said, something I didn't say, what got into her, what didn't, who can she have run off with, who does she love now, is she better off without me, does he love her like I did, I mean do, I mean did, because although I still love her she ain't here to be loved anymore. In the absence of God there's always liquor to turn to. He dived from the street into the liquor store, as though into some tree-shaded pool. The proprietress, beautiful bronzed flesh, big rings in her ears, was talking to someone, resting her elbows on the zinc counter. She saw him come in, without taking much notice, but said,

176

"What's that you've got there, mister? Would that be a shawl?" and addressing herself to the other man, who was breathing his cigarette smoke almost directly into her bosom, she added coquettishly, "Good thing I have a sweetheart to give me presents, because if your sweetheart won't, who will? Husbands think you'll just go fooling around with someone else if they buy you something as nice as that."

"It ain't for sale," Señor Nicho cut in, somewhat sharply, moving up to the counter for his first drink. He drank it down eagerly.

"I thought you were selling it, that you'd brought it in to sell it."

"It's a present, and if you buy something as a present you can't sell it, you mustn't, it ain't right."

"Well, if you find whoever it is you meant it for, you give it to her for me. Sneaky, you've just come from trying to sell it for nothing at the Chinaman's place!"

"If you're thinking of selling it off cheap, let's make a deal, you can't tell me you're here to pawn it for the price of one drink," rejoined the other man, taking his hand out of his pocket and leaving his baggy breeches feeling all empty.

"I'm real sorry to have to turn you down, but it just ain't for sale."

"Well, if you can't sell something you bought as a present, make me a present of it," Aleja Cuevas suggested. "I'd love to have it, the color suits me real well. Still, if you can't . . ."

"No, I can't, otherwise I'd have been only too happy to give it to someone young and pretty like yourself."

"Why, he's even paying me compliments now!"

"Tell you what I'll do, I'll bring you another one just like it, just exactly like it, the same color. I'll be setting off for the capital again in a few days from now, and I'll buy you one like this, if you want, or a different one, just as you please."

"Let's agree on that, then."

"Yes, there was another one where I bought this, and I went to see the Chinaman to ask if it was good quality."

"And I thought you were after selling it . . ."

177

"And instead of telling me whether it was a high-class shawl or not, the brute asked me if I'd stolen it."

"You should have let him have it. He makes too many cracks, that Chinaman."

"Pour me another drink. Don't give me any change, give it to me in liquor."

"What can you be celebrating, I wonder, drinking all by yourself and not inviting anyone?"

"It's more of a wake than a celebration," he laughed at himself with a sniveling laugh. "If you'll have one with me you're both invited, because when you're as poor as I am, everyone looks down on you," his lip trembling, feverish, wet with liquor, "celebrate with me," his voice began to break, "let's celebrate, go on, have one on me, after all, you only live once!"

"Can I get you one?" the proprietress asked her other customer.

"No, it's too early for me. If I drink in the day it tastes like something they give you for toothache. And that stuff you're drinking is even worse," he said, turning back to Aleja Cuevas.

"You don't like my anisette? I bet you wouldn't mind if I wiped it all over your mouth with my lips."

"I wouldn't mind."

"I'm so used to insults, honey, that flattery offends me! Here's to you, mister postman—I don't even know your name —and to those good old days we won't see again."

Señor Nicho stood transfixed by the sound of the flies. The other man had gone, and the woman was talking to him from the back room. Though they weren't really talking, they were somehow always on the point of talking, talking because the other was there, for company, so as not to feel alone, like an ox with its dry maize leaves, while he knocked back the bottle he had bought so as not to keep troubling her for one drink at a time.

But if the truth were told, that kind of conversation is always irksome, even if you stay silent, because you have to be forever

178

looking friendly to show you're attentive to the other person's thoughts, and if Aleja Cuevas kept it up, it wasn't for his pretty face, but on account of the embroidered shawl, which no longer seemed merely attractive, but divine.

Her honeyed eyes missed not a movement of the hand and forearm around which the postman had wound the shawl. For him, in his infatuation, it was as though he were holding it there and the rest were around the shoulders and back of sweet Chagüita Terrón, and her pressed close to his heart. He raised his voice and talked to what, outside him, was like another reality: he addressed the bar-owner, "I won't ask you to have another one, because you're busy at your chores; but if you feel like one you know where it is; don't be afraid to say so."

"If you'll just let me put some salt in this stew I'll come and join you. You're so polite, I've quite taken to you. I've seen you go by, I knew who you were, and I remember we even said hello once, during the fair, remember?"

"Everyone knows me—and thank you for those kind words. Why, some folks find out when it's my turn to take the mail to the capital and wait until then to send their letters, especially if they're sending money in them, cash."

"That's why I don't think you should be drinking so much, mister, if you'll take my advice, because if they see you drunk they ain't going to trust you no more, and anyway you're in danger of being arrested and taken to the barracks for a flogging. It's very risky for a man like you to guzzle down a whole bottle like that. Have you stopped to think what it would mean to lose people's trust, all them foreigners who wait till it's your turn to send all their letters to—to where their families are, to lands across the sea; and all those poor people who have to do without to pay for the stamps; and all those sick folk who think that when the letters you take for them get there, their folks are sure as sure going to come and look after them; and all those mothers who tell their sons about their joys and hardships, and the hopes they have pinned on them. Husbands, wives, sweethearts or loved ones—"

179

"Hee, hee, hee," the postman laughed with the sound of a rattlesnake in the water, "all those letters tell is lies."

"But still, good or bad, truth or lies, it all goes with you, like your shadow, from this tiny corner lost in the mountains."

The postman rubbed one foot over the other, his bare postman's feet which carried so much responsibility, leaning against the bar, a vague expression on his face, foolish and smiling, still holding on to the shawl, talking in a second reality, the one inside, to Chagüita, his woman whose feet took her far, far away, her feet carrying her step after step after step . . .

"I'm going to follow you," he said in his insides, "no matter where you are I'll find you, or my name's not Dionisio, Nicho for short. I think marriage must've locked my love away, and only now, in my sorrow, am I feeling it again, burning, boiling, aching. Without you I'm turning into the same slob I was before, a nobody, because I was alone, and a man alone ain't worth nothing, don't mean nothing, a man needs a woman to make him whole."

The barkeeper, with her eyes still fixed on the bloodlike shine of the shawl, brighter still when the sunbeams entering at an angle through the window began to gleam on it, muttered, "Drunken slob, now he's turning soft! If there's one reason I'd like to get out of this stinking business, it's the way men turn when they get drunk, the stupid nonsense they talk." She raised her voice, which was still just a muttering in the back room, to tell him yet again, "It's not good for you to be guzzling liquor like that, mister."

"What's it to you?"

"I was only trying to stop you from getting yourself—"

"No one tells me what to do."

"No one's telling you what to do."

"I had a mother and a father, and they're both dead and buried. Give me another bottle and shut your gate."

"Don't you be so fresh, do you hear, you great brute, or I'll call the authorities and have you taken away. Ignorant beast,

God knows why you've got your tail between your legs, and why your woman left you, oaf that you are."

Nicho Aquino didn't hear her last words. He tried to lean against the wall, saw it near, and fell on his back. The woman went to the window to see if the street was quiet. Not a soul. Just a mutt, and the one-legged man from the firework-maker's sleeping in a doorway down the road. She locked and barred the door, closed the window, and in the half darkness she began to unroll the shawl from the drunken man's arm. She opened his hand gently, as though she were being affectionate, and little by little she started to—he felt her, gave a start, and changed position. She waited, and then went to her task even more carefully from the other side. The postman shifted again, pulling his arm free and protesting, "Stop assing about, fuck it . . . What a pest . . . No . . . Nothing . . . What in hell's name . . . It's mine . . . You better stop now, before it's too late!"

Aleja Cuevas, hearing him speak, turned her mouth to his face and went shush, shush, shushhhh, until he went back to sleep. But she grew impatient and, having her weapon to hand, it was best to gain time. She went behind the counter and took out a funnel—it was standing in the mouth of a demijohn—stuck it in a flask of the worst liquor, and took it over to where the postman lay. Señor Nicho closed his lips as she, like someone cleaning out a chicken, stuffed her fingers into his mouth to force his teeth apart. The funnel struck against his teeth, chipping them and making his gums bleed, until it was right inside his mouth. Like killing a snake, she thought, and started to pour. The drunk started choking, his throat was insufficient for the passage of the liquid, but she had to keep on pouring it down him. He tried several times to defend himself with his two arms and one hand—he was still hanging onto the shawl with the other one—but then the barkeeper would take the opportunity to try and snatch the precious garment away from him, though without success, for he, it seemed, if he had to choose between letting go of what he so dearly loved and defended, and choking, would rather choke, although he still attempted in the desperation of choking and vomiting to push the funnel out of his mouth by shaking his head from side to side, without managing to do so, since the end of the funnel was hard against the back of his throat. The flask finally emptied and the woman left him in peace. She would just have to wait until the drink had its effect and put him out completely. She opened the door, after rearranging her clothes and hair, brushing off a few threads from the shawl that she saw shining on her petticoat, and returned to the back room, waiting innocently. The sound of a muletrain and horsemen stopping outside made her reappear at the counter. It was the mule drivers. They had finished unloading at Don Deferic's, and now they'd come for a beer to wash away the smell of the road. She wasn't pleased at all, not at all, but what could she do.

"Just as we thought," said Hilario as he walked in, "our Nicho came to get himself good 'n' stewed. Look at the way he's sprawling there like a pig, he might at least have done it in style, to a guitar."

"You, Porfirio, you're the strongest, lift him up," said another, the one who came in just after Hilario. "Poor devil, he must have hurt his mouth as he fell."

"Sure I'll lift him, he's my friend, and even if he wasn't, he's a fellow human being. He don't weigh a thing, lads—that's why he's so fast with the mail."

"If you ask me, it's true he turns into a coyote when he gets outside the town, and that's why when he carries the letters it's as though they'd flown through the air."

So said Hilario, as Porfirio bent over to lift Señor Nicho, with the aid of another muleteer.

"My!" said the latter, "he's as cold as a corpse, feel how icy cold his face is!"

The muleteers put the backs of their sunburnt, earthy hands to his cheeks and forehead. Hilario pinched his ears and rubbed the hand not holding the shawl, whilst the other hand remained a rigid claw hanging on to that piece of glowing silk.

"Why do you think he brought that?" interrupted the barkeeper, now in a very bad temper, referring to the shawl.

"For his woman, poor devil," Hilario replied, looking at her, almost questioning her with his eyes, what could have brought this mood on, she knew very well it wasn't easy to give the other lads the slip when they got back from a drive, nor could he say let's not go to Aleja's place, because even in the company of the others he was the first to suggest the idea, not for the beer, but to see her.

"And the worst of it," said Porfirio, "is that as well as being cold, his heart is nearly stopped, just feel—I can hardly hear a thing here. We'd best report it. You, run and tell, if only for that good news letter he brought you a year ago."

"I'm going, Porfirio, if you'll give me a chance. I'll report it to the commandant. Order me a dark beer, you know it's my medicine."

"What a tale! Drink it now, there's time, more time than life, and this liquor-sick soul can't get no colder, he's like a block of ice already."

"No, I'd best go now, if you're gonna do someone a favor, you should do it properly, a favor done late is no favor at all, and a favor is what I'm doing, as no one's paying me for doing it."

"Poor Señor Nicho, he's even gone cross-eyed," spoke up another muleteer, Olegario his name.

"His eyes must've gotten tongue-tied. Must've been some fall he took. I reckon it's a wonder he didn't break nothing."

"You can reckon all you want, Porfirio, no one's stopping you, but try to sit him up straight, and hold on to him, because if you don't he'll fall over again. It's right what they say about God looking after drunks, though."

The barkeeper, meantime, washed their glasses and set them up, giving no rest to the copal gum she was chewing noisily, nervously, between her teeth. She lined the beer bottles up on the bar, and stopped chewing, to say airily, though with a double meaning, "Right enough, God and all his angels too. I want you all to know that I didn't even notice he'd fallen, because I was busy out back. I went in to scrub some dishes, and when I came back out and didn't see him I said to myself,

Señor Nicho must have gone, and a good thing too, because he was staggering all over the place. He finished off two bottles of pure white rum, just like that, enough to knock anyone over."

"Well, my lads, that's all the invitation we need," said Hilario, raising his voice and his glass, to clink it against the foaming glasses of his comrades, his hat pushed back and his mule blinder dangling over his shoulder.

Porfirio Mansilla, without neglecting the drunk, drank and talked, after taking the first draught, with a frothy moustache over his moustache, "And he even wanted to eat the shawl by the looks of it, 'cause it's all torn and soaked in blood, and it looks as if he's torn himself here, look, in his frustration at not being able to rip it. He tried to give it away to Don Deferic, and the German wouldn't take it."

"He's a decent man, that one. The other day the commandant's sons were playing around with their monkey, and it got in here in the bar. I ran out, he was coming by, and he stopped to get the thing out for me."

"It's a shame to see a fellow in such a poor way," Porfirio went on.

"But he's not in a poor way," laughed Aleja Cuevas, and all the others laughed too.

"Not wanting to hear is worse than mishearing. I meant the poor way that he's in, and if you don't want to understand me you can go shit yourselves."

"Have some respect, you!" snapped Hilario.

"Well, don't make me lose my temper, what with holding up the drunk and defending myself against all of you. What I was trying to say is, it's a shame to see a man in such a bad way, and it's best not to look, 'cause if you do you'll never ever touch another drop, and that's why I don't care for bars where there are mirrors, because mirrors are like your conscience, always watching you."

Hilario cut him short: "And that, my beauty," moving closer to Aleja Cuevas, "is why the only mirrors you've put in here are your own two precious eyes."

"Pardon me while I swoon," said she, laughing gaily, "don't think you're the first one who's told me that."

"But I am the first one to say it sincerely, Alejita."

"Seeing is believing, the rest is just poetry. We'll see if you remember me when you set off on your next trip to the capital, and bring me back a pure silk shawl like this one the postman brought."

"It's as good as yours, my lovely, providing you give me something in exchange—"

"I'm giving you all you want, so stop complaining," and she stretched out her arm, dark firm flesh, to fill Hilario's glass, as he devoured her with his eyes.

"That's the way," Porfirio broke in with word and glass. Olegario called him Porfirios because he was so big and strong he made two of the others. "That's the way to put this stutterer in his place. He's so tricky and gossipy, and such a terrible liar, you'd swear he was rich, but no, poor and barefoot he is."

"I'll have you arrested, you and the postman both, you sober and him drunk, so you can look after him inside."

"He sure did tear at that shawl," the barmaid said, to assure herself against the least suspicion, "he must have ripped it with his teeth. What fault is it of the shawl that his old woman ran off?"

"She took to the road and went, so let someone else have her, for as for me, my name is Hilario, and I've got my own true love as insurance." His sunburnt, hairy arm slipped round the woman's waist, and when she tried to get away he held her tighter.

"Stop playing games, they'll start taking you serious. And you know how jealous Don Porfirio is."

"Over you?"

"Yes, don't you remember, I've been engaged to him since the last time you were here."

"But nothing came of it. Just like a woman. So I'm setting her free to go to Hilario, so they can get married and have a party on their wedding day. And I'll promise to get as drunk with joy that day as Señor Nicho is today. Hilario is a bachelor,

Aleja my girl, and you should always remember that a good husband is a whole lot better than a bad bachelor."

"They must have given Señor Nicho's wife that spider's drink," said another of the muleteers, for something to say, because all he had done up until then was drink and spit.

"I just love hearing old Curlyhead once he gets started," said Hilario, "because he'll believe anything, and no one can get it out of his brain that it's pinole powder spiders have crawled through that makes women turn away from the sanity of their homes to leave and go mad out in the world. He doesn't realize times have changed, and that now instead of getting a tecuna all excited with the old 'spider-spell' powder to put them on the road to ruin, they just give them some thread. Do you all follow me?"

"I follow you," replied the barkeeper, as Hilario continued.

"The long-legged spiders our grandparents used to run over the powder they gave their womenfolk, have all gone, and now they use thread spiders."

The barkeeper pulled herself free, shrugged as if to say, what's it to me, and served some more beer.

"These pals of mine—you, Porfirio, watch out, Señor Nicho's falling over again—never seem to know what I'm talking about. Let me explain. The spider's bite has been brought up to date. Now it's your sewing-machine salesman who turns women into tecunas by turning their heads."

"What a boring sermon!" exclaimed Aleja Cuevas, looking daggers at Hilario for his insinuations.

"You talk too much, you. Keep quiet!" warned Porfirio.

"You're too big and strong, you, I'd best keep quiet!"

"What's all this?" the barkeeper said, parrying Hilario's last words. "Has Don Porfirio lost his girl to a Singer?"

"This idiot just likes to talk about things he knows nothing about."

Aleja Cuevas passed her hand slyly over her bosom, as though she were strumming a guitar, a sign which told Hilario she was grateful to Porfirio Mansilla for the reply which, interpreting her thoughts, he had given. And as she strummed her breast, she said, "By the way, didn't one of you tell me he'd known someone called Nelo, who sold sewing machines, and who left his name carved with a knife on a tree near here?"

"It must have been Hilario, because who and what doesn't he know, he pokes his nose in everywhere. You'd think folk went to him for confession."

"Nelo? Nelo? Anyone would think he was a flea-bitten Indian like us! I can see you haven't had much to do with foreigners. His name was Neill." Hilario interrupted his own explanation. Four soldiers led by a corporal came in to take Nicho Aquino the postman out.

"He ain't dead?" said one of the soldiers.

"No," replied Hilario, "he's drunk."

"Dead drunk," added the soldier, as he touched him.

Soon as he got to the bar the corporal said, "One drink in lines of three."

The barkeeper served him three drinks. The men from the barracks always ordered their drinks like that, to keep up their reputation. One drink in lines of four, was four drinks; one drink in lines of five, five drinks, and so on, through six and seven. But after seven they would say two drinks in lines of four, meaning eight, or two drinks in lines of five, which was ten. But they could take their drink all right, they knew how to "ride" their liquor, and they knew when to halt and retreat, unlike poor Nicho, who had celebrated an Indian fiesta: decorate the house, prepare the fireworks, go for the liquor, drink the lot down, and down goes your Indian too.

"Excuse me—no—hand me the guitar," said Hilario to the barkeeper, playing pushy, almost snatching the bottle from her as she went to serve him more beer, "I like it without too much froth on top."

"With or without?"

"Wiiithout!" replied the waggish muleteer, as he pinched her hands and finally made her let go of the bottle.

"You don't even appreciate me serving you."

"No, Alejita, but that's only because my life hangs by a thread . . . of love!"

"All right, Señor Smooth-Talker, tell us more about your friend Nelo."

"Neill!"

"Neill, then."

"What do you want me to tell you, and why, there are too many people in the calaboose already for telling stories. Porfirio will have to give me permission."

"Since when did you need permission to spin a tale, specially from me, as if I was your father."

"You're more than a father to me."

"You must be drunk!"

"That's right," Hilario spat, "call me a drunk, the young lady a harlot, then speak ill of the government, and you'll end up in jail."

"I never said that, Hilario, you're a devil when you get to talking. What I meant to say was, I'd like you to—"

"Sure you do, and I like you too, but I don't like you to go insulting people, least of all Alejita, because it ain't her fault she runs a liquor house."

"Let's go," suggested Olegario, smoking, with great puffs of smoke beneath his grease-caked hat, "because me, I'm tired of standing up, and at the Black Girls you can sit down."

"Go, then," the barkeeper exploded, "get going, you'll get your salted spider there, all right!"

In the silence that followed, the faces of the muleteers—when they fell serious they looked ferocious—passed round the news that the postman had been carried to the hospital, because he was taken bad, poisoned.

"I don't believe in sewing machines," went on the frizzly-haired muleteer they called Curlyhead, who was still smarting from Hilario's retort and wanted to get back at him, "I'm old-fashioned, I believe in the old 'spider-spell' sting, and I believe in it all the more after what we've seen: Isabra Aquino's been done for, and Nicho's been given a taste of the life to come. There's no knowing the ways of vengeance, that's why I say my prayers, because you can defend yourself against friends you know are your enemies by slipping the noose round them as you dance to their tune; but only the power of God can keep you from the ones you don't know about."

They all left together, as one, leaving Aleja Cuevas to bite her lips in fury, lips livid and thin as fruit peel, though she smiled as she took their money so as not to offer her sorrow for their contempt. Away they went, quarreling, whistling, on a train of machos' feet, to go on with the revelry at the Black Girls, the good ole Black Girls, where they sold cane liquor and maize beer like river water, according to the curlyhead, and where watching the sad river flowing by did more to get you drunk than the liquor.

XIV

 Came a whistle, insistently, incisively, insinuatingly, like front teeth vibrating in the air. The night seemed wet, though it hadn't rained. The bamboo boughs, swung by the strapping young wind, swept the forest silence with brooms of sound softer than feathers, on the edge of the town, toward the graveyard.

"I thought it must be you, your whistle."

"You're late."

"You can talk, you with your whistle still wet. Give me a kiss and stop complaining. What a joy to have one another close, and not have to watch what we say and do in front of the lads."

"Do you love me, my sweet?"

"I do, I do. Where's that muzzle . . . Mmmm . . . Mmmm . . . And another. That's the way to love, and loving me is what you're doing, pinning me down and hog-tying me. Go to it, old friend, I'm your rightful property to do with as you please."

"But you treat me bad, you really do. It makes me feel so miserable. It's hard to think that while you're earning your money your sweetheart's making hay with some other party."

"Someone's been talking."

"No one's been talking. I just sense it, you can tell if something's going on while you're away."

The shadow of the bamboo brought them together, whilst they, it seemed, were moving apart, cutting the ties of love between them. She, full of concern, took his head gently in her arms, and her mysterious eyes gazed deeply into the open eyes of the muleteer, who was weeping.

"Don't be silly," she whispered, "how can you think that because that overgrown ape shows off out by the post on the corner, or because he comes into the bar now and then and starts talking his nonsense to me, about what goes on in town, and the sales he's made with his sewing machines, that I'm going to fall for him instead of you, when you're the only one close to my heart, even though I get the feeling you think I'm your doormat when your muleteer friends are around, I think you're too ashamed to let them know you're mine. But that's a fact, my honey, no matter how much I may love you, adore you, die for you, humble myself for you, anything you ask, if you're ashamed of me being a barkeeper and make me look small in front of the others, it can easily be settled by us not seeing one another again. Love stinks when it isn't freely given, and the more so when your man tries to put you down."

"Men like me don't cry," mumbled the prattling mule driver, reeking of brandy and surrounded by the aroma of guava trees dripping evening dew from each sun-darkened leaf, tiny teardrops from weeping trees, "men like me don't cry, and if they do they cry like the guavas that first wrap their branches all around themselves and twist themselves up, burned inside by their sorrow, burned so bad even the wood turns red; and second—"

"—they cry when they're full of booze."

"I won't say that ain't the truth. But they also cry when their heart tells them they're being betrayed, because then there are only two ways out: either you bring misfortune on yourself by doing away with your rival, or you look the other way, making out you don't care, and do away with your self-respect . . . Let me be, I don't want you giving me the same kisses you give another."

"Look, Hilario, don't be such a fool. Just because you've got beer in your brain doesn't mean . . . My little boy . . . My baby . . ."

"I've told you once, let go of my arm, get away from my face."

"For mercy's sake, I never realized what a favor you're doing me by loving me. Look, even if I was doing what you, because you're such an idiot, think I am, if men cried just on that account the rivers would rise like they do in winter, because not all women are like me, I'm sorry to say."

They fell silent. They could see the lights of the town, close together. Close together and apart, like them. The dew-soaked grass chilled their buttocks. Hilario gazed up at the sky, she pulled the tips off the blades of grass within reach of her dark hand.

"The truth is," she went on after a moment of silence, "that new loves in the city are better than old loves back in the village. Tell me, is she pretty, does she have nice hair, I'll bet she has beautiful eyes."

"What I want to know is why that fellow should spend hours at a time in your bar, I wonder he ain't moved his bed in."

"He was waiting for me to say yes." Hilario stared at her, then started to get up, but she held him back. "But I kept saying no, and said I wanted some proof—"

"Proof of what?" Hilario bellowed.

"Proof of his eternal love," she laughed with all her teeth, throwing back her head so the wind would kiss her hair. "Don't be so silly, the proof that it would only cost me what

191

he said it would." Hilario sat down beside her again, now only half angry. "Sly you are, sneaky, crafty, you know very well he's been trying to sell me that machine, badgering me to buy it, offering it on installments, saying it's not much to pay, and if you make a few things it'll pay for itself, you know because that's why you dropped all those hints this afternoon. Did you think I didn't notice when you said that these days they don't give women 'spider-spell' powder, but threadspiders."

"You can't tell me that's all he was after . . ."

"You're right. One day he turned up with two American women uglier than men, with trousers on, a nice enough pair, though, who wanted to find out what they could about the life of that man you knew, the one who carved his name on a tree somewhere round here. As I didn't know anything about it they went out the same way they came in, without writing a single word in their notebooks, although they stood drinking maize beer until they were fit to bust. 'Curioso,' they said, knocking back glasses of beer as if it was water. Then they said they wanted to drink it from a gourd. Later they caused an uproar in the town, and one of them was thrown from her horse and dragged away, it nearly killed her. You're the only one who knows the story of that mysterious man."

"I know it, but I ain't telling. It's my secret."

"What do I care. I know he was called Nelo, and that he called you Mombin, like I call you honey, and that he put his name on a tree, and that's plenty for me."

From time to time, as drops of dew kept falling like the stellar fragments of a clock, tiny pieces of tinkling glass broken into minutes, mangoes would also fall to the earth, its carpet of grass, with a muffled sound, as if every so often they fell to mark the hours, from the branches of trees visibly sagging beneath the weight of their fruit. Poch, went the mangoes as they fell, followed by the crystals of minute-counting dew, and then after a while poch, poch, poch.

Hilario Sacayón was very young when a salesman who had been recommended to his father came to San Miguel Acatán.

192

Old Sacayón had traveled up and down the country with that man, and when he got back he said that his name was Neill, and that he was a traveling sewing-machine salesman. The next day Neill visited the Sacayón family house and played with a little boy, who was Hilario. Hilario looked and looked at him, then touched him, felt the cloth of his trouser leg, and their friendship was sealed by a coin Señor Neill put in his hand, and a kiss with the smell of tobacco on his cheek.

When he was older Hilario heard his father speak highly of the goodness and learning of Señor Neill, when he advised his sons never to judge a person by the way he looked or the clothes he wore. That man, who in appearance was like all the other sewing-machine salesmen, was one of those men who carry a miniature reproduction of the world in their eyes. There are men whose eyes are like the water in empty fish tanks, but others have pupils with their life's catch gathered inside them, swimming, wriggling, and Señor Neill was one of those.

So strong was his father's affection for the memory of Señor Neill that one day he took Hilario, then in his youth, to a tall tree. On the trunk, carved with a razor, were some letters and figures, which read: O'Neill–191 . . . , with the last figure rubbed out.

Without wasting time the old muleteer, for Hilario's father had been a muleteer also, one of the old kind who used to smoke their cigars as they rode unbroken mules, without dropping the ash, transferred the inscription to his leather breastpiece, copying the characters with his knife, and until the day he died that old man carried on his muleteer's chest the letters and numbers from the tree trunk: O'Neill–191.

This, simply stated, was the secret of Hilario Sacayón. After his father died, the younger Sacayón took over the story, adding all manner of lies from the storehouse of his own imagination. In the mouth of Sacayón the younger, O'Neill had had a passion for a girl from San Miguel Acatán, the famous Miguelita, known to no one but talked of by all thanks to the renown bestowed on her in mule yards, inns, taverns and evening festivities by Hilario Sacayón.

Miguelita was dark as the Bilboes Virgin, a miraculous carved image from the time of the Colony, left forgotten in a niche in the jail at Acatán where rogues, runaway Indians and quarreling spouses were put to torture in the stocks. Miguelita, whose eyes were like two dying coals, dying but with the black fire of coals, dimpled cheeks, hawberry waist, rose-pink mouth, and hair of black crape. Miguelita, who did not return O'Neill's despairing love, because she never cared for him. Hilario called him simply Neill, and the townsfolk Nelo.

He loved her, she loved him not. He adored her but she, on the contrary, detested him. He worshipped her. He told her he would turn to drink, and he did. He told her he would throw himself into the ocean and he became a sailor, to drown his dark sorrow in the blue of the sea, with the same pipe he smoked in front of Miguelita, his blue eyes, his blond hair, his gringo's body and his long arms.

Hilario Sacayón's conscience tormented him after a night on the booze. The things he made up. But where did all that loquacity come from which enabled him to order his words and phrases, ironic or convoluted turns of phrase, as though before he recounted them in his drunkenness they had already been written down, put just as they should be, no less well and maybe better than if all those things he invented really had taken place before his eyes?

He stayed hidden in his house the day after his meeting with Aleja Cuevas, because he and his muleteer pals had carried on their carousing at the Black Girls, and in his drunken stupor he had told many more details about the affair between Neill and Miguelita. He didn't have the face to go out into the street, but right in his house, in his rancho, was the presence of his father who, from the tables and chairs and corners, but most of all from his muleteer's breastpiece, accused Hilario of having stolen the story of his life. Afterwards, quieting remorse, he considered his ingratitude as a natural process of the son

194

annulling the father, that is to say, putting himself in his place, and he even imagined the old man being flattered because he was plagiarizing him in such an artful fashion, telling as his own the stories passed on to him by his progenitor. Later, to quiet his remorse still more, he put the blame on the liquor. Liquor loosens your tongue. You don't know what you're saying. You talk for the sake of talking. However, he ought to return to his father what he stole from him with his chattering whenever he became thus inspired. He would go and say that everything about Señor O'Neill had been told him by his father; but, on reflection, this was a case of the cure being worse than the disease, since it meant pinning the blame for his own deceit on the old muleteer, God bless him.

He swore, as he always did, never to talk about O'Neill or his love for Miguelita of Acatán again, even if his friends begged him to tell more, because, the trouble was, Hilario always had more to tell.

That's why when the gringo women who wanted information on the life of O'Neill returned to the town, Hilario Sacayón was unable to speak. He was sober, and being sober he said nothing about Neill or Miguelita. He took them to the foot of the carved tree, so they could take a photograph, showed them his father's breastpiece, and gave them vague details of childhood memories, but all subject to the truth, just as if he were testifying in court. The gringo women, however, knew a bit about the story of Miguelita, dark as the Bilboes Virgin, marzipan with a touch of anise, feet like pinheads and chubby little hands; but Sacayón was content just to listen conceitedly without saying a word. Before they went away the two Americans left him a portrait of Señor O'Neill, a famous man. Hilario looked at it and hid it away. He looked horrible, all bleary-eyed, thin, and worn. No, that couldn't be the joyful drunkard who died of sleep because he was bitten by a fly on one of his voyages, the man who left Miguelita a sewing machine to remember him by, the one folks hear at night, when the Town Hall clock rings twelve. Who has not heard it in San

Miguel Acatán? Any night after the twelve chimes of the Town Hall clock, if you stop and listen, you will hear someone sewing at a machine. It is Miguelita.

XV

Three weeks later Señor Nicho set off with the mail for the capital, purged of all earthly cares. He'd come so close to death, they had had to give him injections all through the night after his celebration, injections of camphor, they couldn't find the right antidote, camphorated oil, to be exact, and then they gave him a sound flogging which left him aching still. He had to set off with the clothes he was wearing, white no longer but rather the color of the dunghill because when, accompanied by a soldier, he went back home to collect his things, he found that thieves had taken everything he owned. So hardhearted was his woman, not even his going to prison had made her come back. "Tecuna, tecuna, tecuna! . . ."

"Tecuna." With that word on his lips he set off from San Miguel Acatán, shaky, jittery, after stopping by at the church to cross himself and wipe away, with the sleeve of the spare jacket they'd given him, the saliva which the postmaster, fatter than ever, sprayed in his face as he gave him a final warning.

"You'll have to look after yourself now there's no one else to do it for you, now the tecuna has left you short-eared. I'll send a soldier to look the rancho over from time to time. Did you lock it? Did you bar it? Did you sell the hogs, them two hogs you had, and the chickens? Take your dog with you, dog's better'n a woman."

The postman didn't get a chance to explain to that tub of lard who was always spitting as he spoke that he was wearing all he

196

now possessed, that while he was away, first sick, then arrested, they robbed him of everything, everything he had.

"Weighs a bit," he muttered, as he went out of the post office, lifting the mailbags to test their weight, two large canvas sacks and a smaller briefcase with the official documents.

"You're a sly one, you are," the postmaster snorted. "You get your smart remarks in. Of course it's heavy, but that can't be helped, that's how loads are, and you've only yourself to blame, when these stinking monkeys who call themselves citizens know it's Señor Nicho taking the mail, they clog up the letter box in the mailing office."

San Miguel Acatán was left behind. He couldn't wait to be off, to go, to get away, among the spires of eucalyptus trees which cut off lightning and thunderbolts, like the sword of the Archangel beneath whose golden shoe the devil's head lies crushed; the tufts of sweet-smelling pines, providers of good turpentine; and the green mass of other trees.

San Miguel Acatán was lost in a gleam of porcelain beneath the morning sun: porcelain of its roofs, white porcelain of its houses, old porcelain of the church. And Señor Nicho was left alone on the shaded road with his dog, skinny, undernourished, meager, ears cropped because it got distemper as a pup and they'd had to bleed it, eyes golden brown, white-haired with black spots on its front paws.

"What was it you said? She left you asleep? You didn't hear her go? You had no idea?"—the dog wagged its tail—"Ah, Jasmine . . ."—referred to directly by name, the dog danced round him—"Quiet, don't go running on ahead and give me the slip, we're in a hurry."

It was a long day over roads swollen with rain till the earth looked like the peel of a water-sodden potato, and the rivulets played like live animals, everywhere, leaping, running, their activity in contrast with the two travelers who by late afternoon were worn out, ready to drop, in a village of twenty houses where the postmen always stop the night. It was dark before they arrived, but there were still lights in the ranchos when they got in. The dog panting, Señor Nicho somber, like a robot, grinding the soles of his sandals over a street strewn with stones from the river, more of a river, indeed, than a street.

As he took off his hat inside the lodginghouse his hair felt greasy with sweat, sticking to his ears, his forehead, the nape of his neck. He ruffled it a bit with his hand. From his provision bag he took tortillas, salt, coffee powder, golden chili powder, and a strip of jerked beef he threw to the dog, to be devoured in one go.

The old woman who owned the inn came out to greet him, wanted him to do her a favor, besides.

"Right you are," said the postman, setting his provisions down on a step, on the edge of the yard, "long as it ain't too bulky, because I just ain't got room. If it's something small I'd be pleased to, Nana Moncha, you know I'm at your service."

"God bless you. Tell me, Nicho, how's your woman these days, she must be expecting by now because I dare say you've given her what's good for her."

Señor Nicho just grunted. Ever since he married Chagüita, every time he had to pass by Nana Moncha's place the old girl badgered him with hints and indirect questions so he'd make arrangements with her for the birth.

The dog was all expectant, waiting for another slice of beef, but all it got was a kick. If he could have hit the old woman instead he would have done it. Jasmine, after brushing himself and squealing in pain, posted himself in a corner, all eyes and nose.

The old woman pottered about the courtyard, which was more like a small orchard, with fruit trees, a chayote vine, and perches for chickens, and then insisted again, "Well, consider it a deal, Nicho, you only have to call me a day before she bursts, and I'll see to everything. All you have to do is tell me when her time is, you must keep count, and make the calculation more or less according to the moon, that way you'll know, so you can have the things she'll need there to hand, all ready."

Señor Nicho stopped guzzling his cheese tortilla, drank down a gourd of hot water mixed with chili powder, and looked for a place to bed down. But he couldn't get off to sleep. Through the gaps in the rancho, between the ill-fitting canes—the inn was old, like its owner—he could see the stars shining, burnished, almost sharp in the deep of the sky. It's a pleasure just to think some words. Deep . . .

And he went out into the deep, from his petate and his blanket, but to the deepness outside, roaming with his eyes far from his body, in the radius of vision he couldn't reach with his arms, in that intangible world his fingers could no longer touch, but which his pupils brought him like a message from space. There was another deepness inside him, dark, terribly dark since his companion abandoned him; but he only looked into that deep dark place when the weight of his sorrow grew heavy, when the pain he endured snapped the nape of his neck like the neck of a hanged man, and forced him, suspended in the void, to look down at his darkness, his tremendous human darkness, until sleep stole up on him.

That night at the inn he couldn't sleep. Overwhelmed by physical fatigue, crushed, weak legs, tired feet, aching toes, and heels that felt hard as green avocado skin, he might as well go out in the yard. He tried to take hold of the dog but it sneaked away. It too was awake, and must have remembered the kick. He started to call it, he needed its warmth close to him. Finally the animal came up to him, cowing back every time he put out his hand to touch it, the hand that all of a sudden it began to lick, tickling, grateful, until it moved in close, like something his very own.

He couldn't see who he was talking to. Anyone would have said it was a person.

"Tell me, Jasmine, you who are better than people are, more of a person than most of them, tell me and me alone if you happened to notice whether your mistress was pregnant. I'm talking to you, Jasmine, because I think it may have been you she was looking for, what worries and torments me is the blood of my child she carries in her belly, so much so that I can't get her out of my thoughts. And I have had women, Jasmine, just as you've had bitches, that's why we're what we are, males, and I've lost them, or left them, and . . . and all. But this thing that's going through me now, I'd never even imagined it, still less suffered it, it's as though someone was trying to pull my insides out through my mouth, to leave me empty; and just to think I won't see her again, that I've lost her forever, makes me feel ill, as if my blood was stopping, and the fears and anxieties gnawing away like rats make me do things that aren't like me . . ."

The dog nosed in his hands for the distant smell of jerked beef. A form came out of the house to spew saliva. With sort of a croup. The postman thought it was the old midwife and sneaked back to make out he was asleep, while Jasmine ran to bark at the shadow. He barked, grew tired of barking. Went on barking. Other dogs barked out in the street, in other houses, the night was filled with barking.

The form spewed, it was half a cough and half a vomit, and then a thick voice said doubtfully, in the darkness, "I thought I heard someone talking. Funny. Sounded just like folk talking, but they don't look awake to me."

Señor Nicho, hearing the voice of a man, pretended to be waking up, stretched, and said good evening, from his blankets.

"Evening?" rectified the other. "It's almost dawn."

They bade one another good day, though it wasn't day as yet, at that confused hour in which the dead blue color of the fire interred in the kitchens seems to spread in the cold air. Yawns, and hard on the heels of great yawns, the roosters.

The first one to sing out came like a winged shock for Nicho Aquino. Right by him. He couldn't see it properly. He was just starting to yawn when it came, cock-a-doodle-do! He gave an enormous start and turned to take a kick at it, but what was the use if by then another cock was crowing, and another, and then another.

COYOTE-POSTMAN

It was easy to light the stove in the kitchen, a high misshapen room, the highest in the house, a dilapidated oven, chicken crap everywhere, and at the upper parts of the walls, by the roof, soot and cobwebs, and a bat that flew off like a shot the moment the first flame was kindled.

The thick-spoken old man was a real green worm. A clean worm with his noble wrinkles, like hairy navels, two grains of burnt sugar in two very white, very open eyes, flat nose, high cheekbones, wide brow, white down on his head, and big ears he kept touching with his hand whenever anyone talked to him, because he was somewhat hard of hearing.

He stood looking at Nicho, and said, "Don't you go talking to that pooch like you been talking this morning, 'cause one fine day he's gonna talk back at you and you're gonna be left dumb. For every dumb human being there's an animal that can talk. The pooch'll find the words lacking in his intelligence, and you'll find them gone from your mouth. Just a bit of advice I'm giving you that you ain't asked for," and the old man laughed, seemingly in chorus with the cocks, cock-a-doodle-do, "but we old folk enjoy that, we're in our element giving out advice, telling other people to do what we didn't do when we were young and still won't do now we're old, cock-a-doodle-do . . . If only we could stop being old like we stopped being young, cock-a-doodle-do . . ."

The old man shuffled off to milk a goat. Nicho Aquino followed him. He didn't feel so lonely when he was talking. The old man's hands were black, as though he had been cleaning out the oven or were a dyer by trade: two shadowy gloves with shiny yellowing nails, in which the goat's teats, by contrast with the black, showed up like small begonia flowers, and the milk whiter still as it came squirting out in fits and starts.

"You're staring at my charred, sunburnt hands; but you'd do better to look at my geranium inchworm's head. I'm a good measurer, both as a worm and as a person, and last night I measured your sleep, you, your sleep's too short for the grief you're wearing: short, it's cut too short, it only comes up to your neck at the most, cock-a-doodle-do, cock-a-doodle-do. That's why your eyes are left outside and you can't sleep, the sleep don't reach up to your eyes, the most you can do is stretch the fabric of your sleep, which is like a bat's wing, struggling to get comfortable, grinding your head on that jacket you use for a pillow. From so much moving about and stretching the fabric of your sleep you break it, and the weariness of lying down gets in you, and the urge to go out and find it. Hee, hee, hee, looking for the sleep you can't find in yourself is looking in vain. Last night, without going very far, you did your share of walking, you went a good long way looking for sleep, and looking for your sleep is the way to find out that nothing sleeps, that the night is a great wake of stars sounding in the ears of all beings, large and small, and those things that look like the tombs of daytime activity—tables, cupboards, drawers, chairs—don't seem like the furniture of living people during the night, but like pieces of furniture placed alongside a dead man in his grave, so he can keep on living without being himself and without being someone else, because that's the trouble about it, dead men are neither themselves nor others, no one can tell what they are."

The old comadre, her hair, her rags, her scratching—she had barely enough hair to make one little plait on either side, like a schoolgirl, and barely enough fingers to scratch the lice, fleas and ticks all over her—was blowing on the fire when they returned with the milk, followed by Jasmine.

"Señor Nicho will be starting out in a minute," said she, without turning her head, blowing away at the stove. "Can you give me a few pesos so he can bring me back some oil of turpentine?"

"Sure, oil of turpentine for you, and I'd like him to bring me a few pesos' worth of liniment. My fingers get so cramped up with rheumatics when I start milking, and I'm gonna have to start gelding some of the animals soon."

"Didn't you want me to take something for you, Nana Moncha?"

"I did, but it's pretty big, and you ain't got room, maybe

202

next time you come by you'll have less to carry. Every week there's more people in the town and more letters for you to carry in them canvas bags of yours with the stripes painted on them. I wonder why mailbags are like that."

A clamor of cocks, hens and dogs in the houses, and flocks in long lines, like white armies on the move.

The postman set off from the village of Tres Aguas, so named because it was said there were pools of blue water in white earth, green water in red earth, and purple water in black earth, followed by Jasmine, and accompanied by the old man with black hands.

As Nicho Aquino operated his flint-and-steel lighter to light a cigarette, the old midwife repeated what she had already repeated: "Call me in good time, Nicho, because I just know your woman's blood has stopped turning."

Hundreds, thousands, millions of tiny plumes of illusion could be seen waving in the soft breath of the wind, lit up by the sun, and the spots of big yellow daisies with black hearts enlivened their gaze wherever it came to rest, among peaks of majestic volcanoes and hills of steaming stones. Still walking along the plain, little by little the travelers were drawn together, and a blind thirst for roads traveled and still to be traveled took hold of them, after the first exchange of conversation.

"That dog of yours looks good enough to eat."

"Poor thing, he's just a bag of bones."

"But you could feed him up."

"Only savages would do that."

"Everything relating to the food of man is savage. I don't know why they say we've stopped being savages: there's no such thing as civilized food."

"There's maize . . ."

"Maize, you say. But maize costs the sacrifice of the earth, which is also human. I'd like to see you carry a maizefield on your back, like the poor earth does. And what they're doing now is even more uncivilized, growing maize to sell it."

"That's why the misfortunes came . . ."

203

The old man with black hands, hands the color of black maize, inquired before replying, passed his eyes across the postman's face to get a good look at him. Without slowing his pace, he sighed as he spoke, "And the punishment will get worse. Much light in the tribes, many children, but death, because those who sow maize for profit leave the earth empty of bones, because it is the bones of the forefathers that give the maize, and then the earth demands bones, and the softest ones, those of children, pile up on top of her and beneath her black crust, to feed her."

"Yes, the earth is cruel."

"Cruel, cruel . . . But remember, postman, that the earth is only cruel when cruel men inhabit her."

"But let's get down to basics—what do you think maize should be grown for?"

"To eat."

"To eat," Señor Nicho repeated mechanically, thinking more about Chagüita, who came back to him in the aroma of wild anise.

"And it ain't so much what I think—that's the way it ought to be and that's the way it is, because who would ever think of having children just to sell their flesh, to retail the flesh of their children in a butcher's shop."

"That's different."

"At first sight, it is. But underneath, it's the same. We are made of maize, and we can't make a business out of what we're made of, out of what our flesh is. Outward things change, but if we're talking about substances, a child is as much a piece of flesh as a maizefield. In the old days the law authorized a father to eat his children in time of siege, but it never went so far as to authorize him to murder them to sell their flesh. It's one of the obscure things, the fact that we can feed on maize, which is the flesh of our flesh on the cobs, which are like our children; but everything will end up impoverished and scorched by the sun, by the air, by the clearing fires, if we keep sowing maize to make a business of it, as though it weren't sacred, highly sacred."

204

"What you say is right; but it hasn't been explained to all of us. If we knew it, we could never be so mean, and it's also for our own sakes, because maize wears down the soil, it seems to leave it skinned in the long run, and they even have to leave the maizelands to rest."

"You see along the roads, you, and you who are a postman must have seen a lot, because you are obliged to walk, every day there are more lands ruined by the maizegrowers: bare slopes where the water runs only over stones; plots without that vegetable covering made of the hair of dead men who were made of flesh and dead men who were made of wood; stubblefields so full of stones it withers your soul . . ."

"But what I say is, how can they clothe their families if they don't sell the maize?"

"Those that want to clothe their families work: only work clothes, not only families, whole countries. Only idlers go naked. They idle once the maizefield is sown, and they strip the maizefield to eat, to sell, to clothe their families, buy the medicines they need, and even entertainments with music and liquor. If they planted maize, and ate of it, like the forefathers, and worked, it would be a different story."

"How far are you coming? You're a long way from home now."

"I should have turned back before now; but it pains me to let you go on alone, you have so much sorrow in your face, and what you were asking the dog made me feel uneasy."

"So you heard."

"Everything is heard. You may as well tell me. I'm hard of hearing, but when I cough up in the early morning the reverberations seem to stir things up inside my head, and I can hear all right. I can hear when I'm walking, too, when there's some noise around me."

The postman, beneath an amate, the tree whose flower is hidden in its fruit, the flower only blind men see, the woman only lovers see, recounted his grief to the old man with black hands, with no other witnesses than Jasmine and a lot of clouds shaped like dogs, jasmines in the sky.

205

"And the urge to find your woman, does it come from the belly downwards?"

Nicho Aquino hesitated.

"It's the first thing that has to be decided, because if the urge to join with her comes from below the navel it will be the same with any woman you meet. But if it's from the navel up that you feel the longing to fill with her the emptiness you have inside you, then you have her individualized, and the only cure for that is to find her."

"It's both things. At times, thinking about her, a cold fury catches me at the back of my neck and runs down my back, and at the same time in front—in my legs, I think—and I wring my hands and writhe like a liana being wound into a lasso, and I even fly away from myself like the gleam of a machete blade through the tips of my feet."

"And the longing?"

"The longing, I don't know, it punishes my chest, I look on it with fear, because it beats on my head, closes my eyes, wrinkles my hands, dries out my mouth—that's how I look on it."

"All in all, postman, you'd best not go by María Tecún Ridge, and what we're going to do is, I'm going to go with you. I know where your woman is."

The unfortunate postman's coyote eyes filled with gratitude. At last he had heard from the mouth of a human being what he had been longing to hear the night he went into his rancho and found it empty. That night he spent howling like a coyote, as he slept like a person. From the mouth of a human being, because from inanimate objects—stones, hills, trees, bridges, rivers, posts, stars—he had already heard that "I know where your woman is," but they couldn't speak, they couldn't tell him anything. What use was the warrant for her arrest issued by the commandancy. What use were the notices read out at the end of mass, God bless Father Valentín.

"Let's keep going, follow me, I know where your woman is."

The postman, drunk with pleasure, disorientated, didn't notice that he was leaving the high road, the road he ought to have followed with his sacks of correspondence, charged as he was by sacred obligation to take them to their destination, the Central Post Office, and deliver them to that long lean old man, somewhat charred at the edges, like a baker's shovel.

The footpath where they turned off, flat at first with lightly grained soil which looked like coral, took a steep downward slope by the roots of a tree brought down by the storm, rotted by time, hollowed by ants, of which there remained only, like some ghostly monster, a clearing in the undergrowth where it fell and crushed the plants.

XVI

The postmaster thumped his fist on the desk. Don Deferic thumped his harder. Then the postmaster. Then Don Deferic. And behind the blue-eyed German, like pine cones lit from top to bottom by the egg-yolk light of the insipid paraffin lamp, the faces of the important townsfolk who, without hammering on the desk with their fists, kept their eyes fixed on the fat functionary—some their spectacles—and a one-eyed man who was wandering the square came in to gape with his glass eye still and ominous.

Don Deferic stalked out without another word, he'd already called him a "great fat idiot" and the other had called him a "stinking German bastard" in return. Don Deferic's house was lit by lamps which gave white light. It was a different light and in a sense a different world from the murky yellow one which enveloped the postmaster, that "stupid pig in mayonnaise" surrounded by the townsfolk, all shouting, complaining, demanding.

207

The commandant, who had not yet digested his dinner, arrived to see what was happening, cleaning his chipped teeth with a matchstick, and he agreed with the official right from the start. Official means someone who is always right, and he wasn't someone who'd spent his time beating pheasants but someone who had been to war, in the days when Colonel Gonzalo Godoy led the soldiers against the Indians up in the mountains. Musús had been just a second lieutenant then, Second Lieutenant Secundino Musús. Saving a few men of the Expeditionary Force, during the ambush of fire the guerrillas used to trap the colonel in the Earthshaker, had earned him his promotion. They put him up to major.

"Stuff and nonsense," he determined, once he knew what it was all about, "how can you be so foolish as to think such things can happen, what else can you expect from a neurotic German who plays the violin on moonlit nights, wears a flower in his buttonhole all day Sunday because he fancies himself a count, and is married to a woman who mounts a horse like a man. But if he wants to put up the money for a muleteer to follow the postman so the tecuna won't lure him over the edge as he crosses María Tecún Ridge, good luck to him. I wouldn't like to see him go over myself, since I've just sent five hundred pesos to my folks."

A little old woman no bigger than the oil lamp, wrapped in a large shawl she dragged behind her as though she were wearing a dress with a train, stood on tiptoe to say in a Spanish accent that she had sent twenty pesos to her son, a student in the Central Institute for Young Gentlemen; the one-legged man from the firework-maker's kept giving funereal taps on the floor with his crutch, to make it known that he had sent fifty-odd pesos to his sister Flora; and the same to his sick brother; and the same to his brother-in-law in jail; and the same to be deposited in the bank, repeating all the time, "If that money ain't deposited they'll take my home away from me"; and another man, sad as a bone, had sent some money to a friend to buy him a lottery ticket; he said, "It'll all be a matter of luck even if it arrives; if it don't, the tecuna will have robbed me of it."

The postmaster stared at them without blinking, red with fury, his ears like prawn's claws, his short arms in the sleeves of his balloonlike jacket. At times his eyes misted over and he was near to having a fit. So what, he'd be better off dead than twisted up like that. The worst displeasure of his whole life. To take advantage of his friendship, to enclose valuables in their letters without duly declaring them. He said it, he repeated it, he repeated it again, thumping the desk with the tremendous exaltation of a worthy functionary reduced by that gross abuse of his confidence to the condition of an accomplice, under the terms of the prevailing postal code, not noticing the buzzing of the townsfolk which, in a word, was saying, "If you declare it, they steal it."

Don Deferic, meanwhile, was back in his house, in the white light of his house, beside his white wife, among white azaleas and golden cages with white canaries in. But he was like a man possessed. The tecuna would be doing him a bad turn indeed if she lured the postman after her and cast him into the ravine like a human letter into some gigantic letter box. Señor Nicho was carrying his latest composition for piano and violin.

Doña Elda, his wife, tried to calm him, urging him not to be carried away by legends, legends are just stories, they exist only in the imaginings of poets, are believed in by children, and after that only by grandmothers.

The German replied that that way of thinking was completely materialist, and materialism is absurd, because matter is by nature something that passes away. What would Germany be without its legends? Where did the German language drink the better part of its spirit? Did the primary substances not spring from obscure beings? Has the contemplation of infinity not revealed the nullity of all that has limits? Why, without the tales of Hoffmann . . .

Doña Elda agreed that the legends of Germany were true; but not those of that poor settlement of Chuj Indians and louse-infested Ladinos with shoes on. Don Deferic pointed his finger at his wife's breast like the barrel of a pistol and accused her of having a European mentality. Europeans are fools, they think only Europe has ever existed, and that all that isn't Europe may well be interesting in the way an exotic plant is interesting, but doesn't really exist.

He was maddened, beside himself. He raised his white hands, his white fists, everything in him pointed up at the ceiling, amid the aroma of the azaleas, the strong sickening smell of morning-glory, the wet-earth perfume of recently watered quetzal-tail ferns, some with orchid blooms, and boxes and bundles of merchandise stinking of ship's disinfectant like the wax they used to polish their stone floor, where his finger was reflected as if he were playing at making gestures and faces like some grotesque dancer, only to see himself as a giraffe's head down on the floor, and the figure of his wife like the cutout silhouette of a cardboard swan with folded paper feathers.

Father Valentín came to call, first the black reflection of his cassock on the mirror of the floor, then the contrast with the white blur of a cane rocking chair in which he sat to make himself comfortable.

The presence of the priest obliged Don Deferic to abandon his own language and express himself in Spanish. The priest explained that although he rarely left the convent house at night except in cases of urgent confession or grave illness, he had come because of a person gravely sick who was going to die without confession if someone wasn't sent to accompany him past María Tecún Ridge.

"I am prepared to volunteer myself," said Father Valentín, "to leave at once. It is my duty to be wherever there is a soul at risk, *parvus error in principio, magnus in fine*. I will fight the devil . . ."

The German interrupted him, "You needn't worry, father, one of my most trusted men is going after him. It would be a sad thing indeed if our best postman threw himself into the gorge—"

The German was interrupted by his wife: "Bravo!" she said, clapping loudly, "how heroic, how poetic!"

She too was interrupted, by Hilario Sacayón. He was ready to ride, judging by his garb. The boss paid so well and treated them so well that none of them minded going out at all hours, after all, for a man who is really a man there are no good or bad times for setting out, any time's a good time if it's necessary.

Don Deferic embraced him, gave him a cigar to light up on the way, and some money for expenses. Father Valentín handed him a rosary and told him to pray the moment he began the climb up to the ridge. And Doña Elda gave him some black bread and some diabolical-smelling cheese wrapped in a napkin. Hilario jumped onto his gray mule, an animal greedy for the road which set off almost at the gallop as they left the dark street behind. His mission was to overtake Nicho Aquino before he reached María Tecún Ridge, escort him past that place, and then turn back.

Father Valentín accepted a glass of eggnog to keep company with Don Deferic, who was drinking cognac. Doña Elda settled for a sip of sherry.

"Of all the causes of marital instability," the priest intoned, this being the heart of the matter which had kept him from his bed, "none is remotely as serious as the one which makes wives the victims of an ambulatory madness provoked by 'spider-spell' powders, with the result that they abandon their homes, never to be heard of again. This hand you now see holding a glass of eggnog, holds rosary and pen by turns, I pray or write to my superiors, in order that the Lord and the Church may come to our aid in preventing homes from being destroyed, families divided, men and women wandering the roads and tumbling into ravines like sheep."

"Those people are sacrificed so the legend may live," suggested the German, whose blue eyes were not transparent: glassy at that moment, they looked, on the contrary, like two small blue disks, of a dry pewterlike inexpressiveness.

"Unconsciously," said Doña Elda, "because none of them

knows he is moved, attracted by a hidden force, to such an end," and then, looking her husband in the face, she added, "sometimes I detest you!"

"The devil, madam, the devil."

"The victims aren't important, are they, Deferic, as long as they feed the monster of popular poetry. A man who can coldly say that people are sacrificed so the legend may live, is a detestable man."

"If by not saying it I could stop the legend from claiming its victims, I would keep quiet, but that's the way it is, Elda, and it must be coldly acknowledged, however detestable it may seem to you. The gods have disappeared, but the legends remain and they, like the gods before them, demand sacrifices. Gone too are the obsidian knives which tore out the hearts of sacrificial victims, but the knives of absence which wound and madden, remain."

Father Valentín woke up just then. Don Deferic was speaking in German. He took his leave of them and asked them to send news of the postman when Hilario Sacayón returned. It was so dark out in the street that he had to accept the lantern they offered him. Once alone he quickened his step, but something like the body of an animal floated on his feet. He lifted his cassock and almost saw the shadow of a coyote. "Is that you, Nichón, you who they say are a coyote?" he cried out. But it couldn't be.

Half an hour later the twelve chimes of the Town Hall clock rang out. Don Deferic, accompanied by Doña Elda at the piano, was completing a performance of the composition which, if the postman passed safely over María Tecún Ridge, would reach Germany. The German was just putting the bow of his violin down on the baby grand piano, when his wife came toward him full of dread. In the silence of the night a sewing machine could be heard, the machine of Miguelita of Acatán.

At twelve o'clock
Miguelita sews

212

COYOTE-POSTMAN

buttons and bows
in Acatán-tan.

Sewing, sewing
through the night
until the light
in Acatán-tan.

And when she sews
the whole town knows
it's twelve o'clock
in Acatán-tan.

Tan-tan, tan-tan.
Tan-tan, tan-tan.
Tan-tan, tan-tan.
Twelve bells chime
to end this rhyme
in Acatán-tan.

Hilario Sacayón made a stop in the village of Tres Aguas. Smoked a cigarette. The forest smelled of mint and watercress. Two eyes peered out to see who was passing by so early, two eyes set in a fleshy pumpkin with a nose and mouth beneath a strawlike fringe of hair, and a mass of petticoats and underskirts. It was old Ramona Corzantes, midwife, curer, and marriage-maker, on the right side of the coin, though on the other side it was said she was a witch, a soothsayer, and a mixer of potions to send folk mad, make them fall in love, give their souls up to God, and bring any baby out of its mother's belly before her time. But the worst, the very worst they said against her was that she knew how to prepare 'spider-spell' powders.

It was a job to make him out, he was in the sun, dazzling her.

"Oh, it's you, half-breed, no wonder the dogs didn't hear you!"

"What do you mean—half-breed? The dogs don't howl at

213

me 'cause they know I'm part of the family, Nana Monchita, and because if they do they know they're done for."

"You're mean-hearted, you. Get down from your horse, if you're going to, and let me get back in the dark, I'm gonna close my eyes for a moment, because the glare of the sun has left me seeing little golden dregs."

"That would just suit you, wouldn't it, old lady—a coffeepot that left you dregs made of gold when you'd finished drinking. I won't get down, I'm in a hurry. I just stopped for a moment to see you and smoke this cigarette in the shade of your eaves. The house's beard is growing real long and you still ain't had it shaved, you ought to call in the barber."

"You notice everything, don't you, but you ain't noticed I'm poor, and no one says: here, take this, have the house painted. I used to tidy it up myself, I'd clamber up the ladder and knock all the upstairs garden down, the filthy spider's webs, and once I even found a boa. We had to slice it up because the damned thing wouldn't come down from the roof: half of it stayed up there and the other half crawled away. It was that that made people start saying I was a witch."

"Don't see much movement these days."

"It's dead, there's no business at all, except for regular customers like Señor Nicho the postman."

"Has he been by?"

"Went by last night. Must be well on his way by now. I was going to get him to take something for me, but he had no room, it was pretty big, and anyway, I just had a funny feeling about it."

"He's very reliable."

"Yes, but you know about his woman. I kept dropping hints to see if he'd let anything slip: would you believe it, Hilario, he said not a thing, and I'm sorry for it, because I wanted to advise him not to go along the high road. Get down and have some coffee."

"I must keep going, Nana Monchita, another time, I'm in a hurry and if I stop now I'll fall too far behind. Thank you for

214

the coffee anyway. Why were you going to advise him to take another road?"

"Because of the grave risk that even though he's a man sworn to deliver the mail, his woman will appear and send out her tecuna calls to him, up there on the ridge, and if she does he won't get past, he'll stay there, he'll go straight over the ravine and bury his head. If you catch up with him thereabouts, you be sure and warn him."

"All those things can't be true, Nana Monchona, they're just made up: it's not enough for people to slander their neighbors, so they slander the rocks, which are not at all to blame for what happens to us. Of course there's something mysterious up on that ridge, you feel strange as you pass by there, your hair stands on end, your eyes mist over, palpitations flutter in your nostrils which turn as cold as hailstones, and your bones stick out of your flesh with the icy cold, as if you were wearing your skeleton on the outside. But all that is natural enough given the altitude and the raininess of the place, the road turns just like soapberries when the sun fails to enter through the clouds, and then it's easy to go over the edge. I can tell you this much, Nana Moncha, I've crossed María Tecún Ridge by day and by night, in the afternoon and in the early morning, and I've never seen or heard a thing."

"You told me you were in a hurry . . ."

"I am, but that don't mean nothing; have a smoke."

Hilario handed her a purple cornhusk cigarette. The old woman looked at it, and after a good long puff, she said, "The maize comes up with purple leaves when it's from round here, round the well of purple water. You're an unbeliever because you're conceited. In every conceited person there's an unbeliever. To believe you have to be humble. And only humble things grow and endure: see it on the mountainside."

They both of them gathered their thoughts in silence as if they were drawing them from their cigarettes, inhaling the smoke and passing it through their mouths and nostrils with a sigh of satisfaction. The old innkeeper blew out the smoke of her cigarette which made puffballs in the clear springlike mountain air before her gaze, and tapping the butt she still had left to smoke with her little finger, she went on chiding the muleteer for being so disbelieving.

Hilario, meantime, was thinking about "his" Miguelita of Acatán. He, in one of his drunken fits, after weeping, because he always started weeping, as if he drank liquor tapped from weeping willows, invented the love affair between Miguelita and Señor O'Neill, and that machine which can be heard sewing in the town after the Town Hall bell chimes at midnight.

Who did not repeat that legend which he, Hilario Sacayón, had made up in his head, as if it had happened? Had he not been present at a mass where they had prayed to God for peace and eternal rest for the soul of Miguelita of Acatán? Had they not been through the old ledgers of the parish register, searching for that miraculous child's birth certificate? Were nursery rhymes not sung to frighten children and trouble lovers, threatening the children with her sleepwalking machine, if they misbehaved, and assuring lovers that the sewing of that machine in love with the impossible accompanies their serenades, making possible their love? How could he, who had invented a legend, believe in tecunas?

"I told you what I think last time you consulted me, Hilario. As my name is Ramona Corzantes, I heard my grandmother, Venancia Corzantes San Ramón, tell that story about Miguelita, and it was even put to music, how did it go now, I can't remember, maybe if I hum the tune the words will come back to me. Like I say, it was a song."

> *I ask of the Bilboes Virgin,*
> *may the rural guard come and take me,*
> *surround me and tie me and take me,*
> *in prison I'll find consolation.*
> *Miguelita's the name they baptized her,*
> *Acatán is her glorious surname,*
> *in prison the dark Bilboes Virgin*
> *lay abandoned in sad isolation.*

"It can't be, Nana Moncha, as my name is Hilario Sacayón. I made that story up, I swear by the blessed bones of my father, in the name of God, I made it up. It was when I was drunk, it came down from my head to my mouth and into words, like a reality: it's as if you were to tell me the saliva which filled my mouth at that moment wasn't mine, because that's what talking is, turning spittle into words."

"You don't feel any need to defend this fabrication of yours?"

"Of course I don't."

"Then listen to me. We often think we've invented things that other people have forgotten. When you tell a story that no one else tells anymore, you say: I invented this, it's mine. But what you're really doing is remembering—you, through your drunkenness, remembered what the memory of your forefathers left in your blood, because you must realize that you're a part not only of Hilario Sacayón, but of all the Sacayones that have ever lived, and on your mother's side, of all the Arriazas, all folks from round these parts."

The old woman seemed to go on speaking with her eyelids, so swiftly did she blink, before continuing, "The story of Miguelita of Acatán was in your head, as in a book, and your eyes read it there, and you started repeating it with the drunken clapper of your tongue, and if it hadn't been you it would have been someone else; someone would have told it, so it wouldn't be forgotten, because its existence, true or false, is part of the life, part of the nature of these places, and life cannot be lost, it's eternally at risk but it cannot be lost eternally."

"Well, what's certainly true is that I arranged it in my own way, because in the time of that song Señor O'Neill didn't exist. I joined the name of the girl to the memory of what my father told me about him. Many strange things come together when you've been drinking."

"So the bit about that man and the sewing machine don't belong; but it doesn't matter, it's been saved from forgetfulness to go on like a river. Tales are like rivers, they pick up what they can as they flow past, and if they can't pick up something and carry it along, they carry its reflection. That man and the sewing machine are the reflection of Miguelita."

Hilario lit another cigarette with the glow of the one he was finishing, a wretched little stub between his fingers, spat, and let his eyes wander across the plain, until they jolted against torrents of balanced rock. It seemed to him that the mountains were tumbling rocks which suddenly froze into equilibrium, temporarily still.

"I'll be on my way, Nana Moncha, and we'll have another talk on my way back. I'll leave you to your troupial."

"Take care, don't go astray."

An old dog which had just stood itself up, tired of sleep, and was stretching, raised high on the fur onions of its paws, cowered back against the wall as the rider went by, then barked low and hoarse and without conviction. Old Ramona-Mona or Monchona-Mona, as she was called by those who took her for a witch, looked again at the troupial with its delicate plumage and infinitely small and pretty eyes, like two sparks of fire.

"Come on down, my little one," said she to the hopping bird, "your millet pap soaked in water from the blue well is all ready and waiting for you. Mind you don't drink from the green well because you'll die and become grass that doesn't sing, still less from the purple well because you'll get dizzy and they'll hunt you down with a blowpipe! Beneath your feathers are your little brains, and your little brains think it's nice to go for a walk, and your little brains think it's nice to come down and see old Moncha! Come, little one, come! Don't you want me to look after you?"

Moncha's shadow appeared in the henhouse. Pigs with their necks in wooden triangles to stop them getting through the fence, rooted, grunted, squealed as though they were being slaughtered, while hens followed by their chicks ran spindle-legged with hollow bodies between half-open wings, clucking; the cocks pushed their way through with thrusting breasts leaving their spurred feet behind them as they ran; and above the laborious approach of the ducks and their intolerable quack, quack, quacking, not running but rowing, doves and pigeons flew in to peck at the maize in the old woman's apron.

Who would ever believe how hungry these birds get! Just like our hunger when we eat them; and like the hunger of worms when they eat us!

The troupial jumped up with a worm in its beak.

"There you are!" She lifted her hand to her forehead and tasted something like a worm which dropped from her memory onto the tip of her tongue. But what was the use of remembering the rest of the song, when Hilario was already well on his way.

> *The muleteers carried the loads,*
> *pieces of eight by the hundred,*
> *and carried them off to the Gulf*
> *with no thought for their Heavenly Queen.*
> *In Acatán's prison she moldered*
> *until Miguelita was born,*
> *that girl who was coined in her image,*
> *the most beautiful girl ever seen.*
> *Sparkling coals for her eyes,*
> *her mouth a carnation,*
> *when the Virgin was moved to the church,*
> *she vanished, departed the town.*

She tried to go on, but her wheels got stuck. She stood there for a long while with her fingers poised on the strings of her dry hair: she needed a guitar. The troupial, after gobbling down its worm, flew up into the branches of a suquinay whose intoxicating aroma attracted bees, butterflies and devil's-needles to its blossoms.

And it went on, the song went on, but she couldn't remember anymore. She scratched a buttock, muttered, and looked for something to do. Her broom, her duster. Her sprig for fending off lightning was still behind the picture of the Holy

Trinity. A spotted cat, the color of a butterfly, started to mew. She looked for her ointment against buboes. Though maybe it was nausea. She lay down. Why did she have to drink chocolate? But wedding chocolate was so delicious. Christening chocolate. All great occasions are celebrated with chocolate and bird-cake. The little birds Baby Jesus was making with breadcrumbs when the Jew came and tried to crush them with his foot. Baby Jesus blew on them, and the little birds flew away.

Hilario Sacayón could tell by the way the mule was going that he was near María Tecún Ridge. Even animals have their moods, he thought, pulling his hat forward a bit—he usually wore it on the back of his head for effect—for it was better now to look with his eyes hidden, concealed, just in case.

He thought he saw fireflies, so present in his mind was the story of that horseman, Machojón, who had been turned into a star in the sky as he rode to ask the hand of his intended. That fellow who leaned his whole weight into the glowing wind of fiery sparks and the evil which was filling him with terror.

"Up, mule!" shouted Sacayón as the beast stumbled, pulling it over to one side with the rein.

The mist, clinging like frozen smoke, got in his hair, under his hat, in his clothing, under his coarse woolen jacket, beneath his shirt, up his sleeves, over his chest, chilling his bare feet, his leggings, his breeches.

The truth of the matter was that the fireflies were trying to unhorse that fellow and they still haven't unhorsed him, he is riding still as a star up there in the sky, and year after year he comes down to the earth and is seen wherever people are slashing and burning, in the clearing fires, clothed in an outfit of gold from his riding sombrero down to the hoofs of his black horse, which appears to be an uncastrated stallion.

Sacayón wiped his hand across his face. His face was like ice. He rubbed his nose. Breathing in mist isn't good for you. But what choice was there in that white world of drifting clouds which made not the slightest sound, colliding, repulsing one another, merging, falling, rising, or staying suddenly still, paralyzed with fear?

The first golden pockmarks began to fly, sporadically, somewhat faint in the daylight and the dense mist, making him hug his arms round his body to fasten his spirit within his bones, his spirit which was so attentive to what was going on outside as he thought of Machojón. He concentrated his mind and made himself look straight ahead at them, lest he become dizzy. Feet in the stirrups. That's the main thing. He too would stay firm in the saddle. The cloud of fireflies soon passed. A tulle veil dotted with spangles, like the one which covers the hair of the Bilboes Virgin.

The rein slipped through his hands, the beast's trot felt ungainly, jarring his nerves, he gesticulated to take breath, they were winding their way up to the peak where the bronzed earth journeyed through the clouds between mutilated pines more swiftly than the mule. He urged it onwards—"Gray mule! Get going, mule!"—spurred it, lashed it with the rein to make it quicken its step and not be left behind by the earth escaping beneath its hoofs. Horrible, he was falling back, hanging in the void, riding through the clouds, changed into a Machojón made of hailstones. He was shaking cold, his teeth were chat, chat, chattering, and his spurs in the stirrups were like two flowers on a metal daisy plant at the time of an earth tremor. Better to die there, deep in the ravine, than be changed for all eternity into a man made of hailstones, a cloud rider. He felt for his pistol. There were five seeds of salvation dust in the chamber. Better they should find him dead from a bullet with his mule wandering loose nearby, than spend centuries and centuries, till the world's end, turned into some white vegetable, a potato with roots instead of hair, an onion with a goat's beard, or a bald turnip.

María Tecúúú ÚÚ Ún! . . . María Tecúúú ÚÚ Ún! . . .

The cry was lost with the name beneath a storm of accents deep in the chasms of his ears. He covered them over, but still he heard it. It came not from outside, but from within. A woman's name which all men shout to call that María Tecún lost in their consciousness.

María TecúúúÚÚÚn! . . . María TecúúúÚÚÚn! . . .

Who has never called, never shouted the name of a woman lost in his yesterdays? Who has not pursued like a blind man that being who went away from his being, when he came to himself, who kept on going and still keeps on going from his side, a runaway, a tecuna, impossible to hold because if she stops time turns her into stone?

María TecúúúÚÚÚn! . . . María TecúúúÚÚÚn! . . .

At the peak the name took on all its tragic meaning. The "T" of Tecún, lofty, erect, between two sheer abysses, never more deep than in the ravine of the "U" at the end.

He crossed the highest part of the ridge, before María Tecún's rock, rooted in the vertigo of a precipice whose edge no one approached, where the clouds fell, pruned by the invisible hand of mystery.

Rock of María Tecún, image of absence, love ever present and moving away, traveler always standing still, tall as the towers, opaque with forgetfulness, stone flute for the wind and, like the moon, with no light of its own.

María TecúúúÚÚÚn! . . . María TecúúúÚÚÚn! . . .

The blind voice of that blind man who, so folks say, left the clouds of his eyes behind when he regained his sight up there in that place, only to lose it again with that soapy water which allows no image to stand still, fix itself in one place, they all go sliding by, marching away, erasing one another like those great slate blackboards down in rocky hollows where the stones look like the bodies of petrified lizards, or like those abandoned trees, stripped of leaves, which look less like trees than the antlers of giant animals sunk in glaciers.

A coyote passed up ahead of him, among the "rounds" of

the pines that don't climb all the way to the top. He saw it very close, almost in front of him, but lost sight of it at once in a pall of rain and brushwood thickets which seemed made of rubber, elastic, easy to bend but impossible to break. Behind the coyote he could hear the splashing of a waterfall without much water.

He started to whistle, extracting all that was metallic from within his bones to give that ocarina note. He was out of danger, in a landscape of inflamed dahlias, green pastures, shivering poplars, small marshland flowers, sheep in deep flocks, small red birds, wild ducks, and a few huts with kitchen smoke along their flanks.

Still whistling he undid the sodden hat cord which had been throttling him under his chin, and remembered Father Valentín's rosary and Don Deferic's cigar. Smoke a cigar as you recite the rosary. He gave the mule its head. He didn't know how to smoke a cigar, nor how to recite the rosary. His whistle rattled somewhere between a whistle and a laugh.

Was it or was it not a coyote? How could he doubt that it was, when he saw it so clearly. But that was it, he clearly saw it and saw that it wasn't a coyote, because as he looked he had the impression it was a person, and a person he knew. He sucked the skin of his cheek down into the hollow of an old tooth. They'll laugh in my face if I tell them I arrived in good time at María Tecún Ridge and saw Aquino the postman in the form of a coyote, howling—that would be my own contribution—at the mother rock of the tecunas which, in its hard sandstone soaked always in tears, holds the soul of runaway women, those fugitives who carry deserts of ash beneath the soles of their feet, on their shoulders storms which tear down nests, on the ends of their arms hands which have become broken pieces of pottery, in their eyes the anguished muteness of coconuts split in two, empty of water and empty of flesh, on their lips the thorny betrayal of their laughter, shame in their shameful parts and in their hearts the mockery of spite. All they yearn for is denied them.

He shook his head—so many foolish thoughts—and harnessed himself with the hat cord again, he was having to hold on to his hat, which the wind was intent on turning into a bird, spurred the mule forward and was soon well beyond that small settlement which, now that he came to think about it, was the only sign of human life in the region around the peak.

Overtake Nicho Aquino, escort him through the bad stretch and return to San Miguel, those were his instructions. But had he overtaken him? Had he seen him? Up on the ridge, apart from that accursed coyote, not a single living creature had he seen.

The mule would be his guide. He would keep going until he caught him up, rather than return to San Miguel with his colors lowered, until he caught him up, even if it was to be in the post office itself.

He met a train of oxcarts. The carters were sprawled on their backs, not moving, with their eyes open. He greeted them, not because he liked their looks, but to ask them about Señor Nicho. They hadn't seen him. Sure they knew him, but they hadn't seen him. They didn't even raise their heads to find out who they were talking to.

"You must think you're on the telephone. Idle slobs, you can't even answer a question like decent folk! Wake up, only no-good trash sleep with their eyes open, like horses!"

All this and more he would have liked to have shouted. Some little red birds landed ahead of him, only to take to the air as he came near, as if they had laid bets as to which of them would face the danger of being trampled by the mule the longest.

A man and a woman on horseback. He didn't see them until they were on top of him because he was looking at the scarlet birds and because they met on a sharp bend. The mare the woman was riding climbed up the roadside, then backed out across the road, and Hilario pulled his mule to one side to avoid a collision. As it was, she very nearly dropped a birdcage she was holding carefully in front of her. A fluttering in the cage, a fluttering in her breast. Her doll's plaits swinging, her green eyes, her pale face. The man's horse reared up, too, as he gave a sharp tug on the reins. They bade one another good day. They greeted one another although they'd never met before, as wayfarers, which gave the muleteer the opportunity to ask them about the postman, if by any chance they'd seen him. They were on their way back from the city, and they couldn't rightly remember, though they hadn't bumped into anyone like a postman. Those fellows are always taking back roads, was the last thing he heard them say, amid the dust raised by the animals as they rode off, soon to be out of sight.

"Well, this is the way he came," thought Hilario, "whether he's lost or whether he's turned into a coyote, which folks say is his trick for getting there more quickly, and God forbid he's that coyote that came out to take a look at me on María Tecún Ridge. Best not even think about it, scare myself stiff, for whenever I start imagining things they seem to turn out real. Though if that's the case, who knows what can happen, let's hope it ain't so and I find him down at the post office doing what he ought to be doing, delivering the mail. I'll take a good look at him all right, to be sure it really is the same Señor Nicho who left Acatán, even if he did turn into a coyote along the way, though it couldn't really have been the one I came across up on the ridge because that one seemed a bit lost, and then I'll shoot back to the town with the news that he arrived, because all that matters to them is the cash they all put in with their letters, no one can tell me it's the fancy words they care about—what's written ain't blown by the wind, but eaten by time."

With his eyes like two cherries at the bottom of a liquor flask from lack of sleep and food, and from drinking in long distances, his legs cramped from riding, bowed at the waist, head sagging with weariness, he rode into the capital, submerged in noise and silence in the early hours of the day, with a dark sleep of volcanoes on one side and plains of fiery sand to the east.

Steaming mugs of coffee and the breath of early risers coming to drink it beneath a ceiba mingled their vapors. Nearby a woman stood serving behind a table by a wood fire whose glow awoke the grackles up in the branches of the tree, spread for more than six arm's-lengths around.

The woman took the bubbling pot off the fire with the tips of her fingers, stretching her arm right out in order not to singe a face already blackened by sun and smoke. Dishing out coffee, half naked, clothes thin as tomato skins, blue with cold, and a sleeping baby on her back.

Seeing the muleteer arrive and ask for coffee, she asked him if he was Justo Carpio. Because if you are, she said, make a run for it, they're after you, and when she found out he was someone else she saw fit to explain that they were looking for Carpio because he'd cheated the government. He delivered ash instead of lime, and they'd had to stop work all day yesterday.

A plumber came to attention in front of the table. Good morning, Fauna, he could be heard to say from beneath a towel which covered his neck and part of his face. He put his master key down on the ground. She served him. After the first draught—it burned its way right down his windpipe, it was scalding hot—he took out a roll of cigarettes made with yellow paper, fat as boa constrictors, and put one in his mouth straight from the roll. The muleteer stared at him. He was almost the same height as himself, though his French-style trousers made him look taller, but then again, his hat covered him down to his shoulders and flattened him out a bit. The serving woman and the plumber were talking about a gold tooth. Finally, after pushing his towel down around his neck to drink the coffee, and after a suck on his cigarette, blowing the smoke out through his nose like a double-barreled shotgun after it's been fired, he half opened a mouth the color of raw meat to show her a gold fang. Suits me, don't it, he said, half as a statement and half as a question. It flatters you, she said, I'm glad for you, where are you off to now. The hippodrum, he replied. I'm going to pump out a pipe they say's blocked up, it's the water, it's coming down like mud. What with drinking that water and going through all the calamities we have these days, and things the price they are, said she, as she rinsed out the mugs in an old pot, we won't die even if the blackest of black widows bites us, because we've all eaten the remedy by the cartful in advance. The plumber showed his gold tooth as he laughed.

A little old man whose name or nickname was Sóstenes came up for his coffee. The woman knew him, if you can call it knowing someone to see them only in the early morning, somewhere between the sleep in your half-open eyes and the foraging light of the fire as it mingles with the blur coming down from the sky. Yes, she knew him: goodness knows how long he'd been stopping by to have his coffee there with her; but she always called him mister, just in case Sóstenes was a nickname.

The old man drank his coffee and after each sip his tiny eyes peered all around him through his spectacles, as if he were only now discovering the ceiba, the church, the houses which had been standing there for hundreds of years. As he took the last sip he paid, stopped, seemingly disoriented for a moment, rubbed his hands, and walked off. The woman shouted after him. Don't forget I won't be here tomorrow, mister, maybe you can have your breakfast in the market instead. Don Sóstenes turned back, asking what she had said, and when he found out he shook his head in annoyance and informed her that professors could not take breakfast in the market without diminishing their professional decorum. And who knows, who knows, he said, perhaps it will be as well if I don't have breakfast tomorrow, since I am to speak on the great Plato himself: we love only that which we cannot have!

Three men with the faces of all-night revelers, stinking of sweat and onions, arrived at the stand. Coffee, coffee, coffee, they ordered. Did you play last night, the woman asked them, as she planted a row of three steaming mugs in front of them. The tallest of them, a big mulatto with very black eyes, answered: a serenade, but now they want us to start playing the marimba at nine in the morning, night and day's gonna be one

227

long shift. Have you changed your instrument, she asked. No, replied the same one who answered before, looking for the handle of his coffee mug so as not to burn his fingers. Another of the marimba players took a handkerchief from his pocket, and blew his nose and sneezed at the same time. Now you've woken up the baby, there's a fine way to sneeze, I hope that's not the way you play the marimba. The baby started to cry and before the first great shriek she pulled it round to the front with the shawl she used to carry it on her back and took a breast full of milk out from under her shift. Fauna could sell white coffee, too, said another of the three musicians. She retorted: so could that housekeeper of yours, only then it wouldn't be milky coffee, it'd be filthy coffee.

An Italian came up whistling, with his jacket collar turned up. He was accompanied by several hunting dogs. From the bell tower of the nearby church the sacristan was shouting: Fauna, my coffee . . . My, it's nearly time for mass, she exclaimed, looking up. The marimba players and the man with the dogs moved off in conversation.

Hilario paid her. As he unknotted the coins from his handkerchief he said: so you won't be here tomorrow. No, because —but on reflecting that there was no reason why she should account to some nosy country fellow for her movements, she changed her friendly, chatty tone for a mocking one: so you've been and gone, then?

The bells all pealed out together and put a stop to further talk. The muleteer, who had tied his mount to a large stone when he arrived, replied that he hadn't moved from the spot, because he didn't catch the sarcasm in the question, and led the animal away to continue his journey along with all the other people coming in, some with loads, others with animals, others with carts: men, women, children, scattering through the city, quickly if they were riding, trotting if they were carrying loads on tumplines or on their chests, others at walking pace, and others, those who were driving hogs, hardly advancing at all, as though they were walking through a swamp. Automobiles went by like rockets, bicycles with wheels like blades, motorcycles even faster than rockets, and trucks bloated with sawn-up firewood, so loaded down they were farting.

Hilario was at once irritable and gay, irritable because of the fright a dog on one of those trucks gave him as it rushed across and barked at him, barked in his face, right in his ear, so close did the great truck pass by the mule, and gay because it was such fun to be among so many people, people from all over, all ages, all sizes, people he didn't know, dressed in many colors, moving in so many different directions that instead of having things to do they seemed to have places to go, to have to keep on walking and walking forever, so the city would be busy all day. He stopped in a doorway. They were selling hay inside, in the cobbled hallway. He took a look at the bales of hay stacked up against the wall. Big ones. He shouted for someone to come and attend to him. A man as nervous as a young colt took his money and set his hay aside. The hay's for the mule, said Hilario, to show that he was no poor yokel. He was always glad to be back in the city, but as he moved through the streets with his eyes and mouth wide open, his skin ruffled like wind-swept water as he readied himself for anything he thought might endanger his self-esteem. At the same time, beneath that skin-deep feeling—the anxiousness of a bought chicken—and by way of compensation, he felt a distinct sense of superiority which came out in the way he kept using the word "poor." A brass band came marching down the middle of the street. The muleteer saw them coming and pulled to the side as they passed right by him, tubby, uniformed, marching with their instruments, sweating. He sat looking at them and from deep down inside, commiseratingly, he said, "Poor devils!" Further on he came across a traffic policeman stuck up in a thing like a pulpit, directing the traffic with his two white hands, he looked a bit like the judge in a bull ring, and after a long look at him the comment was just the same: "Poor devil!" And as for a platoon of soldiers who marched past with pipes and drums, they were doubly to be pitied. A little man selling newspapers, shouting like a lunatic, a team of Indian street sweepers, some silent schoolchildren all dressed in the same color, made him hold on with both hands, furtively— they don't miss a thing in the city—to his pommel, to remind himself he wasn't staying, only passing through that horde of sedentary folk, buzzards who would never ever turn into eagles. Poor, poor devils.

Further on he went into a lodginghouse—about time he watered the mule—in case someone he knew was stopping over there, to ask them about Señor Nicho. He gave the mule its drink and set off at the gallop—there was the stink of squashed bedbugs coming out of every room. Everyone piled on top of everyone else, poor devils.

The clothes stores were a fine sight, really poetical, just like altars, with breeches, jackets, petticoats, shawls and children's clothes all hanging on display in the doorways. Lengths of cloth lay sleeping on the shelves in rolls, until the assistants spread them out expertly along the counter when someone was buying by the yard. On their feet all day behind that counter. Poor fellows, their legs were bound to get overloaded. They were becoming fat as capons, the lot of them, always smiling, neat and tidy, carefully brushed and combed—poor devils, they didn't know what it was to be out in a high wind. And among the tailors and other stores were the pharmacists. When a man goes into a pharmacy with toothache and comes out feeling better, it seems a place of enchantment, like it did to him the time before last. And to think that all those poisons are lying there hidden in little jars that shine like snake's eyes. The poison they used to kill Gaspar Ilóm, the chief of Ilóm, the first time Gaspar drank the river dry in order to live again—and he lived again. Afterwards he threw himself back into the river on purpose, when he saw his men cut to pieces. Right next door to the pharmacy, a shoemaker's, where the shoes seemed to be walking for all those folk who have no shoes, himself among them, because although he pulled them on when he got near the city, he always took them off again in the country, and went

230

deliciously barefoot. Hardware stores. All the tools you could think of. Machetes, knives, scythes. Just like a village meeting. Shotgun slugs in deep pans, from the tiniest birdshot to the biggest balls of lead. And plows, and lamps. In the public squares there were statues like saints' images, only made of stone, and as he turned the corner to go up to the market, the same old question: I wonder why they made a statue of that horse? Poor thing, it too was turned to stone, presiding over the festivities in the streets, with half its body embedded in a wall which was like time turned to stone and mortar. But the horse was outside of time. Everyone grew old around it. From seeing it so often they no longer saw it at all. A mere point of reference on the city map, only the children noticed it. The children and new arrivals.

A thousand times his mule had ground its way up that climb from the Street of the Sun to the market gate, but he'd always had Porfirio Mansilla with him. He had come without telling him. He wouldn't have let him come alone. You have to watch how you go. But as he was on a special errand it didn't do to bring company, and anyway Porfirio was busy, he was supposed to be going down to the coast to buy a pair of white mules.

Hilario was feeling gloomy when he got in from the country, and now here he was with his eye out for a good time. He slowed as he passed by a carver's workshop. He didn't like seeing saints which hadn't been consecrated and perhaps that was why the devil excited his curiosity. Fact is, it ain't right for images to be treated like puppets or pieces of furniture. An Indian Hilario knew in a village up in the mountains, who was also given to making saints, disappeared whenever he was commissioned to make an image, and stayed in hiding until he had given form to it with his tools, and only when it was built did he let them bring out the flowers and prayers and put it on show. Perhaps it was because of that example that he didn't like it when he saw the men who made those saints through a glass screen which looked out over the balcony rail, smoking, spit-

231

ting, whistling, and the saints all around them, with no clothes, no legs, as though they were just blocks of wood. So now those city-made saints, too, came in for the same remark: poor things!

A friend of his, Mincho Lobos, rushed up to greet him. The moment he saw him he threw his arms round his waist, above his legs, to half embrace him as he was, on horseback.

"What are you up to, pal?" his friend asked. "Miracle to see you."

"You and your miracles," answered Hilario, delighted to have someone to exchange a few words with, and edging the mule close in to the curb he added, "Well, well, Mincho Lobos! What are you up to? What have you been doing with yourself? I haven't seen you since that last time."

"I'm here in the city, as you see; I haven't seen you in a long while either, you old twister, where've you been? I'm going in here to hand back an image of the Virgin Mary that's all entirely wrong, it doesn't inspire respect."

"No good, then . . ."

"It's got real wild eyes. Come in with me, get down, I'm gonna take it back right now."

"I got to fly to the post office. You don't happen to have seen or heard whether Nicho Aquino the postman got in?"

"Postman, you say. I ain't heard anything, I couldn't tell you. If you come with me for a moment, I'll go with you afterwards. All I'm going to do is hand this image over."

Sacayón dismounted, who could refuse Mincho Lobos—the eager way he invited you, and his wholesome fresh-baked face.

An Indian porter was carrying the sacred image wrapped in a sheet. All three went into the workshop, treading on shavings which silenced their steps, and welcomed by the aroma of cedars, paints, and a varnish that smelled like perfumed bananas.

Although Mincho Lobos was a peaceable and kindly sort of fellow, and one not given to making trouble, he set about the master carver with a vengeance, a pale long-haired gentleman with an eyebrow across his lips in the shape of a moustache, and a bow tie. Hilario moved gingerly, feeling clumsier than usual in that emporium filled with delicate objects, trying not to knock over any of the things lying covered in dust and forgotten on work benches, tables and shelves, far from the sun shining out in the patio on shady plots, fresh and fragrant, and upon the fur of cats.

"No, no, no, even if you offer it us for nothing, we don't want it," clamored Mincho Lobos. "Very pretty it may be, whatever you say, but we don't like the eyes."

"And what's wrong with the eyes, may I ask?"

"Well, I don't know . . . I can't explain it, because it's a matter of feeling. If the soul comes out of a person's eyes, you can't tell me it's Our Lady's soul that's coming out of those eyes."

"But if you can't tell me why you want them changed, how can I change them, it would mean a lot of work, like making the face up all over again. The dearest thing of all would be having to paint her again, you don't know what it costs, the patience you need to cover all the pores over, to shine it up, to make up her skin with saliva and using a pig's bladder. Or do you believe there's nothing to it?"

"I believe what I see, I'm the one who's paying for it, and I don't like the eyes."

"They're saint's eyes," declared the master carver, his voice overcast with consumption, cavernous, "and nothing has been written about saint's eyes. Look at that Saint Joachim, that Saint Anthony, a Saint Francis we have over there, that figure of Christ bearing the Cross—"

"Well, there ain't nothing written about taste neither, so either you change those eyes or you don't get the rest of the payment, and we'll find another sculptor who will, because you ain't the only one, after all."

"That wouldn't be fair, the deal was in good faith, that's why I agreed, even though you only paid me half in advance. We always have trouble with orders from the villages. If making a suit can cost a tailor more headaches than stitches, sir, what do you think it costs me to make images to suit the taste of hillbillies like you!"

"You don't have to insult me, all you have to do is change the eyes—"

"The eyes! The eyes!"

"Yes, sir, the eyes, because—may God forgive me—the eyes you gave it were animal's eyes." Mincho Lobos shuddered as he uttered those words, but did so as a last resort to back up his argument. His lips trembled, the hat he was holding trembled, he was ashen from the horror of having said it.

A young apprentice came in from the street whistling the "Merry Widow Waltz." Seeing strangers in the workshop, he stopped whistling, put two packets wrapped in rice paper down on a table and, taking advantage of the silence brought on by his entry, said, "I've brought you deer's eyes. He says to keep using them because there aren't any others about. There's some jaguar's eyes in the other packet, see how you like them. You can have parrot's eyes, too, but they're so round and light."

"Did you see any donkey's eyes, so I can put them on you!" shouted the sculptor, advancing toward the apprentice, who was already backing his thoughtless form away from the green rage of his master, he went like a quivering leaf on a tree whenever he lost his temper. "That storekeeper's been deceiving me," he said, " 'Eyes for saints' images,' it said in the catalogue, and what does an animal have to do with a saint?"

"The man who attended me," said the apprentice timidly, "told the girl at the cash desk that wild beasts and saints have the same eyes because they're all just pure animals."

"He's the animal, the idiot. They'll be bringing their Saint Agnes back from Pueblo Nuevo, for who would want a Saint Agnes with deer's eyes, and the Nazarene from San Juan . . ."

The post office wasn't far away. Lobos discharged the Indian who had brought Nana Mary down from the village. He ex-

234

plained that they were leaving her in the workshop because they were going to repair her and make her prettier. Hilario almost leaped onto his mule, and followed by Lobos, who was riding a dark brown horse, they swallowed up two or three streets in a flash, stopping round the corner from the main entrance to the post office in a long narrow lane.

"In and out in no time," Hilario told Mincho Lobos, who stayed outside to look after the animals or, as they say, hold up the rancho.

Spurs and hat in hand, hat, spurs and saddlebags, he went along to a large door where there were a large number of surly-looking men in light green uniforms, some seated on long benches, tunics unbuttoned, sweaty feet half out of their shoes, others passing backwards and forwards; none of them answered his question. They paid no attention because they were too busy laughing, yawning, massaging their legs, which became crippled with walking by the end of each shift, or getting ready to start delivering the sacks of mail presently arriving from everywhere, in carriages, carts, official vans or, quite simply, on man-back. Finally a man as tall as a ladder, and just as thin, took some notice of him. He listened to the question and shook his head from one bony shoulder to another, just like a skull. He tried to say something, but was electrified by the beginnings of a sneeze and started waving his hands about until he could sneeze at leisure, with a handkerchief ready in his hand to blow and wipe his nose. Sacayón repeated his question and the man, the color of tar, confirmed in words what he had already said with his head. The postman from San Miguel Acatán, Dionisio Aquino, had not arrived. He should have arrived last night, or this morning at the latest. He's presumed to have run away.

"It's always the same," the old man grumbled—his words rattled a bit because his false teeth were loose—"they put too much trust in a man who, after all, isn't a bank teller to be carrying money back and forth without even a peso of it for himself, risking being attacked on the road, a postman travels in lonely places, travels alone, some of them don't even carry a machete. This one's escaped and paid his way across the border"—as he said this he made the gesture of sliding the palm of one hand over the other—"there's nothing like a bit of palm oil to make a fellow look the other way."

Hilario stood looking at him with his breathing troubled, choking, painful. Through the hot poultice of his body flowed the anguish of a root which can find no earth, a river which improvises beds in the sleep of sleeping plants, the anguish of what he suspected, the tremendous foreboding which had just emerged into the sea of reality, not because of the news, the news wasn't important, he'd almost known it in advance, but now he was convinced of what he didn't want to be convinced of, what his human condition rejected, his human flesh, his human soul, the man that was in him, the idea that just such a being, born to a woman, given birth to, suckled with a woman's milk, bathed in a woman's tears, could change at will into an animal, turn himself into a beast, put his intelligence into the body of an inferior creature, stronger, but inferior.

Señor Nicho and the coyote he ran across up on María Tecún Ridge were the same person: he had him just a few paces away, he had had the impression it was a person, a person he knew.

He went out without uttering a word, wiping beads of cold sweat from his brow with his sleeve. He put his hat on as best he could, he was in the street now, the lane covered over with grass and prickly weeds, bluish leaves like tinplate and pale yellow flowers like butterflies.

"You've had a rough time!" Mincho Lobos said when he saw the look of shock on his face. Hilario took the mule's halter from Mincho's hand, rolled it up and mounted. "But you can't feel worse than I do," added Lobos, busying himself adjusting the horse's girth. "You know, I ain't looking forward to arriving back at the village, everyone'll be waiting to hear what happened about the Virgin. When I came the first time to collect her, I noticed she had a queer pair of eyes, but in all the fuss and excitement of taking her back I didn't pay it much attention. Imagine what they're gonna say about me now, to my face: they'll say I'm a brute. What have saint's eyes got to do with eyes for stuffed animals?"

"Look, Mincho, thinking about all this from another point of view, and without beating round the bush, because I know I don't have to with you, let's go and get ourselves a drink, and I'll tell you what happened to me: I've had such a shock, there really are animals with people's eyes."

"Stuffed, you mean?"

"Alive! And if so, why should you be surprised that a saint should have the eyes of—a coyote, say . . . ?"

"Don't be ridiculous, whoever heard of such a thing—unless you've turned Protestant?"

"God forbid!"

"Thanks for your invitation, but another time. If they see me arrive back in the village full of drink, telling them they've put deer's eyes on the Virgin Mary, I'll be strung up, that's how wild they are up there."

"Who asked you to get drunk. One drink, I said."

"Not even one, Hilario, thanks all the same. You must tell me about your tricks and dodges to turn people into animals with people's eyes some other time. They exist, you bet your life they do, my grandfather told me he clearly saw a curer who could change himself into a deer, the Deer of the Seventh Fire; but that was all so long ago."

Mincho Lobos held out his hand. They said goodbye. Each went his own way, and each took his own thoughts with him. The muleteer was almost run down by a car, which made the mule jump as it had never jumped before. Lucky it was obedient and used to obeying in a flash.

The barber ushered him as usual into a riding saddle without a horse. He made himself comfortable. He sneezed with his spurs, already seated. The barber, Don Trinidad Estrada de León Morales, gave him a courteous welcome, slapping him affectionately on the back.

"My usual trim and a shave," he ordered as he walked in, hanging up his hat, and now he was covered by a bib down to his feet, below his knees anyway, and repeated, "My usual trim and a shave."

"That hurt?" Don Trinis asked, as he moved the clippers over the back of his neck toward his ears.

"That blasted machine of yours is hopeless, I'm gonna end up with toothache like I did last time, and I'll have to go to the pharmacy for a remedy."

"Not much more down here, if I don't do it it won't turn out as you like it, Don Hilario. How are things in your part of the country; what news, the roads must be in good condition for you to be back so soon, are you here for a few days or in and out in one day?"

"I'll be away soon."

"You didn't come for provisions, then. I suppose Don Porfirio stayed behind, stayed up in the village. I was thinking you'd both have come, you're just like brothers, always together, I like to see that. I'm told that last time you lost a mule, or had one stolen or something."

"We found it. It got loose and went for a stroll, having a look at all these fine city sights."

"You like the city, do you?"

"I like it, but I'd never get used to it. There's too much for a person to watch out for, and too many people watching out for a person. You people have a lot, but it's mostly bad; up there where I'm from there ain't much, but what there is is good. And it seems to me we are freer out in the country— you poor folk here live like prisoners, and you have to ask permission to do everything: with your permission and by your leave, and excuse me, I'm sorry, that's all life comes down to here. Up there we don't have all that palaver, and you don't have to keep apologizing for breathing."

"I got you that thing you wanted."

"It was Porfirio wanted it, but it makes no difference."

"It worked out a bit dear, but there aren't many about, you

see; it's a beauty and what's more you can easily get ammunition for it, because that's something you have to take into
consideration. Now, hold still a moment . . ."

Don Trinidad was gabbing almost in his ear as he took the
fuzz off with his close-shaver, bending over him, peering
through the hair falling to the floor, cut to pieces, like the hair
on a black coconut.

"I'll show it you when I've finished tidying you up," Don
Trinis continued, clip-a-clip-a-clip-a-clip, "I'm sure you're not
in that much of a hurry. You can take a look, and if you like
it we can make a deal. I thought of you two, you and Don
Porfirio, soon as they brought it in, a friend of mine knew I
was after something of the sort—I hadn't ordered one from
him, but he brought it in and left it for you to see. They'll be
along any day now, I told him, and here you are."

Hilario remained silent and looked at himself in the mirror:
dark face, big velvet eyes, well-formed lips, a fine forehead,
and an aquiline nose. Not so very ugly. Aleja Cuevas, his
country belle, had told him as much. She's going to dance with
joy when she sees the shawl, because before he went to the
barber's he'd been down to the Chinese quarter and bought
a shawl, the silken twin sister of the one poor Nicho Aquino
took home for his wife, the one Aleja Cuevas had taken such
a fancy to.

"If you want, I'm certain you're going to like it, you can take
it with you now and pay me later, no need for you to give me
the cash today."

Porfirio Mansilla was right, mirrors are like our consciences.
In them we can see what we're like and what we're not like,
because a man who looks deep into a mirror tries to hide his
ugly features and fix things so he'll look his best, just as he does
with his own conscience.

The barber finished with the clippers and blew on them a
few times to clear away the hairs, before putting them back in
their place.

"There you are, now the comb and scissors to finish the trim, and leave you with a forelock you can easily comb whichever way you want."

A moment later he was finished. Hilario's buttocks felt hard as hearthstones, he got tired sitting anywhere except on a horse.

"Comb it this side, if you please."

The barber combed him with a brush so hard it made him close his eyes, quickly took off the great bib, shaking it loudly, and hung it over a rickety old armchair.

"Look, Don Hilario," he took the revolver out of a drawer and handed it to the muleteer, "it's a real beauty, and the best part is there's no shortage of bullets for that caliber. Here are the boxes of ammunition."

"I've got mine with me, but like I said last time, it ain't much good anymore. It's a deal if we make a swap and you give me a good trade-in on my old gun."

"You sell yours somewhere else, or I'll sell it for you, but you'll have to pay me cash for this one, because the person who's selling it needs some 'ready.' Take it, I'll give the fellow his money myself, and you can pay me later, and if you like, if it suits you, you can leave me yours and I'll try and sell it, tell me how much you want for it, we're bound to get something. Think it over, you won't regret it, it's a good deal, that way you get yourself a new pistol, and you're laughing, even if the coyote comes to get you."

The barber, who was examining some bullets he'd taken out of a box, failed to notice the expression of profound displeasure on Hilario Sacayón's face when he mentioned the word "coyote." For a moment he saw himself, pistol in hand, aiming at the hide of that coyote up on María Tecún Ridge, which was not a coyote, which was no coyote at all, he knew it, with all the faculties of the soul which are not in the senses, he knew it, his consciousness had accepted as irremediably real something which previously had been a mere story as far as he was concerned. Shoot the coyote and Nicho Aquino falls wounded or dead, heaven knows where, and how would I bury the coyote if he fell down the mountainside, and how would I return Nicho Aquino's soul to him? The beautiful gun was still in his hand. He put it down quickly and asked for his hat.

"Take it, Don Hilario, you'll only be sorry!"

"Only those who get themselves chopped up are sorry they didn't buy a pistol. If you've still got it next time I'm here, maybe we'll make a deal. I almost went without paying you . . ."

He lit a cigarette as he stood waiting for his change, spat in a spittoon by the door, shook hands with Don Trinidad Estrada de León Morales, and out into the street he went, where his sleepy mule was waiting.

The noise in the street was so loud you could have cut it up and eaten it, or licked it just as if the air were a plate and the din a jelly. It stuck to you. He always left the city feeling as though there was something sticky on his hands and face, on his clothing. His eyes opened wide as he rode past a high-class saddlery. In one of the windows was an enormous horse; and in the doorway, as though welcoming the customers, another one the same size with the same stance, both harnessed with silver and gold-lined trappings, saddles, gleaming bridles, and stirrups glittering almost like fireflies. Whenever he went by there, and although the horses never had riders, he always imagined he could see Machojón, like they say he looks when they're setting fires in the forest. Like a star in the sky. They don't let anyone ride them, he thought, but they seem to be moving even though they're quite still, like the sun and the stars; but who would climb onto them anyway and risk being fixed there, turned into a statue, and besides, I expect they're hollow like that pony Don Deferic gave the commandant's eldest son on his saint's day. I like the stone horse better, he's more solid, more like a horse, that milky-colored mane of his, and the way his eyes shine when the sun falls on him, held back by the wall, and held down by little boys' bottoms, because they all ran to sit on his back when school was out.

He returned to the place where he had bought the hay, and

241

went into the courtyard. The afternoon had befuddled everyone there, all wandering up and down the passageways as if
they were lost. Someone was picking at a guitar, and a voice
was singing:

> *A prisoner am I and unhappy,*
> *in love with a cruel woman,*
> *and as long as I live in this world,*
> *I'll never wish to see her again.*
> *The things she told me weren't true, not a one,*
> *they were all false promises, false coin she gave*
> *in exchange for my true, true love.*
>
> *And every man who loves a cruel woman,*
> *and like a cruel woman would treat her,*
> *let him do as the wind when it lifts up leaves,*
> *and drops them where it first took them up.*
> *The things she told me weren't true, not a one,*
> *they were all false promises, false coin she gave*
> *in exchange for my true, true love.*
>
> *Now suppose that we two were just rubbish,*
> *and a whirlwind carried us high,*
> *and though for a time we were walking on air,*
> *the power of that same wind forced us apart.*
> *The things she told me weren't true . . .*

After hitching up the mule where he'd be out of the way,
watering him and putting down his hay, Hilario went on in
with his gear, only to meet up with Benito Ramos and one
Casimiro Solares, who were unloading maizecobs carried in
nets from a string of mules. They were both friends of his, but
he was none too fond of one of them, Ramos, and Ramos
didn't exactly worship at his shrine either. They just didn't get
on. Ramos greeted him, but straight off with bantering, nick-
names, "Your shirt's hanging out."

"What's this, half-breed, do my eyes deceive me, fancy see-ing you!"

"Pardon me while I cross myself," Hilario gave as good as he got, "because you turn up where I least expect to see you."

"Out with it, half-breed, why don't you tell me straight you think I have a pact with the devil, we ain't gonna fight over that."

"Truth's no lie!"

Once the mules were unloaded, and while some women were asking Ramos and his companion whether the maize was for sale, Hilario stood listening to the sound of the guitars. He took off his hat. If just one of the many stars shining in the sky fell in his hat, he would be happy.

> *The things she told me weren't true, not a one,*
> *they were all false promises, false coin she gave*
> *in exchange for my true, true love.*

Sitting on the steps to the verandah, talking in the half darkness, Benito Ramos told him he was very sick, the effects of an old hernia which not only hurt, but threatened to kill him at any time if it became strangulated.

"Well, go to confession if you ain't been already, that's if you can find anyone to hear your confessions," joked Hilario, keeping up the offensive to fend off any further attack; but when he heard Benito fall quiet, embedded in a heavy silence, he was sorry for his stupidity, softened his voice, and said, "What you ought to do, before anything else, Benito, is see a doctor and stop worrying, plenty of people have been cured of hernia—they can operate on you in hospital, and there are other cures too: some sicknesses you have to catch them in time, else they get worse."

"That's what I've been thinking, and that's why I'm here. I was hoping Señor Chigüichón Culebro's remedies would do the trick, but they didn't work for me: he made me fast and drink some astringent herbs, the worst medicine I ever drank in my whole life, and he prescribed some grease that stank of cloves."

"Your illness is the operating kind, they're gonna have to take the saw to you; it's lucky you're tough enough to take it."

"Why are you here?" asked Ramos between moans. The pain was affecting his voice, you could hear it breaking.

"It ain't the canker, is it . . . ?" Hilario hesitated for a long time before uttering that black word, which even as you're saying it leaves your mouth feeling like you've spat out a toad.

"No, it ain't canker; if it had been that Chigüichón Culebro would have cured me—it's a congenital hernia. Believe me, I trembled, I was sure that was what was wrong with me, and I told the herbalist so. If it was that, he replied, I could cure it. And in fact I did see a sick woman cured. Imagine, to cure the canker he takes a poisonous snake and gives it injections of colchicum. The reptile turns monstrous, but then, the way Chigüichón told it me, it turns vegetable, starts going like wood, and ends up dead as a living creature, but alive as a vegetable one. And the poison from that vegetable snake is dosed out to the person with canker, who turns into a monster too, his teeth fall out, sometimes his hair, but he's cured, radically cured. What are you doing here, you still ain't told me."

"I'm on an errand, I'll soon be heading back."

"I envy you your health, half-breed. When a man's fit like you are, the saddle rests you from getting tired in bed. I can tell you, when I was your age standing on my feet used to tire me. I got bored, that's why I took part in the campaign against the Indians of Ilóm under Colonel Godoy and a fellow called Secundino Musús, who they tell me is a major today, he was just a second lieutenant at that time. He was like a plucked chicken, malarial, and real mean-hearted."

"Yes, he's boss of San Miguel now, he's commandant of the garrison. He's fat now, but his character seems kind of dry, the man seems real sour."

"Well, you can ask him. We used to change horses and ride

straight on, whatever the roads, up until we all got out of it after the death of Colonel Chalo Godoy. That man was real good for war, because he was real bad in every other way. Trapped by the wizards in the Earthshaker, he was, they burned him alive. Some of us saved our skins because we'd gone up to the Cattle Pass with an Indian carrier we found in a coffin. The son-of-a-bitch had tucked himself up in there real cosy, thinking he'd go on with his journey the next day. The colonel decided it was a trick worked out by the cattle thieves who were all over the place round there, they were always laying out so-called dead men in ambushes, and now instead of a man pretending to be dead, all there was was a coffin—"

"The boat you'll be rowing someday, brother—"

"Yeah, but not from this illness. Like I was saying, the colonel thought that deserted coffin lying out in the forest was a snare, right out in the heart of the forest it was, where no one passed by for days at a time. You can imagine the shock he got when he opened it and found an Indian inside all dressed in white, with his hat over his face. And do you think he'd wake up? Colonel had to poke him with a pistol. Then we saw the dead man was alive all right, he really shot out of there, told us the coffin was for someone else, some curer up in the Cattle Pass. I could tell you some stories. When I talk about all that it helps me forget the pain. Maybe that's why history was invented, so we could forget the present . . ."

Benito Ramos, sometimes known as Benigno, and sometimes Pedrito, sat tapping on the knuckles of his left hand with the fingertips of his right hand, timing his own silence, which was curdled by the thoughts gnawing away at him. And he refused the cigarette Hilario offered him.

"I'll tell you more about that time in my life, if only to take my mind off this bastard pain. I will have that cigarette, if you insist, and because maybe if I smoke—it's a dull pain, blocked, like the gripes, like I had rheumatism in the guts. Give me a light, I won't ask you to spit for me, I've got more than enough bile of my own—when the pain comes I find heaps of the stuff suddenly there in my mouth. Well, like I was saying, half-breed, Second Lieutenant Musús led us up from the Earth-shaker to the Cattle Pass, with the Indian carrying the coffin on his back, the one he'd used as a bed, and us with our mausers ready to sling lead. And we had special orders: if the coffin wasn't for the curer or for a dead man who really was dead, we were to put the Indian in it and shoot him on the spot with the coffin nailed down, ready to shovel earth straight over him.''

He drew on the cigarette and blew the smoke out through his nose in short bursts, after spitting out a few particles of tobacco which had stuck to the end of his tongue, and went on, in a calmer voice, "We didn't shoot the Indian, and we didn't see Colonel Godoy again. Real good for war, he was, because he was real bad in every other way. And''—he took another drag—''to cut a long story short, before Musús and the lads in the escort realized there was a fire—there wasn't even any smell, things were completely normal, like tonight—I had a vision of what was happening down there in the Earthshaker. You've seen the miracle plays, haven't you?''

Hilario started to laugh, a laugh that grew bigger and yet bigger, as he tried to explain the cause of his untimely out-burst. "Ha, ha, ha, the miracle plays, ho, ho, ho, the miracle plays, hee, hee, hee, hee, the main player in them tableaus is your friend, ha, ha, ha, ha, your friend with the eleven thou-sand horns!''

The words and phrases, fragmented between roars of laugh-ter, followed one another without thread: miracle plays, friend, eleven thousand horns, main player, friend, eleven thousand . . .

"Your friend fights, ha, ha, ha, and fights with the Angel of the Golden Ball,'' Hilario laughed on, twisting himself up with laughter as he spoke, as if he'd been wound up, and waving his hands like a drowning swimmer, after dropping his hat, he couldn't stop it falling because he was searching for his hand-kerchief, for tears were beginning to form in his eyes.

"Have you finished?''

"Go on with the story, I'll stop laughing in a minute."

" 'Laughing,' he says, and he's crying his eyes out."

"Go on, go on with the story," and back came the irrepressible laughter, born of the imagination of Hilario, who saw Benito Ramos in his mind's eye, dressed up as the devil, with the holy pain of his hernia getting worse every time he had to stamp his foot and proclaim his pedigree as the King of Hell, in battle, first with the Moor of Austria-Hungary, and after defeating that Moor, who has foam in his mouth and butter up his arse, then with the Angel of the Golden Ball, all in order to carry off as his prize, if he wins the duel, a drunken Indian.

"You're mistaken, I never took part in that tableau, all I've ever done is watch. You're just laughing at the idea, so laugh on."

"Go on with the story, you should be grateful. There's nothing like laughter to frighten pain away. So, you saw what happened as if you were watching a miracle play, before it even took place . . ."

"Not only did I see it, I informed Musús and the lads. I saw it as clear as I see you now, Colonel Godoy and his men surrounded by three deadly circles down in the funnel of the Earthshaker. Counting from where he and the soldiers were standing talking, not realizing the danger they were in, the first circle was just owl's eyes, without owls, just the eyes, the owls weren't there, and if they were they looked like unwrapped tamales; the second one was formed out of the faces of wizards without bodies, thousands and thousands of faces hanging in the air like the face of the moon in the sky; and the third was made up of rounds of Spanish daggers with bloodstained tips."

"A tippler's nightmare!"

"Sure, except it turned out to be true. The report the government put out just said that Colonel Godoy and his troop, returning from a reconnaissance mission, perished in a forest fire; but the truth is—"

"The truth is what you saw, you saw him burn to death or die fighting, nothing is hidden between heaven and earth."

"He didn't burn to death and he didn't die in combat. The

firefly wizards, after turning the cold fire of despair on him, reduced him to the size of a puppet, and multiplied him in the form of a poor child's toy, a wooden doll carved with a machete blade. You see, what they were keeping him for—"

"No, you saw it . . ."

"Yes, I saw it—but now I'm telling you about it you're seeing it too. They were keeping him for a punishment worse than death. The Indians were more advanced than us, I reckon, because they'd even surpassed death itself as a punishment."

A boy from the street, tousled and wretched, one shoe on and the other half on, came in selling newspapers, shouting. Ramos bought one and because he was so slow in unfolding that sheet of paper with printed letters on, a little at a time, the pain from his hernia didn't allow him much movement, Hilario said, "Now you've bought it, let's read it."

"Read it, you say, as if a man can read the paper in the dark. Let's get under that light bulb there."

"I thought you could see in the dark."

"Don't push me too far, half-breed, if you don't want a smack in the teeth. Look here, there's news from your town— 'Post-man-dis-ap-pears . . .' I can't read very fast, you take over."

Hilario snatched the paper from Benito's hands, but Ramos, who would not be despoiled in that manner, took it back, holding on tightly, to continue reading: "San-Mi-guel-Aca-tán-we-have-re-ceived-tele-gra-phic-in-for-mation-that-the-reg-u-lar-post-man-Dio-ni-sio-Aqui-no-Co- . . . ," he uncrossed his eyes, whenever he said anything his eyes went crossed, "that's all it says, you, dopey, the postman's disappeared, not a word more. They might have said . . . Did you know him? . . . What a question if it was you they sent after him! My pact ain't with the devil, it's with the newspaper, and that's how I guess things."

"Is that what it says there—that I came after the postman?"

"You're saying it, half-breed. All the paper says is what I read out to you. They've lost their postman. He's become invisible. He's turned into nobody. He must have found out he was carrying a lot of money in those letters. It's risky to send dough by mail. Money's paper that talks, but it don't talk friendly: that's why when I've got some bill to settle I go along myself and avoid the loss and the annoyance. Bank notes ain't love notes."

He spat. His throat was suddenly full of saliva. Saliva which was the very excrescence of his pain. A gentle tremor shook him beneath his skin, as if the whole earth were trembling, not just him.

"Well, Benito Ramos, I'm going to lay my body down, I'm wore out. I'd like to keep on talking, but I ain't laid down nor had a wink of sleep since I left San Miguel. I should have caught the postman up before María Tecún Ridge, but he must have taken a back road and got himself lost: such odd things happen that you end up thinking you must be dreaming it all" —he gave a long yawn—"Well, now, I'm almost out on my feet, if you happen to find out where Señor Nicho is, let me know, why else do you have that pact with the . . ."

"If we're talking miracles, what amazes me is that you are still exactly like yourself—no good! One of these days I'll have had enough of you and"—he pushed his arm out as if to run Hilario through—"they'll have to pick you up with a spoon."

"And you, where have you been?"

"Out on the town . . ."

"Good time?" asked Hilario, spreading out his mule-warmed bedclothes on a cold rush petate.

"I sure did, they know they'll enjoy themselves when I turn up. It's like half a life going to see the girls—you don't win nothing but you have a good time; and it's nice to be loved, even if you have to pay for it—Ow, blast it, I've given myself pins and needles! Stupid pillar, and stupid me to jerk my elbow back like that. Oooh, it's like a swarm of ants, ooh, ooh, ooh, right down through my fingers, it's the Lord's punishment for saying what I shouldn't."

Stretched out on their mats, with their jackets as pillows,

Hilario and Benito kept up their conversation for a while, before putting their heads under their blankets, as Casimiro Solares had done long since. A drowsy conversation, somewhat forced, a flimsy rope bridge across the roaring river of snores flowing from the fortunate Solares.

"The point of what I was telling you when the newspaper boy came in—"

"Yes," mumbled Hilario, more asleep than awake, "and then Casimiro came in . . ."

"The point was that from that day I became famous for having a pact with the devil, because I knew in advance what was going to happen to the colonel, what was happening to him—you see, I didn't know whether I was seeing it before it happened, or at the very same moment, only from a great distance. Of course many people have the ability to anticipate events; but as there will never be enough of them, they always seem to be rare. But they have it without ever needing to make any pacts with the devil, it's something natural, or supernatural, like thinking. You tell me what's more wondrous in man than his thinking. So why couldn't it have been God who gave me my divine gift? I don't have it anymore. At first it was something that just suddenly came to me, where from I don't know, as though on the wings of a bird I couldn't see that got in my nose, my eyes, my ears, my head, and possessed me. Later I had to concentrate a bit to hit the nail on the head. Not anymore, I've lost it, everything comes to an end with the passing of the years—Are you listening, Hilario?"

"Yes, that's interest . . . pity . . . you . . . lost . . . gift . . ."

"You're not paying attention."

"It must be a real treat," the words followed one after another, then became spaced out again, "to know in . . . ad . . . vance . . . what's . . . gonna . . . happen . . . to . . . you . . . that . . . way . . . you . . . can . . . get yourself out of trouble before you even get in it," he was talking normally again, "if the wall's going to fall on you and you know it in advance, you can get out of the way and even spit on it before it can make

250

a pancake of you. Now I've woken up. My sleep's gone away . . ."

"That's how it ought to have been. But experience has taught me that it's a thousand times better not to know what's going to happen. I need only tell you I saw my lady mother die before they brought me the news that a mango branch had fallen on top of her. I saw the old girl fall to the ground like a crushed leaf and I stretched out my hand, but how could my arm reach out to help her, when I was twenty leagues away, high in the forest."

"Your woman?" asked Hilario, as he rolled over on his petate, his back looked like a piece of molasses-dipped candy on a maize leaf, he wasn't going to be allowed to sleep off his tiredness—all that gabbing from the devil's disciple, Casimiro snoring and smelling like a rotten egg, the postman walking all over his body, an ache that started off as a man and ended up as a coyote, images of saints with the eyes of stuffed animals . . . "Brute of a sculptor—putting deer's eyes on the Blessed Virgin, I'd have punched his nose in Mincho Lobos' place."

"My woman," Ramos pulled in his legs, groaning, "we parted some time ago, she took it into her head to move to Aguazarca with her children, she's a bandit . . ."

"And were you left alone—didn't you have any children by her?"

"No, I didn't. And it's clear that's why her blood has dragged her away. All that love nonsense comes from the urge to have children: you see a woman you fancy and you feel the urge to grab a hold of her, and in that urge lies the child; so you take hold of her and squeeze her, and the child is there, in the warmth of your bodies and the jerking of your brain, in the saliva of the kisses you give her, in the affection that comes out in her words . . . She ran off with her children, that's what always happens when you shack up with a woman who's already had a litter, when you get old they leave you whistling on the wind . . . Want a cigarette?"

"I don't like to smoke lying down."

"I spent my time with her, and I've no regrets, Hilario—
though maybe I have, because you always end up with regrets:
good or bad, however life treats you, as time goes by you
always get the feeling you've lost life in the very living of it."

"Smoke to keep the smell of Casimiro away. You're rotting,
you, Casifart!"

"That's what children are for, you, Hilario, so that when
you're old you ain't left with the uneasy feeling you've lost life
in the very living of it, that time slipped away from you day
by day. Life passes by you like a muletrain, as you live it, and
only children can give you the illusion of a muletrain that's
gonna keep on going, and the best thing is you can't eat them
or sell them, they endure . . ."

"You, Casifartarse, listen to Father Ripalda sermonizing at
me! You're talking too difficult for me, the only thing I can
make out is you ain't got no children, why's that?"

"Because of the accursed curse of the cursed firefly wizards.
All of us who were in the attack against the Indians of Gaspar
Ilóm, when we made mincemeat of them without leaving even
one of them to tell the tale, we were all done for. The daylight
that morning broke the light of life in our bodies, it was light
salted with sorcerer's curses, and those who had children saw
them die, and their grandchildren too, and old Machojón's son
was carried away by the fireflies themselves, to become a star
in the sky, and those of us without children, our spring ran dry.
I sent one no-good woman I set up house with packing when
she told me she was pregnant. How could the merchandise be
mine, if the wizards left us all with one ball apiece, rotten
eggs."

"But Major Musús has a son . . ."

"Then it's his by another man, because at that time Musús
was a second lieutenant of the line, and what was so special
about him that the curse shouldn't fall on him, when it fell even
on the forest, even on the stones, everything fell withered to
the ground, and the stones looked like they'd been scorched.
To this day it's known as the Place of Curses."

"You brought the maize in nets, I see—"

"Those nets—the Indians were even right about that, curse them! You should have seen what this land was like when they were cultivating it rationally. You don't need much arithmetic to work it out. You can do it with your fingers. Maize should be planted as they used to plant it, as they still do, to give the family its grub, and not for business. Maize is sustenance, it allows you to get by, more than get by. You show me a rich maizegrower, Hilario. It seems crazy, but we're all worse off. There've been times in my house when we haven't even had money for candles. It's the folk who own chocolate trees, cattle, orchards, beehives, who are rich. Small-town rich folk, maybe, but rich for all that, ain't so very bad being the biggest fish in a small pool. Now the Indians used to have all those things, as well as the maize that forms our daily bread. They did things in a small way, if you like, but they had all they needed, they weren't greedy like us because now, Hilario, greed has become a way of life to us. You just take maize itself: poverty sown and harvested until the very earth is worn out . . . Wake up, Hilario, don't leave me with my Bible in my mouth, it's rude to go off to sleep like that—what's there to choose between a dead man and a man asleep, they both look the same . . . The maizegrower leaves the land in the end because he's beaten it to death, like killing a snake, with his planting and planting, over and over, after all he knows it ain't his, it belongs to the boss, and if they give him leave to set fire to the forest, heaven help us all! . . . I saw the forests of Ilóm burning at the turn of the century. It's progress advancing with the tread of the conqueror, Colonel Godoy used to explain, real poetical, as he stood before all those rows of precious timber being turned into flaming brands, smoke and ash, because it was progress that was turning trees into firewood— mahoganies, primaveras, sapodillas, ceibas, pines, eucalyptuses, cedars—and because justice had come to the forest with the authority of the sword, as blows rained everywhere and on everyone . . ."

253

The memory of so many good things brought to ruin merged in his mind with the ache of his hernia, which was more painful than ever in the cold of three o'clock in the morning, a cold asphyxiating pain, as though he'd been stung by a hangman wasp.

Sure enough, the coffee vendor had gone from beneath the ceiba. The table lay with its legs in the air, and inside it some hearthstones on a piece of burnt sacking, a heap of ash where she lit her fire, all swept by the cold of the morning. Hilario gave the mule its head on the outskirts of the city, to let himself wake up at leisure, numb more than tired after listening to Benito Ramos talk and Casimiro Solares snore, all through the night. His body was like a bruised mango. His head hollow. That was why all those long hollow yawns kept forcing their way out of his mouth. From a few houses electric lights were shining out into the blue haze of the morning through the seams of the doors. The bakers were busy opening their shutters. Time had caught up on him. Luckily the newspaper would have let everyone in San Miguel know about the runaway postman. He had the paper in his bag. Benito Ramos kindly gave it to him. He took breakfast in a rancho when he was well clear of the city, hot coffee and toasted tortillas, frijoles and fresh cheese, pity they had no chili. Two girls attended him. One was very pretty even though she hadn't combed her hair and her clothes were still crumpled from sleeping. The older one caught on to the fact that Hilario fancied her younger sister, and didn't move from their side. Better to carry the memory of that young beauty than the painful impression left by the hernia and the philosophy of Benito Ramos, the man who had a pact with the devil.

Without effort, as trees, stone walls, plains, rocks, stretches of river went by, Sacayón saw the delightful face of that young girl at the rancho as though she were superimposed on the air. Over everything traveling with him, keeping up with him, wherever he laid his eyes she appeared. The soul is so given to what the body wants, when you're young. It's the reverse with old folk. In old folk, it's the body that's inclined toward what the soul wants, and the soul, when the years have gone by you, starts wanting to fly.

Lovely little rancho girl. Trim and tasty. He was tempted to turn back and ask her to marry him. It was just a matter of turning the mule round and carrying on, only instead of his face heading the way it was going now, it would be heading in the opposite direction, and at the end of the ride he would find the rancho again, with a few clay pots and gasoline cans planted with flowers and creepers which sent curtains of leaves and blossoms climbing up to the thatched roof.

He couldn't make up his mind. The mule stopped by a broad river to drink water, he didn't actually stop it but he did move the rein a little, and it stopped. Be nice to let the mule take him back and pass by where that young miss lived again. Pass the miss, pass a kiss, kiss and pass, kiss her arse—he used foul language to talk himself out of the idea. Rancho girl or no rancho girl, the bond between him and Aleja Cuevas was not a joke. He was taking her a shawl. She was from his village. Not badly off, besides the bar she owned a bit of land down by the river. And she had something about her that was worth more than all the gold in the world, something of Miguelita of Acatán, not in her looks—Miguelita was beautiful, and Aleja was pretty ugly—but in the fact that both of them were from Acatán. There was something, too, in the fact that she was the very opposite of a tecuna, because she was long-suffering, and because she liked to stay at home. Miguelita sews when everyone is sleeping, stays up at night to earn her daily bread, never leaves her house and if she does, returns. He commended himself to the Bilboes Virgin, while the mule, satisfied, breathed contentedly and brushed its nostrils over the surface of the water.

After swallowing down the swift-flowing water of the river the mule began to move more swiftly along an unmade road that was more stones than road, until some leagues later it started to flag and went virtually lame. Still following the stony

river, above the rumbling of the current as it formed eddies at
the bends, he turned off along a trail that meandered between
ash-blue mountains and came out on the shores of a lake with
twelve villages seated on the surrounding slopes, twelve apostles hewn out of mountain rocks in whose nets the ranchos and
their dark inhabitants with fishlike eyes lay trapped.

He was taking the long way round so he wouldn't have to
pass María Tecún Ridge. The peaks clashed together in mid-air
like rams. When he'd been riding down alongside the fast-
running river he'd had the impression his beast wasn't moving,
and now its climbing was annulled by the vision of the peaks
growing sheer before his eyes. The steps of the mule heaving
up that steep slope meant so little in the face of mounds which
rose more and more steeply until they cut the clouds. A waterfall he couldn't see was splashing down below, a deep echo in
his ears, audible proof that the earth was not only climbing as
he was, quicker than he was, toward the peaks, but falling,
diving headlong into somnolent abysses.

The river fell away into a confused rumbling, like a flight of
birds with liquid feathers. The girth of the back path through
which he was cutting was pulled tight round the belly of a
mountain which he imagined to be a wild stallion, between
young saplings which bowed obsequiously as the wind blew,
and the silence was greater when a mockingbird sang, because
you could hear the mockingbird and you could hear the silence. He shielded himself against brambles by raising his arm
and keeping his head well down beneath his wide-brimmed
hat. He heard a deer go by. The sound of claws up in the trees.
Further ahead the plains would begin, the flies and the black
honeybees. He raised himself high in the saddle to look back.
He had climbed enough, made it to a stretch of good road
across a wide plain. Muletrains, Indian carriers, oxcarts, men
on horseback. Some going in his direction. Others coming the
other way. They approached, met him and greeted him. No
one he knew. The lake dazzled him. The mule kept its four
clappers chiming, after toiling so hard on the steep back road,

where one step today and another tomorrow was good going. He too straightened up to throw off the weariness of the climb and shifted the position of his fingers on the reins, his feet in the stirrups. He stopped to light a cornhusk cigarette which had been hanging dead between his sunburnt lips. Flocks of wild birds settled on the pastures, rising at once after pecking at the cow dung, unconcerned by the huge-headed oxen, calves drowsy with sleep and ticks. Some mule drivers passed by like a rush of warm air, and Hilario Sacayón felt a sudden surge of desire to go back with them. So long, they said. They were whistling. It's hard to believe some folk just lie, or sit, or move, in only one place.

A woman's voice made him turn his head: "It's a sad thing to be poor!"

"Why, I didn't see you there in the doorway! How are you, Miss Cande? Still at the stall? Though I see you're nearly sold out. Only the other day I was thinking how much I enjoy a nice piece of pork. Got any crackling left? I'll buy you out. So how are you?"

"Well, thanks be to God. And you, where are you headed? You were going past me without even saying hello."

"San Miguel."

"Didn't you bring any mules?"

"No, I didn't."

"Traveling alone. Porfirio and Olegario are around, I don't know if they're inside."

"You don't say. How about your brothers?"

"They're here too at the moment. They came down from the mountains about nine days ago. Why don't you get down and come in, it's late now and there's nowhere for you to stop further on. Besides, we're having a party here tonight."

"Better to be early than invited, I always say. If you'll excuse me I'll go on in."

"I'll see you in a moment, I'm glad you came."

Candelaria Reinosa was still selling pigmeat at her stall by the wayside. She had filled out a lot, dressed almost always in yellow, with her thick black plaits flowing over the faded gold huipile like the perennial stream of mourning she carried in her soul. Her gentle eyes still gazed down the trail with the same lively anxiety there was in them the day Machojón was to come and ask her hand. The trail was her life. Time and again her brothers had tried to drag her away from the pigmeat stall, now they were men of means; but she wouldn't hear of leaving that lookout post, as if it were really true that waiting feeds the fires of hope. By waiting she was feeding her hope. A castor-oil lamp at the foot of an image of the Virgin of Good Hope was the only luxury in her stall for pigmeat, sausages, and crackling. Her brothers sold the lard in the capital now. Better price, and they had a regular buyer there for their firewood, besides. Candelaria Reinosa, it's silly, but without knowing why, fell sad until she got chills and started to lose weight, the day her brothers told her they'd be taking the lard with them. It was as though they had taken away the white dress she was to have worn on her wedding day. A plain white dress licked around the wildflower stalk of her body. She was not quite eighteen years old. Machojón, whenever he arrived to see her, took her hand without a word, and they would stay silent for long periods at a time, and if they spoke it was to point out what was going on around them. Listen to the chickens, Machojón would say, so she would notice the clucking of some broody hen, for the truth was he had barely heard it himself, that noise from outside which was so remote from the mysterious language in which they two spoke, merely by holding hands. The flame, she would say, when a candle lit at the foot of Christ Crucified suddenly began to flicker. Damn them dogs, they bark at everyone who goes by just for the sake of barking, they'd do better keeping quiet. The leaf, she breathed, when the wind carried off a leaf. Everything was important. In those days everything was important. Machojón's sombrero. It used to smell for eight or ten days wherever he left it. Phew, sometimes it made the whole house stink. His jingling spurs in the depth of his manly stride. He used to bury his heels in the ground as he walked, like a real man does. And his calm voice, with a man's loneliness in it.

Candelaria Reinosa pushed through the canvas cloth she used to cover the entrance to her pigmeat stall, to appear out in the courtyard of the house, where her brothers were having a celebration, accompanied by their women, their children and their friends. The cup of cane brandy was filled for each guest in turn and passed from hand to hand. The marimba called them to the dance. The guitars were waiting over in a corner. They all talked for talk's sake. They laughed. Embraced one another. Porfirio Mansilla came in with his arm around Hilario Sacayón, followed by Olegario, who was lashing the ground to kick up the dust with a whip as long as a monkey's tail.

A saffron-colored old man was attracting attention. He was nicknamed "White-Louse." Started off as a curer, and now he just loved folk to call him "doctor." He was surrounded by guests. Miss Candelaria realized they were talking about her. What did she care. The "doctor" was still clinging tight to his hobby horse, like a white louse. He wanted to marry her. And their ages, according to her brothers, were just right, only she didn't want it.

Porfirio, Hilario and Olegario, the muleteers, went up to Candelaria, full of their own mischievous gossip, laughing and joking.

"Don't just stand there watching, why don't you dance!" Hilario asked, a little behind Porfirio, who was already shaking hands with her.

"Not me, I'd rather die!"

"Take my arm," said Porfirio, giving her his hand, "and we'll show these two how to blow up a storm."

"You must be joking!" she exclaimed, slipping her arm free of his.

"What are we celebrating here, anyway?" intervened Hilario.

"The betrothal of one of Andrés my brother's daughters."

"It's Chonita who's getting married," added Porfirio. "It

was all kept very quiet, just like it will be when you come out and surprise us all, Canducha."

"Only if you decide to marry me, Don Porfirio, because no one else would have such bad taste."

They stopped talking to listen to the marimba. By now the guitars were being tuned up, too. A lame dog started howling, fled yelping out into the street from the kitchen, where it had caught a solid swipe with a stick.

"That Javiera's real mean-hearted!" said Candelaria Reinosa, smoothing out the apron over her plump, spinster's belly with her white hands, and she moved through the guests to scold the Indian grinderwoman, forever stinking of green cobs, pregnant by God knows who, a scrounger, a tippler, and even a harlot on the side, so they said. There was nothing she couldn't do, but she was a bit light-fingered and her devotion to other people's property condemned her to the gentle torture of the grinding stone.

She didn't reply to the telling-off, didn't even lift her eyes, until she'd finished pounding the maize she had on the stone. Then she dropped the pestle and straightened up at once.

"Your brothers told me they wasn't gonna let you come out to the kitchen, and what's more they—they said a lot, your brothers did. And what's more . . . you look for any excuse . . . There's a party going on, go back inside, stop gaping at the fire . . ."

Candelaria Reinosa stood motionless, eyes fixed on the heart of a small furnace full of burning wood, flames, smoke. From the smoke to the flames, from the flames to the wood, the wood to the trees, trees to earth, earth to sleep, sleep to dream. Her two eyebrows together. Still closer together. Her apron ready in her trembling hand to put out the secret, elemental weeping. From the smoke to the flames, from the flames to the wood . . .

The grinderwoman touched her arm with cold fingers roughened by goat's-water. Candelaria didn't even notice, but went out of the kitchen, she had to attend to the guests, no one

260

else was, all they were interested in was the quarrel going on between the Hilarios, as she affectionately called the muleteers.

"If I'd been in Olegario's place, Porfirio, I never would have let you buy that pair of mules, even though you do fancy yourself an expert on animals. And you paid far too much for them, in any case."

"Don't you go blaming me, Hilario, I told him not to buy them, he can tell you so himself. As my name is Olegario, I pointed out it would never do to buy them so damned dear, 'cause they were damned dear, those mules, you, Porfirio. And—"

"What you all need is a drink," said Candelaria, as she went up to them and held out a tray to Porfirio, with three glasses of good liquor on it.

Porfirio didn't have to be asked, though he was still put out that Hilario should call him to account about the mules, the moment he'd got him to say what had happened in San Miguel after the disappearance of the postman Nicho Aquino.

It was a public scandal. Father Valentín announced that the Archangel Saint Michael, the archangelest of all the archangels, was going to unleash the tempest of his sword up on María Tecún Ridge, come the Saint Francis Day storms. Rumor had it the postman had been carrying a wax-sealed envelope with funds for the archdiocese. The postmaster had been called to testify, but had suffered an apoplectic fit on the way, and was left all contorted and unable to speak. Don Deferic tried to organize a demonstration in protest against the patent negligence of the local authorities in having sent a man who was the victim of an unparalleled case of mythomania . . .

"Jehoshaphat, where did you get them fu . . . nny words from?"

"That's what Don Deferic said. He must have said it ninety times: an unparalleled case of mythomania. But there wasn't no such protest. Major Secundino Musús, even although he's his

261

compadre, threatened to have him thrown in jail. The only one who didn't care was the Chinaman, everyone was complaining except him, even the prisoners—but then, their very liberty depends on what the postman brings. Even Aleja Cuevas was asking, though not about the postman but about some loud-mouth who set off after him at breakneck speed, but didn't catch him up because the postman evaporated along the trail, surely turned into a coyote."

"I'll evaporate you if you keep on, Porfirio!"

"And look here, you, Adelaido, it ain't right to leave that girl alone to go round wandering loose, let us know next time you're going away—someone else might gobble her up . . ."

"It'd be a pig's dinner, then! And anyway I'd still have Miss Candelaria, who's in her prime and deserves the best, after all. Here's to you, Miss Cande, lots of happiness to you!"

A slight tremor of her hand made the glasses tinkle on the tray. That toast sent a shiver through Candelaria Reinosa's body, her inner being which was crushed to pulp by sorrows. But none of the three muleteers noticed, Porfirio, Hilario, Olegario, because they were too busy knocking back their drinks. Elbows up, drink down, and head forward to spit out the dregs at the bottom.

White-Louse, the "doctor," was on his way over to the marimba, but joined the group instead, took a glass from the tray almost without looking, because he was gazing straight into Candelaria's eyes, and drank it like water, didn't even spit, but tasted it in both cheeks, saying, "The lady likes the company of horsemen, they are so agreeable, so plain-spoken . . ."

They thanked him for his compliments. Very nice of him. Only Porfirio took it the wrong way, the drink was going to his head, and it sure was fighting liquor, or maybe it was just because he was so tough he wanted to cross swords with White-Louse, an interfering fellow, the kind that take on airs in the city and afterwards, because they're from the country, they don't really fit in either place.

"But we horse-riding men, mister, we don't like lice hanging on us, and Miss Cande stayed a miss because she wanted to, she's turned down suitors by the dozen. Julián Socavalle committed suicide for her, to name only one. He was a horse-riding man, all right, but not as much of one as the man who was her own true love."

"Is," ventured Candelaria, much flattered, lowering her pretty eyes to the empty glasses the muleteers and the doctor had placed back on the tray.

"Is, she says, and rightly so, because she loved him then, she loves him now, and she always will! Someone who is loved, my friend, is never absent. Dead, vanished, whatever, but always present as long as the person who loved him still lives! That's how things are with a man who really was a man, as Machojón was!"

"Was? Is!"

"Yes, Miss Cande," Hilario broke in, "is and will be, as long as there's a woman who loves him—a man on horseback and a star in the sky."

"That's the way," Porfirio went on, the alcohol making him merrier still, and Olegario had already shouted "bravo!" "If there's heading off to be done, it's best to do it while there's still time, and as these drinks are here for the drinking, by your leave, Miss Cande—you, too, Mr. Doctor . . ."

The marimba, the guitar players, the whirling dancers, Candelaria Reinosa with flecks of ash in the black cascade of her plaits, her yellow party blouse, the jacket lifting her breasts a little, and the Hilarios who by now could scarcely keep still, such was their eagerness to bring the star-filled sky down at the feet of their loves.

The betrothed couple went up to them: Chonita Reinosa, daughter of Andrés, brother of Candelaria, and Zacarías Mencos, her with her full little mouth like a heliotrope, him reeking of rabbits and the farmyard in spite of the social air he acquired when he had boots on, though they got in his way so much he seemed to be horse-shoed. They went up to the group of muleteers and the "doctor" to hear what their Aunt Candelaria was telling them.

"Sometimes I'm woken by the trotting of his horse at night.

I go out to see, and down the trail there's a dust-storm of fireflies . . . He passes close by me, but as the fireflies left him blind he doesn't know I've stayed awake waiting for him just like the leaves of the leaden evergreen oak stay awake when the moon's out. He passes by so close and so far away, physically close but far away, because he can't see me. It's horrible but simple"—she talked on without seeing anyone and without looking at anything—"things that maybe never happen, and if they do it's once in ten centuries—what can I do, it's my fate to be pierced by flying sparks: that's why I was and am the image of the one who really was wounded, because that's how love must be understood. A man can be many things, a woman must only be the true image of the man she loves . . ." The last words were a stutter, her lip quivered, she was about to burst into tears, but it turned into the laugh of a woman who has remained a child. "I remember once we were dancing out here in the yard. Let's dance a fox trot, he said, and tried to trip me up, not to make me fall, but to have an excuse to touch my arse. I gave him a good slap—"

"And a kiss too, right, auntie?" said her niece. Family and friends all knew the story by heart.

"What I wonder, in my foolishness," said Olegario, smoking the last of a cigar and eyeing the future bride, who looked just made for fox-trotting, "is if all the stars up in the sky were horse-riding men."

Porfirio butted in before the "doctor" could reply and elbowed him in the ribs, not because of the question itself, but because of its hidden meaning, laughing and saying, "Someone should slip Zacarías the whisper that Olegario here is after his intended. Eat her up now, Zacarías, don't let this braggart take too much of a fancy to her, or she'll slip through your fingers!"

"Seems like you're some fruit, you, Chon," rejoined Zacarías Mencos, struggling to get his hands free of the sleeves of his new jacket, they were too long for him, with his moustache all orange because he'd been mixing his cane juice with pinole.

"A forbidden fruit, but a tasty one, if you ask me," added Hilario.

"Forbidden to others, but not to I," said Zacarías, managing to liberate one hand, with which he fingered his hairy moustache, "because when you get married you each get what's coming to you."

"You're forgetting we ain't married yet, Zaca," said Chonita, and blushed all over.

The voice of a guitarist could be heard singing:

Unhappy tree, without branches or blossoms,
you too have been withered by sorrow . . .

The Moratayas, Benigno and Eduviges, and other friends, formed a circle round them, without moving, savoring the song. Eduviges was the older brother. Beneath his skin lay his bones and in his bones lay the sadness of his importance. Six times he'd been mayor, and the last time everything went wrong, because a fellow they named treasurer made off with the municipal funds and even filed off the silver from the handles of the local officers' staffs.

The mineralized ears of old neighbors, sunk in years, prevented them from speaking quietly. They shouted secrets to one another, and had it not been for the marimba everyone there would have heard their comments on Señor Eduviges Morataya, and now, his turn having come, on the "doctor."

"A graveyard worm, like everyone who lives in the city."

"Graveyard worm, you say—a moth that feeds on dowries and wills, more like it!"

"I may be wrong, but I get the idea he's after Candelaria's money. Hah, if pigs could fly!"

"Try this aniseed brandy—and look, they're passing round slices of egg-bread. They're generous folks, these Reinosas, the old grandparents were just the same."

"Are these Reinosas or Reinosos?"

"What's the difference? The grandparents were the kind of folk who used to really go to town when they had a celebration

—I was here where we're sitting now when they were getting ready for Candelaria's betrothal, she was their favorite daughter. Gabriel was her father's name, Gabriel Reinoso. They killed a steer, heap of pigs, sixteen turkeys—"

"Stop exaggerating and drink your anise. Maybe it was all that partying fouled things up for them."

"Misfortunes are never lacking: Machojón rode out of his house and never arrived to ask her hand."

"He was coming right here to do it."

"Yes, right here where you and me are, all these years later, at Chonita's betrothal—fate, just fate . . ."

"A star he may be," Candelaria was saying to a group of pigmeat vendors, some of them fat and pockmarked, "but I've heard him crying like a baby! Those great golden dots we see lighting up the night aren't happy, I can assure you. On the contrary, when I stare at them and stare at them and become almost one of them through so much staring at them, I can tell they are lights of longing. The infinite vault is full of absences—"

"Auntie," the bride-to-be came to take her away, "the guests want to have a drink with the family, in the other room."

"Is your father there?"

"He's there with Mamma, they're all waiting for you—the 'doctor' is going to say a few words."

"Now the turtledove no longer fears the kite; now the genteel youth a fair companion takes, to build with him a nest; now the cup of life o'erflows with bubbling rejoicing . . ."

Porfirio Mansilla's loud voice could be heard above the hushings and shushings of the guests, filled with indignation at the bad manners of that muleteer, for a muleteer he must be, and calling for silence. Hilario almost dragged his friend outside.

"Come on, Porfirio, stop putting your foot in things. Come with me, man, for heaven's sake, let's see if those guitarists from Juan Rosendo's fields will sing us a song."

The applause for the end of the toast could be heard coming from the reception room.

"Look, Olegario's on the floor already," Hilario pointed out, to take Porfirio's mind off the idea of fighting with White-Louse, "he's a bandit even when he's dancing. He sticks his leg right between the legs of his partner. And the way he stinks of tobacco. I'm glad I ain't a woman just so I don't have to dance with him."

Porfirio rubbed his hairy ear, furious, not saying a word. He didn't like to be thwarted. That White-Louse rubbed him the wrong way, right from the word go, right from his nickname —White-Louse—and that alone was reason enough to pick a quarrel with him and, if he wasn't careful, throw a few punches at him, or cold steel if he liked, give him a good sharp poke and see if he could patch himself up if he really was a doctor, because a doctor was the last thing he looked like, just some sharpster who was after what Candelaria had got.

"What's it to you," Hilario objected, "you're getting like those deaf old girls who bring everything—love, friendship, life itself—down to victuals and hard cash."

"Sing something, Flaviano, you know we're all waiting, you just want to be asked," said a girl dressed in red to a swarthy young man with very white teeth, whom they called "Cheese-Sandwich," because his face was like a lump of brown bread with a piece of cheese inside.

One of the guitar players bent at the waist, bowing his head to put his ear to the face of the guitar he had rested on his knees, and while bent upside down like that he adjusted the pegs, tightening and loosening them. When he was satisfied with the tone he started strumming it, then lifted his head and nodded to Flaviano, to let him know he was ready.

"See if you like this one," he said, showing all those white teeth set in that swarthy face, "it's a song from your own town, gents—a waltz . . . ."

Porfirio's face lit up, and he rested his arm on the shoulders of Hilario, who closed his eyes to hear the song better.

I ask of the Bilboes Virgin,
may the rural guard come and take me,
surround me and tie me and take me,
in prison I'll find consolation.
Miguelita's the name they baptized her,
Acatán is her glorious surname,
in prison the dark Bilboes Virgin
lay abandoned in sad isolation.
The muleteers carried the loads,
pieces of eight by the hundred,
and carried them off to the Gulf,
with no thought for their Heavenly Queen.
In Acatán's prison she moldered
until Miguelita was born,
that girl who was coined in her image,
the most beautiful girl ever seen.
Sparkling coals for her eyes,
her mouth a carnation,
when the Virgin was moved to the church,
she vanished, departed the town.
San Miguel Acatán still remembers,
that seamstress is heard in the night,
giving warning with lights that she's watching
over virtuous girls all around.
Love is love when it waits and remembers,
kiss by kiss she constructed my chains,
in heaven Miguelita sits sewing,
while I lie alone with my pain.

XVII

It's sad to move off the next day from a place where there's been a fiesta. That foul taste in your mouth, your stomach stewed in alcohol, and that sad feeling inside you like the ashes of your happiness. They'd agreed to set off at four in the morning, but at half past six they were still tramping about the house, in which the only other creatures awake were the pigs, chickens and dogs. If only there'd been a nice chilate, all they had was some coffee boiled up from the dregs of the night before. Hilario would have given anything to hear the song about Miguelita of Acatán again, but the musicians from Juan Rosendo's fields had left long before, and all that remained of it was the tune and a few wisps of words, like the steam rising from the ground as the sun peeped through without shining properly, because of a light shower that soon started to come down heavily. Goodbye, they shouted to Miss Candelaria from the outer gate, but no one answered. The sun was shining in the distance, the crests of the mountains basting in blue oil. But there where they were everything was slippery mud, and the air was soaked to its skin and damp with the smell of moss. They leaned forward to protect themselves a little from what began as drizzle but quickly became a downpour. Live animals were standing among the rain-soaked dream of the trees, but they too were like dreams.

At the end of a short but very steep hill, a real devil of a hill —it had the right name: Bad Thief's Rise—in a chalk-covered spot, the muleteers agreed to wait for the rain to pass, for it was growing heavier all the time. One after the other they shot beneath the eaves of a nearby house, mules and all. You almost never saw anyone around there, but now it looked as if the

269

owners were in, or rather the owner, because the man who lived in the house on and off was Don Casualidón the Spaniard, Spanish as they come, though of Irish ancestry, an ancestry betrayed by his eyes of blue porcelain in a face burned copper red by the cold of those regions, and the blond locks which turned his forehead, his ears and his bull neck to honey. His extraordinary physique, together with his height, distinguished him from his neighbors, who were runty to a man, with big heads and the eyes of hungry soldiers, eyes which bulged from the poor quality of the water, which also accounted for their tendency to goiters, swellings of the veins, and cowardliness.

Garlic-colored hills and fields swept by winds whose oceanic thrust from the Atlantic to the Pacific allowed no vegetation to prosper but the hardiest creeping plants and the shapeless claw-lined limbs of a few cactus plants.

The commotion of the five mules, the chattering of the muleteers once they were under cover, almost intentional, to let it be known that people had arrived, brought a group of men stretching and yawning from Don Casualidón the Spaniard's house, all dazzled from being in the semi-darkness with their eyes fixed on one point. They were all people Porfirio knew.

"My, my, so you fellows really are working for the devil now!"

"Look who's talking, you've all dismounted so's to go more slowly," replied one of the others, One-Arm Melgar.

As Don Casualidón the Spaniard came out he dug his two long-nailed hands into his trouser pockets. He left only his thumbs out, like two pistol triggers.

"We thought it was the mounted patrol," he said, "the troops get their noses in every crack and crevice up here, like bats."

One-Arm Melgar stepped in front of him. "You're all invited to my rancho, it ain't so smart as this, but it's safer. The patrol's already on to Don Casualidón. Besides, I've got my rooster."

270

"Sorry, we're in a real hurry," Porfirio informed him, uneasy at the way this meeting was turning out, "so we'd best leave the challenge for another day, there's more time than life."

"Suit yourselves," said One-Arm Melgar, scowling, with the face of one doing penance.

"Ain't right to go testing a man like that," growled Olegario, "if men weren't given to vice they wouldn't be men. If we weren't careful you'd have our mules off us. Not likely . . ."

"Or you'd win mine," replied Melgar.

"Now he's trying to tempt us!" exclaimed Hilario, as Olegario asked, "Where did you get them from, you, One-Arm?"

" 'Where' ain't a question that's asked among gents, and the same goes for 'when' and 'how.' I got them from where I got them from, right, Frankie, ain't that plain Spanish?" This was directed to Don Casualidón, on whom the nickname Frankie fell like a kick up the behind. "They're there, they're mules, and they're there for the taking, if you want to take them."

"What the hell, here goes. Here's for the other mule, the biggest one."

These words sprang from deep in Hilario's throat and fell into the silence of a group of men who were no longer speaking, who only breathed, all jammed round a table, heads down, oblivious to the rain pecking away at the roof and the wattle walls, in an atmosphere damp and heavy with tobacco, gazing with their eyes lit up with longing for what was about to take shape in the strange world of dots, as those tiny, fateful dice started to roll. Threes, fives, or 'tops,' win; aces, twos, fours, or 'bottoms,' lose, in that mysterious world of what was not yet in being but would come into being in a moment, as though the property and ownership of things really were just arbitrary combinations of luck.

"Here, let me throw," said Olegario, taking hold of the arm of Hilario, who already had the dice in his hand, he was gambling the second of the two mules they'd bought down on the coast to take back to San Miguel Acatán.

271

"Why should you throw?" Hilario protected his arm and the closed fist in which he was gripping the dice, and they struggled: "Let go of my wrist first."

"Because you've got someone who loves you, and that won't do. I ain't got no one. If you love her that's waiting for you, you'll give me them dice." Among themselves they never spoke the name of the woman they accepted as their true love, they alluded to her indirectly, to speak her name was to possess her in a certain magical way, a show of caution in sharp contrast to the nonchalant way they mentioned the names of women who served only as entertainment in the hammock. "Give me the dice, listen to what I say, you'll lose the mule—"

"Let me be, Olegario!"

"I will not let you be!"

"I know I'm going to win."

"And I know you're going to lose. Two mules just thrown away. Let me throw, if not for her sake, for the sake of Miguelita of Acatán."

As he heard the maid of his fantasy invoked, a being for him as real and living a person as any other, Hilario let the sweat-soaked dice fall from his trembling hand.

"Still the same with him? You betting the mule?" asked Don Casualidón the Spaniard, hunched up alongside One-Arm Melgar on the side where his arm was missing.

"Of course," replied Porfirio, sounding frightened stiff. He was a big tough man with plenty of guts, the last to turn tail when there was a fight on, and when he hit he hit hard; but he was a hopeless gambler and turned coward for the lack of someone to face up to, someone to take hold of and crush with his two hands. Chance—bah!—only those who aren't man enough to face up to work, that enemy who becomes your friend in the long run, only they seek out that heap of crap to pass the time, and they're the kind who always play dirty.

"Well, if the same goes for him," said One-Arm, "let's get started, we ain't none of us got much to lose."

"Right!" shouted Olegario, thumping the table, but just as

272

he was about to throw he stopped, and turned up the brim of his hat, alarmed by the presence of a spindle-legged rooster, all featherless and fidgety.

"It's this rooster that's got us knotted up. Ugly-looking bird! Get it out of here! Throw it out! With our bad luck, all we need is that shitty bird wandering backwards and forwards!"

One-Arm Melgar replied at once, "No, man, leave the rooster alone, it ain't doing no harm."

"Who knows if the bird ain't my real opponent. If you've got a pact with the rooster, say so once and for all, I won't shoot and you can keep the mule—I'd have brought my own cock if I'd known."

"Pull yourself together and stop acting so soft. You're a pain in the neck, leave the rooster alone!"

"Arseholes!"

"Go stuff yourself!"

"Horrible bird, it gives me the shivers, I won't throw until you get it out of the yard, why does it have to be here with us?"

"Because it does."

"Because it brings you luck."

"Shoot, and shut that mouth!"

"I won't shoot while that cock stays."

"You can bet," exclaimed Hilario, "it would've been a different story if that starving bird hadn't been here."

"Explain, you, Frankie!" shrieked the one-armed man with fury glittering on his eye teeth, which were the only top ones he had.

Don Casualidón the Spaniard, on whom the nickname Frankie descended once more like a boot, tried to cool things down by explaining that the cock had to be there in case the army patrol should turn up.

"Rubbish," said Olegario, "what does one thing have to do with the other? No, friend, I'm a mule driver because I drive mules, not ducks, still less with gourdfuls of water!"

One-Arm Melgar, still baring his nicotine-stained fangs, felt obliged to explain further, "The soil is soft around here, more so today when it's wet, and horses make no more sound than if they were walking on a carpet, so the patrol can fall on you without giving you a chance to save your skin."

"And the rooster warns you, I suppose?" Olegario asked sarcastically.

"Put the dice down on the table."

"Look, I want to go on playing, you've already won a mule off us, and I might get it back."

At Melgar's insistence Olegario obeyed and put the dice on the table, he didn't want to, but he did it, on the understanding that they would keep on going until they or Melgar and Don Casualidón the Spaniard were left with all the mules.

But just as Olegario put them down the one-arm swept them to the ground with the stump of his missing arm before anyone could make a move to stop him, and the moment they fell the cock rushed forward, snap, snap, snap, and left not a one, they disappeared.

"How did you do that? How did you teach the rooster?" inquired Porfirio, to whom the whole business seemed the living work of the devil.

"How did I do it? How did I teach the rooster?" Melgar laughed in his face, "I keep it hungry, so when the dice fall he thinks they're grains of maize."

Despite the practical demonstration and the respect won by that starving accomplice, an invaluable skeleton who would move into action with the voracity of fire should the mounted troopers arrive, soundlessly, carbines at the ready, just waiting to give way to their fingers, he had to be taken away. Away with the cock. Don Casualidón put a fresh pair of dice on the table and Olegario and the one-arm were left face to face to go on shooting. Olegario won back the lost mule and in total silence, without much fuss, he won the other two off One-Arm, who had no option but to "stand," the contest being over. In the last round Melgar threw a "top" dice, and not even that could save him. When Fortune gives, she gives, and when she takes away, she takes away. If God wills it, the sun shines and the rain falls, as it was doing at that very moment.

"I, my lads, have got a dry throat after what you've just put me through; there was a moment back there when I thought old One-Arm had us over a barrel," said Porfirio, spurring his horse up a short slope, beneath a shower of thorns turned silver by the sunlight, washing over low nearby hills the color of summer squashes. "And the worst of it was that it was the mules we'd only just bought the one-arm was after, the beggar already had one of them, and we'd paid so much for them."

"Blame this crazy clown, Hilario, who has turned gambler and wild man both!" Olegario talked as though he'd have liked to scorch him with his voice, half in joy and half in anger.

"Ha, ha, ha!" laughed Hilario, "hee, hee, hee, it was booting out his rooster fouled him up—he was so furious that if he'd made the sign of the cross he'd have scratched himself."

"Now you can laugh, but if my saint hadn't straightened up we'd all be tramping home on foot right now, because after losing those two mules we'd have put up our own ones too, what do three more mean when you've lost two already . . . Imagine us winning the whole lot, even though he'd started slipping in the loaded one."

"Serves him right!" cried Porfirio, "for wanting to try a fiddle. God shows you the ones you have to watch out for, right enough."

"I liked Hilario better when he just used to drink, than now he's turned into a mad gambler," Olegario went on. "He used to put down his drinks, knock back his bottles, and set to telling a great long sausage of verses he knows by heart, a string of riddles enough to drive anyone insane . . . But it's wrong of me to talk this way, because one of those rhymes made him let go of the dice: he's got more affection for fiction than fact, he's a poet. If I hadn't had the brainwave of demanding them in the name of Miguelita of Acatán, we'd have lost our shirts."

Hilario went on laughing, "It was that rooster fouled him up. The rooster and Miguelita between them. One-armed fool! One-armed brute!"

"That's right, now start insulting him—you gambler!"

"What happens is, if I see a mule I feel like hitting the trail;

if I see saints I turn holy and pray, even if they've got the kind of eyes they're giving them these days, ones that aren't saint's eyes at all; if I see dice I gamble, and don't show me no crutches because I start feeling crippled, and don't let me see a woman, because I'm telling you . . ."

Don Casualidón the Spaniard caught them up, riding a horse with a white spot on its forehead. The halter, bridle, Arabian stirrups, all the very best, his light eyes the color of caramel moist with saliva, the high-flying brim of his hat; it was said he was a priest who'd left the cloth, and certainly there was a priestly air about him beneath his felt hat, with his dark riding jacket buttoned up to the collar, those blond locks behind his ears, and so fresh of face despite his age.

Priest, filibuster, or both, Don Casualidón had come to bury his last days in that region of dry sandhills, terribly harmful to a man's lungs, where anyone who arrived with the idea of settling soon left in fear of slow asphyxiation, and no one stayed longer than the time it took them to ride on through.

Don Casualidón grew agitated and bristled all over every time the one-arm called him Frankie. The seven letters of the word shook him through and through, just like the tamer's whip does to a caged beast. In his day-to-day life he forgot his past, but under the spell of that word he would feel his mouth filling with the bitter sweetness of vomit, remembering why it was he had condemned himself to spend his last days in a place where life could only be an endless punishment, where the animals turned scrawny and indolent, the earth lay stripped and scorched by the air, the vegetation charred, creeping, fugitive, and game was scarce. He hung up his cassock, why try to conceal it, when his rapacious greed made him unworthy of his sacred ministry, and he brought upon himself a black Irish remorse. Irish he was on his mother's side. If he had been a Spaniard, only a Spaniard—he said it slowly, word by word: only a Spaniard—he would have taken hold of his ambition and rubbed it over his body like perfumed oil, with no fear of the Irishman in him who condemned and perverted his greed in a struggle between inflamed passions which reduced him to a mean and base condition. For that reason, for his meanness of spirit, he sentenced himself to die in a place where even death could not take root, because the skeletons of men and beasts that passed away there soon became fleshless and wasted until they turned into flakes of bone swept away by the hurricane wind like the leaves of some sepulchral autumn.

But perhaps it will be as well to tell his story, from that day once upon a time when he was made parish priest of a fine town of poor Ladinos, of whom there are so many in the cold lands, though few as pretentious as these, owing to their education, which was not considerable, to be sure, but enough for them to call themselves educated, people of consequence, sad and important. That gentle small-town poverty which is concealed behind good manners, soap, water, and small gifts, surrounded the newly arrived priest with good food, books for study and leisure, visits, tea parties, card games, checkers, and picnics.

Sitting back in his rocking chair before retiring, and savoring a cup of tea sip by sip, Don Casualidón learned from one of his visitors that a colleague of his who had charge of an Indian parish where the locals worked panning gold, was thinking of retiring for reasons of health. The Irishman, drowsy with tea, was powerless to stop the Spaniard, who swallowed down in an instant all the water passing through the placer, to catch a gold nugget between his teeth, on his tongue, beneath the sky of his mouth.

"Hens, chocolate, pieces of eight!"

He was no longer Don Casualidón, but the notorious Don Bernardino Villalpando, bishop of the diocese in 1567, with his Portuguese and Genoan priests, his nephew, and his housekeeper.

Paper will bear with anything. Don Casualidón wrote to the sick priest proposing that they should exchange their posts, complaining greatly at not having been informed earlier of his colleague's breakdown in health, since otherwise he would have made the suggestion long before, it not mattering to him in the least that he should have to give up the comforts of his parish with its fertile lands and good Christians.

The priest from the Indian town, a hardwood saint worn down by time, wrote to thank him for his kindness, his most generous gesture, without accepting the proposed exchange because, he said, his parish was one of fifty thousand apathetic Indians entirely neglected by the hand of charity, poor, poor, poor.

The Spaniard, as he read the letter, buried his free hand in the pocket of his cassock, searching for a pinch of snuff down in the lining. In his greed he took what the sick priest said as an exaggeration, the better to cover up the fifty thousand Indians whose occupation, however apathetic they might be, was to labor in a placer. In his imagination the nuggets and golden sands leaped like a fountain, as in a pan of laughing water. He could see the dark-skinned Indians, muscled like gods, bringing him as a gift, Sunday after Sunday, one of those nuggets. Heretical as they may be, they're worth more than my highly Catholic, wholly mortgaged, Ladinos.

In a second letter the priest from the Indian parish wrote that the exchange proposed by his worthy friend would lie heavy on his conscience, and that he therefore preferred to leave the negotiations with the archdiocese to him.

Don Casualidón the Spaniard journeyed to the capital, talked to His Grace the Archbishop, who commended him for his selflessness and sense of sacrifice, and one fine day in March he made his entry into the town of Indians with gold nuggets, and to his colleague he left the gilded poverty of a spacious convent house, richly furnished, with windows onto the main square, electric lighting, water in clay pitchers out in the court-yard, a bath, a parrot, and an effeminate sacristan.

No sooner had Don Casualidón arrived at his new residence than he looked out over the square, poking his head through a bull's-eye in which he very nearly got himself stuck, a misera-ble window which gave light to the room, whose appearance was more that of a dungeon: a floor with stones from the river set in ordinary mortar, grimy walls, smoke-stained beams. The bed was a cot strung with strips of leather. A lame table. Nobody came. He shouted. Everything seemed neglected. The muleteer who had accompanied him with his baggage had set off again at once. Finally, after a good deal of crying in the wilderness, an Indian appeared, bade him good afternoon, though by now it was late evening, and asked him what he wanted.

"Someone to serve me something," replied the Spaniard.

"Ain't no one," the Indian told him.

"I want something to eat. I want a fire lit."

"Ain't no one," the Indian repeated.

"But I'm the new priest. Tell the people. Who used to wait on the other father?"

"Ain't no one did," answered the Indian.

"What about the church, the sacristan?"

"Ain't one."

Don Casualidón the Spaniard unpacked his things, with the help of the Indian. This was impossible. The most brutal conquistador surged up inside him, and he climbed a creaking stairway up to the bell tower. A violent pealing of bells, like a fire alarm, announced his arrival. As he came down from the tower, among cobwebs and bats, he met the Indian whom he had sent to tell the neighbors of his coming.

"Did you give them the news?" he asked.

"Yes."

"Did you tell them, did you say I was here?"

"Yes."

"And what did they say?"

"That they knew you'd arrived."

"And aren't they going to come and greet me, bid me welcome, see if I need anything?"

"No."

Darkness descended at a tortoiselike pace down the buttressed walls of a church which had been an architectural showpiece of the sixteenth century. The fifty thousand inhabitants, scattered on hills and in hollows, indifferent to the world which blinked outside, beneath the stars, were sleeping out the weariness of a conquered race. The streets were like wolves' tongues beneath the feet of Don Casualidón the Spaniard. He went round knocking at doors in person. They answered him from their beds, in a strange language made up of stammers, and from some houses, as he called despairingly for help, copper-colored faces emerged to greet him, without affection or hatred.

That night he understood all. The stars glittered in the sky like gold nuggets. It was all he needed. From the map of Europe leaped Catholic countries, piling on top of his shoulders till they forced him to his knees. The Spanish beast struggled not to bend the knee, like a wounded bull, snorting, swinging its head to look from side to side, eyes ember-red with rage, glowering. But kneel he did, on the stones of his bedroom, bent double by the weight of remorse, and there he remained throughout the night. Pearls of frozen sunlight on the tall ovens of his temples, on his forehead; canals of cold sweat down his humbled back. As the dawn came up he climbed to the bell tower to call mass, opened the church, lit the two candles at the altar, dressed himself, and went out. No introit ever carried more force of conviction onto the *mea culpa*. He wiped away his tears before beginning, *Confiteor deo* . . . The "ain't no one" Indian came in. Don Casualidón made signs for him to come and help. He knew a bit. How to hold out the cruets, pass the missal, kneel, stand up, make the sign of the cross. He finished the mass and they had to light a fire to prepare breakfast. The Indian went for coffee. It was more like toasted maize. The bread was only half baked. A few oranges. That was all the food he had until midday, when back came the coffee, the unbaked bread, and as a variation, instead of oranges, two small bananas. Nothing in the afternoon, and worse than nothing in the evening: cold coffee. The penance was long—hunger, silence, solitude—but he profited spiritually: all the pride of the Spanish Catholic shriveled away within the Christian blood of the Irishman. Privation made him humble. He adapted to a primitive existence far from that civilization which his abstemiousness and sobriety taught him was merely an accumulation of useless things. The natives were poverty-stricken Indians who wanted for everything because their families were large, and the wealth which passed through their hands in the placers or in the fields did not belong to them. Wretched wages kept them sick and feeble, always drunk. At first Don Casualidón would have liked to inject them with energy, with the health that he himself was lacking, as Don Quixote would have said, shake them like puppets to bring them out of their contemplative renunciation, their meditative silence, their indifference to the earthly world in which they lived. But now, with the passing of time, he not only understood them, but had come to share their attitude, half dream and half reality, in which existence was a continuous rhythm of physical needs, without complications.

An obscure vision, obscure because he dared not lift it too far into his consciousness to examine it, content merely to sense it, without explanation; an unstable vision, composed of spots which would keep coming together and moving apart, like the horses they were now riding through a tangle of rainbows fallen from stormclouds heavy with water, had made him share in the happiness of those good folk, tied to the earth, to their goats, their maize, their silence, their water, the stones, scorners of the golden nuggets, because they knew their real worth.

It seemed a contradiction to know the worth of a gold nugget and yet scorn it. The naked Indians, standing in rivulets which formed webs of water, capillary manes of liquid systems, were blind forces hurling onto the bonfire of worldly interests hundreds of glowing embers, whose true value was the total ruination of man. The Indians avenged themselves on their oppressors by putting the means of perdition in their hands. Gold and more gold to create useless things, factories full of stinking slaves in the cities, torments, anxieties, violence, without ever remembering to live. Don Casualidón would put his hands over his ears, horrified at the thought that he might ever again hear the disgusting confessions of civilized people. Better his Indians, their fiestas at the solstices, their drunkenness, their devilish dances.

Night after night Don Casualidón would repeat the words of Saint Remigius as he baptized King Clovis in the cathedral at Rheims: "Bow your head, proud Frank, worship what you have burned, and burn what you have worshipped," and he would close his eyes tight until the tears came, they were like black ink in the darkness, to blot out all visions of treasure from the blue porcelain of his eyes, content with his poverty among those poor children of God, whom he called natural, to differentiate them from civilized men, who should be called artificial.

"I can't give you anything for baptizing my lad Juan, but I'm going to leave you this for yourself," an Indian told him one morning, one Sunday.

Don Casualidón the Spaniard was about to refuse the round container, shaped like a giant pear, which the Indian was offering him, and was now taking out of a bundle of handkerchiefs, when he heard, for his woe, that something like coins was clinking inside.

And Villalpando, Villalpando, Villalpando, with ten nephews instead of one, he stretched his fingers out to take the offering. It was heavy. It couldn't be anything other than money, silver pesos, or . . . gold nuggets. He shook it harder and a metallic chinking made his eager curiosity more eager yet to know what was inside. He baptized the baby in the arms of a long-haired, bran-colored Indian girl, dark around the eyes, and when the couple left the baptistery, followed by a cretinous Indian who had acted as godfather, without even taking off his surplice he hastened to shake the tortilla gourd again. There wasn't the slightest doubt. Silver, silver coins. The sound of silver coins chinking together. He wedged his nails in the round, tight-fitting lid, to see what was inside. The whole machinery of his joyful face shifted into the most bitter gesture of frustration. He put away his find and went directly outside for a horse to take him on a journey. There were none to be had. So he pretended to be ill to get the Indians to organize his removal on a stretcher to the first town where there was a doctor or a horse. And thus it was, lying on a stretcher of leaves, that he left that town of Indians, Don Casualidón the Spaniard, carried by four young men who kept panting, talking, panting, talking, accompanied by a moustachioed old man who would come up to feel him from time to time to be sure he wasn't catching cold. They put him down in the first town where there was a doctor. I don't want a doctor, he told the Indians, who kissed his hand before turning back, I'd rather have a horse. Spaniard that he was, he imagined that he had traveled like one of the dead kings on their way to the Escorial. While for the Indians he had journeyed like one of the lords borne to the Great Pyramid on a litter. He abandoned the stretcher, dismissed the Indians, and hired a horse to take him to his former parish. His shoes, the upper part at least, for they no longer had soles, thudded opaquely over the shining tiles of his old house. There stood the old priest with whom, intending to deceive him, he had exchanged a parish of Ladinos up to their ears in debt for a parish of wealthy Indians.

The old priest slapped him on the back with delight by way of welcome, hastened to urge him to make himself "at home," and ordered the housekeeper to make some hot chocolate and get a room ready. He must stay the night.

Don Casualidón the Spaniard, bearded, sickly, with shadows around his eyes, would accept none of this, beyond the affection, until he had first explained the reason for his visit. A long, long journey, half on a stretcher, half on horseback, to ask a great favor of the holy father. Anything, said the Creole priest, so long as it is to the greater glory of God.

With no little difficulty Don Casualidón the Spaniard began to draw from the gourd something which had to be turned the right way round for it to come out, during which time his colleague, who could not understand what all this was about, stood wondering what the object might be. Finally, Don Casualidón held it out to him. His friend understood still less. It was a steel bit. Don Casualidón handed it to him, pleading, "Put it on me, father! Put it on me!" and he opened his mouth wide and moved it closer for him to insert the bit. "I deserve it for being an ass! A beast! For my ambition!"

Don Casualidón hung up his cassock and fled, with the name Frankie, convinced that he had not burned what he had always worshipped, to those ash-covered lands where nothing was stable or lasting, because the strong wind swept everything away.

Truly it was a grand thing to ride the trails together, and Don Casualidón, on his white-starred horse, still had the stamp of a bandit about him. He left them before they reached San Miguel Acatán, after a brief farewell. Still searching for the frontier, thought Hilario Sacayón, and what's beyond, thought Porfirio Mansilla: the navigable rivers, lumber camps full of men and howler monkeys, the pull of paddles pushing canoes, forest turkeys peculiar to that region, black plumage, red crests, sea turtles, the chutes which despatch the precious logs, hurling them headlong into the divine hands of the foam. Olegario was thinking the same. They only thought it. No one spoke. The silence of men who are coming close to their home-land had entered into them. Hilario sat looking at Porfirio alongside him. Few men could have more admiration for a friend. Porfirio Mansilla was perfect. How was he to know that the reason Hilario hadn't caught Nicho Aquino up was be-cause he had turned into a coyote. But whenever there was talk about it, he only listened, and said nothing. He said nothing to anyone, not even Aleja Cuevas, for fear that if he disclosed having come across Señor Nicho turned into his nagual up on María Tecún Ridge, something bad might happen, it would bring him bad luck. So sacred, so intimate was the link estab-lished between them by that furtive encounter that to reveal it would bring misfortune, because it would break the mystery, violate the secret nature of certain profound and remote relations. He babbled the odd word when he was alone, and he stopped drinking so much for fear his tongue would run away with him. Six anisettes and a couple of beers, no more. That was all he would have. He even changed his character. He no longer laughed out loud like before, and he ceased to be the life and soul of every party. Possessor of a hidden truth, he kept silent, silent, and in his eyes, as he fell asleep, the image of the lost postman, of whom no more was heard in San Miguel, merged with his sleep which was a kind of soft coyote, a fluid coyote, a coyote of darkness in whose shadow were lost, on four paws, the two feet of the postman.

XVIII

Instead of hair, fur like the music from a cane flute, a coat of fine threads which his hand, a leaf with fingers, combed softly, because when he sank his nails in deep the sound would change and come splashing over him like a torrent. He witnessed great spillings of rock with a feeling of ferocity in his flesh of unripened sapodilla, the icy down wrapped about his limbs like grass. A prison of tight muscular fibers, rejuvenated, washed by lava with a raging of blood, though only the purest red of it, the solar voracity of amalgamated metal reducing to impotence the gentle brother who had joined with him in search of protection. With a leap of his nostrils he rose from a cushioning cloud of ipecac aroma. He needed to arrive, to get across that tangle of presences to where she was, his woman, whose scent was in his nostrils. The woven cloth of his jacket gave way and fell in stained tatters carried away by the current of coal-black water. The ground scratched itself without hands, like him, just by shaking itself. The region of the pines, where everything itches. He bared his long teeth, his glorious watermelon gums, and with a movement of clippers scratched his belly, his back, his paws, and around his tail the color of a rotting quince. His scratching was like the laugh of a man. Strange to be like him, an animal, purely animal. The round pupil of his eye, too round perhaps, painfully round. Round vision. Inexplicable. And for that reason he always moved in circles. He didn't go straight as he ran, but in little circles. Talking, talking, with a kind of deep sucking, or gasp, of amazement, he swallowed his own throat, as though he were a city. Mute, with no other soliloquy than his long amorous howl, he came to know the alertness of elemental instinct, that fierce appetite he kept hidden in the sheath of his pointed muzzle. Strands of shining saliva from seas of appetite deeper and more sensual than the darkness held within the black pips of fruits. And the tenacity to sharpen his claws, ivories hidden in onions of rubber. His head fashioned into an axe looked all around him, striking blows to left and right. What animals were stumbling after him? Two heavy monsters with neither heads nor paws. He seized them with his teeth, sniffing all round them as though he were bathing them in laughter. Their presence irritated him. Shake himself free. Get them off. Animals without extremities, without heads, without tails. Only bodies, hee, hee, hee ... Hee, hee, hee ... He took a kick at the air, just as though he had suddenly snapped an elastic band, kicked out his paw, and tried to run away, but the mailbags were tied round his neck, animals with neither heads nor tails, only bodies, hee, hee, hee.

He noticed that although his run of zigzagging onions was fast as lightning, every so often he would take a few clumsy steps with misshapen feet made of sand, and one of those uncertain steps sent him rolling down a hillside, only instead of banging his head and body all the way down he found himself running on little paws of tiny zigzagging onions.

Alongside him was the man with black hands, the one who

came with him from the village of Tres Aguas, the one who promised to tell him where he might find his woman. He was alongside him, but hazy, half disappearing, in the midst of a thick cloud of dust. Stop him, speak to him, help him, tell him he was disappearing. He could do nothing. All he saw was that the man was leading his dog and making signs that they were to enter a cave which lay before them.

He was afraid. His feet had been torn as he walked through brambles, and now they were hurting. But he ran no more than a few steps, for suddenly the old man with black hands beckoned him and his dog toward the entrance to the cave. Did he not run? He ran hard and far. He sat down on a crag the color of fire. The frozen fire of the earth. He sat down to decide what to do. The high road. It was like the memory of some distant happiness, and he vaguely recalled having walked it all the way up to María Tecún Ridge. He had been through places where he didn't want the old man to go, while he was with the old man. A rapid coming and going, coming, looking out, and going. He sat down between the mouth of the cave and the thorn thicket. The shadows of sharp-peaked hills, stretched out one after another across sheets of sand, stood measuring like the needles of gigantic sundials the time which for Señor Nicho would count no more. A crow the color of an old key flew down to peck his shoulder. It was surprised to find him alive. He was sleeping beside the mailbags with his eyes open wide. He decided to enter the cave. But as he took the first steps he was afraid that the jaws of that toothless beast might close and swallow him up. He lifted his head to look up at the crow in search of enlightenment. His hunger dripped flavors: roast meat, tortillas, beans like black letters imprinted on maize-cake primers, sugared anise, cinnamon and rose water. He measured by distances of hunger into what misery he had fallen through wandering after his woman. He was paying for his stupidity. It wasn't stupidity. For his whim? It wasn't a whim. Then for his desire to have her beneath his hot breath again. But then why not look for another woman? Because it wouldn't be the same. Aha, that was the secret! Why wouldn't it be the same?

The tecuna runs away, but leaves her sting behind her, which is why the saying "out of sight, out of mind" does not apply to her. She is searched for with the passion of a thirsty man dreaming of water, a drunkard who would go to the ends of the earth for another drink, a smoker just dying for one more cigarette. He dragged the mailbags behind him and advanced further into the cave, looking for another stone to sit down on. He sure was tired. Yet he couldn't remember having gone far that day. From the village of Tres Aguas to the place on the high road where he and the old man with black hands turned off along a narrow gully. Though he vaguely recalled having climbed to María Tecún Ridge. A rock more like a small tamale provided a seat. He was going to think out, away from the light, alone, beneath the earth, why it was he couldn't do without his woman.

Tecunas—it's less direct to think of them in the plural— some have within their secret parts the bodies of small palpitating birds, others the downiness of aquatic plants which begin vibrating as the current of the male swirls through; and the magic ones have sexes like pleated bundles which gradually fold and unfold in the ecstasy of love, there where the blood drives its last living distances in an organism that is possessed, then leaps to become the beginning of another living distance. In the final plunge, love is inhuman like a tecuna. Its hidden snout seeks out the root of life. You exist more. In those moments you exist more. The tecuna weeps, struggles, bites, squeezes, tries to get up, gasps, mouthes, sweats, scratches, and is left like a wasp unable to buzz, as though she were dead from suffering. But she has left her sting in the man who had her beneath the breathing of his desire. Liberation ties them together!

Now, now finally the stones know why he seeks her. Now, now the trees know why he seeks her. Now, now the stars know why he seeks her. The rivers why he seeks her.

COYOTE-POSTMAN

Using stones of red-black clay he found scattered on the ground, he painted eyes on his face, hands and feet, the soles of his feet, under the direction of the old man with black hands and the face of a geranium worm, who went off with the dog, and tattooed thus with eyes he followed them toward the interior with the mailbags on his back, among white crabs, bats and blind beetles with immensely long feelers.

Nicho Aquino, where are you going, he heard himself say, beneath the earth, beneath the dripping crags, as he listened to a concert of roots whose little tips of desire sucked the life of the soils from the sexes of tecunas, perfumed ones and stinking ones, sweet ones and bitter ones, stinging ones, poisonous ones, burning ones, sour ones, greasy ones. A fluid of hidden meteors pushed him on like witchcraft, like the speeding letter carriers of the chiefs, who used to travel along underground trails which connected cities. Postmen are sons of the chayote. Chayote vines run and run and run. Their suckers travel here, there, everywhere, from one day to the next, swifter than the darkness. He had arrived. The man with the face of a worm explained that they were close to the Painted House, the hall of solitary light. He backed away in surprise, his mouth open wide, his feet uncertain. The sunlight was spilling into the interior through an immensely high gorge like falling water, and as it fell further inside, over his head, it was still like water, water, water, but static water, water frozen in diamonds, an ecstasy of diamonds. And not only from above, from below too there came a strange vegetation of crystals. It was like being inside a pearl. At times the light from the gorge, no doubt as the sun shone more strongly outside, passed through the densely woven dome of trees covering the lofty skylights, and that world which only a moment before was formed of diamonds turned into the green night of the emerald, night of lizards, and the cold sleep of lianas. First spirals of lime green, and then pure emeralds.

Señor Nicho pushed the mailbags aside, took off his hat, as if he were in church, and continued to stare, stupefied. Some-

289

one ought to live down here. All this beauty going to waste. Why not go back to San Miguel Acatán and get everyone to come and live here instead. It wasn't a grotto from a children's story. It was real. He put out his fingers hastily, like one who fears that what he believes to be a dream will fall apart in his hands, to touch the luminous needles. They felt colder than the earth itself, because they looked like white-hot solar bodies. The sun must be at its highest point in the sky, and that was why it was giving so much light. Señor Nicho went on touching them, hundreds, thousands of stones of precious glass buried there, though now they were turning slightly orange, the color of the moon. He felt cold. He turned up the collar of his jacket. He had to do something, get out of there, find the high road and continue on his way to deliver the mailbags at the Central Post Office. If his woman lived in such an exquisitely beautiful place, she was hardly likely to want to go back with him to live in a town piled high with ugly houses and a sad church. Why shouldn't everyone come and live down in the caves, and have this Painted House as their church? Here God's altar really would look its best. And Father Valentín, and Don Deferic's piano, and his white wife who was just made for these reflecting walls, and the great fat postmaster reeking of candle-grease, and the muleteers with their horses dripping majesty, if they were harnessed up with some of these beautiful things.

A man with blue—or, rather, black—hair, in any case it was shining, and soot-stained hands like the hands of the old man who showed him the way to come in search of his woman along these hidden paths, fingernails agleam like fireflies, took him out of his thoughts. If he liked it so much, why not stay there?

"Do you think I should?" the postman hastened to say, eager for someone to talk to, to hear what a human voice would sound like in that enclosed zone. Same as in any other vaulted place. Still another proof that he wasn't dreaming or living out a fairy tale.

The mysterious apparition told him to follow, and he went

after him to the opposite end of the Painted House, where they could distinctly hear the calls of birds, warblers, guardas, mockingbirds, so close they seemed to be singing right there, though they were singing outside, far away: where? And he could hear people jabbering away to one another like parrots, and the beat of oars conveying vessels like the wings of enormous birds.

The Painted House looked out over the edge of an underground lake. In the dark water floated small islands formed by millions of green algae, masses moving together and parting on the gentle swell of the current. Down there, however much Señor Nicho might touch the water, the reality was more of a dream than dreams themselves. Through a delicately carved opening, arches covered with stalactites and stalagmites were reflected in the lake like oranges cut in half. Down inside the liquid, the deep blue of a gleaming feather, all the glittering necklaces and fantastic gems collected by the most Indian of Indian women, the earth, were on show, as if in a jewelry case. Grains of incandescent maize shed from the most resplendent of cobs.

"First," said his companion, "you must know who I am. You must also know where you are."

A small vessel floated past full of ghostly men and women wrapped in white blankets.

"I am one of the great firefly wizards, descendants of the great clashers of flint stones, who dwell in tents of virgin doeskin, who sow seeds of light in the black air of the night to be sure there will be guiding stars in the winter, who light bonfires to speak with them of the heat that will parch the earth if it beats down with all its yellow might, of the ticks that make the cattle thin, the locusts that dry out the moisture in the sky, the empty streams where the mud grows more wrinkled year by year, like the face of a kindly old man."

Another boat went past, full of fruit: golden bananas, golden sugar cane, hog plums whose hard flesh is the color of blood, honey of blood, striped cucumbers to feed to zebras, sweetsops of most immaculate flesh, star apples more like amethyst flowers than fruits, baskets of mangoes like a geography of lands in eruption, nance cherries like the tears wept by some golden god . . .

"The substances," whispered Señor Nicho, as those igneous volcanic substances flowed by in their vegetable present through that preterite world of twinkling, resplendent minerals, scattered in reality and in reflection, everywhere, high and low, everywhere.

"And now that you know who I am, I will tell you where you are. You have journeyed toward the West across lands full of wisdom and maizefields, you have passed beneath the tombs of the Lords of Chamá, and now you are on your way to the mouths of the rivers . . ."

"I am looking for my woman . . ."

"The whole world journeys after her with you, but before we move on we must destroy what you are carrying in those canvas bags . . ."

The postman, obligated as he was by his duty, instinctively shielded the mailbags with his body, refusing to let them be burned. Better to go on. They moved toward the West, to come upon an immense window opened in the blackness of the rocks, and gaze from there upon the milky blue void of the mist coming up from the sea. Little clouds on spider's legs drifted by them on the wind through the luminous powder of the sunlight, powder that would be mixed with water to make it clean, drinkable, tearful. A tearful bearer of nostalgia is the rainwater. Those who drink it, men and women, dream of greens they have never seen, journeys they have never made, paradises they have had and lost. The true man, the true woman which there is, that is to say, there was, in each man and each woman, has departed from them for ever, and all that is left is the outside, the puppet, puppets with the duties of sedentary folk. The duty of the postman as a puppet is to defend the mail with his life, that is why he carries a machete, and deliver it with all due safety and security. But the puppet comes to an end, the duty of the puppet, when from beneath the shell appears what is bitterly human, what is instinctively animal.

His companion, in whose face was the solitude of roots uprooted, stretched out his hands of black mud with his nails sparkling with fireflies to the immense green shadow which began at the earth and ended in the sea, and said:

"Brother to the postman is the horizon of the sea, lost to infinity when it delivers the correspondence of the parakeets and the flowers of the fields to the planets and the clouds! Brothers to the postman, the meteors that fetch and carry the correspondence of the stars, godmothers to the tecunas, and tecunas themselves, for after drinking down space as they scurry by like clouds, they go, disappear, are lost like shooting stars! Brothers to the postman the winds that fetch and carry the missives of the seasons! The season of honey, Spring; the season of salt, Summer; the season of fishes, Winter; and Autumn, the season of the earth that counts the year's dead in the graveyard: one, two, three, ten, a hundred, a thousand, here, there, further away, and so many, many more in other places. Man's flesh has tasted the drink of migration, a powder with the crawl of spiders, and sooner or later it too migrates, like a shooting star, like a runaway wife, it escapes from the skeleton to which it stayed fixed for a life, it goes, it cannot stay: our flesh, too, is a tecuna . . ."

Señor Nicho was struck dumb with horror as he saw that the wizard had stopped talking and was advancing toward him, and he leaned back against the mailbags to defend the letters as though they were his own flesh. But it was useless. There are other fatalities than death. His urge, the urge of the male to find his partner, the faint tickle of a woman in some distant part of his body, made him give way, and the canvas mailbags tattooed with cabalistic symbols fell into a fire of dry logs.

The bonfire was slow to bite into the bags. Its teeth of fire could not sink into the canvas, which was as damp and sticky as if it had absorbed all the sweat and anguish of Señor Nicho caught between his duty as a puppet postman, and the tickle of his woman. But flames like jaguar's fangs, flames the color of tapirs with probing tongues, flames with tangled manes of gold like little lions, wore down the resistance of the striped canvas sacks, and as the first piece of cloth gave way, a bite opened in black and gold, they penetrated to the inside, from which leaped handfuls of burning paper, letters in square envelopes, rectangular envelopes, packets of colored paper, pieces of molten sealing wax like clots of blood, bits of cardboard, stamps . . .

Señor Nicho closed his eyes. He didn't want to see what he had abandoned: the tip of the score Don Deferic was sending to Germany emerging like the ear of a white rabbit, a portrait of one of the soldiers, some officer at the barracks, writhing in the flames as though he were being burned alive, bank notes slow to catch fire, then burning along the edges worn and soiled by the hands of all the thousands of people who had counted them, spat on them, defended them, and, finally, lost them, documents from the court of justice on sheets of paper like strips of bone, letters in Father Valentín's spidery writing asking for help against the plague of tecunas . . .

Señor Nicho, eyes closed, heard the ashes of the correspondence being hurled to the four corners of the sky. It was the ash of ignominy. The wizards met, crooked, enigmatic, hair and beards, more like vegetables than men, ageless, sexless. From their lips Señor Nicho was to hear what had become of his woman, vanished without trace from her rancho.

Bub, bub, bubble, bub, bub, bubble, a pot of boiling water. A piece of white cloth hanging out on the line, after the last faint call to prayer. A dog searching anxiously for the person it was with, round the spot where she disappeared, runs up and down, stops, sniffs, emits little weeping howls, turns its head, sits up on its hindlegs to see up ahead, scratches itself, turns round and round, runs one way, then the other, but cannot find what it has lost: a woman who left her house with an earthen pitcher on her head, her white roundlet, and whom it followed close behind, nosing at her heels, her skirts. She vanished, she was gone, it couldn't see her anymore, much as it searched, not even the jar, not even the pieces, jar and all she was suddenly gone from the face of the earth. At first the dog thought she had stopped and bent down to look for something, pick up something she had dropped, or simply scratch her foot, but not so. Her form was missing, she was missing. For a long time it continued to look for her, after those first moments of doubt, with the most anguished unease, the anxiety of a weaver's shuttle, jumpy, not knowing what to do. It went nosing along the ground, a little at a time, then it would lift its head and sniff out her absence on the wind, that person who had been walking with it and then, all of a sudden, in a matter of a moment, deserted it, left it alone, as though she were hiding from it. Jumping about, with the barking and yelping of a dog confused and fearing for the life of its mistress, it remained there, disoriented, and only when the night was well advanced did it return to the house, where the water had boiled over and put out the fire. The cloth was still hanging outside like a white stain in the dark yard.

Señor Nicho summoned all his courage to face up to his misfortune. "The dog, after all," was all he said, acknowledging Jasmine's fidelity, the only one to see the tragedy in that field surrounded by barbed-wire fencing, and return to the rancho alone. And it never found her, it looked all round the house, just to hear her voice, feel her clean warm shadow when she went out to comb herself in the sunshine. That night it howled inconsolably.

The postman's pupils filled with pieces of obsidian which began liquefying in the bottomless wells of his eyes. He too had to swallow her. Swallow her beloved image just like the earth which had devoured her without trace, without even lifting from the damp muddy ground the fragile dust raised by someone who falls. Nothing. She fell down a well who knows how many feet deep, those wells they sink in search of water and leave open when they don't find it, with no sign of danger, not even a brick shield. A hundred, two hundred, three hundred feet deep, round there the water is a deep root. A well hidden in the undergrowth like a reptile with a hollow body and toothless jaws. His words turned to weeping and took her from his living memory, pretty and graceful, as she was, and he let her fall through his wet eyes into his grieving body, unable to get used, although he was already getting used, to the idea that never again would he see her, hear her, touch her hands, catch the smell of her hair bathed in soft water and dried in the morning sun, squeeze her as he lifted her playfully from the cruel earth that swallowed her, to carry her from one place to another. She would kick, become angry and upset, but then the laughter would start to peck at the dimples on either side of her mouth. And still more pain was caused him—sorrow is a world of roots which ache—by the loss of that gentle companion in white cotton clothing which smelled of warm napkins wrapped around tortillas, the docile and manageable companion of his nights made wild by the warmth of their blankets, his urge to put her body beneath his breathing. Weeping formed at the edge of his eyelids, among his lashes, liquid circles, shining, a trembling world of concentric circles. He had been turning the color of a thorn. He cast off his human shell, a rag doll with dripping eyes, his tragic human mourning inseparable from the memory of his woman changed into a pile of bones, and flesh, and hair, and clothes, and pieces of broken jar, and cold of bracelets and earrings, and a tangled roundlet at the bottom of a well in which she, through going for water, went to meet her darkness. He cast off his human shell and leaped up on to a sandbank warm but rough beneath his four extremities of howl with hairs. The firefly wizard who had accompanied him since they met in the Painted House was still at his side, and told him he was the Curer-Deer of the Seventh Fire. And indeed, if one looked at him closely, his body was like a deer's, his head was a deer's head, his tail, his rump, the way he moved. A deer with seven ashes on its crown, seven white volcanic eruptions between its little needle horns, and golden honey leaping from its eyes of dark gold.

And he, without saying it, proclaims himself a coyote, with

teeth from a cob of white maize, his far-fetching body like a handsaw sawing, pitched forever forward, four paws of running rain, blazing eyes of liquid fire, his tongue, his panting—as he panted he went suffa, suffa, suffa, suffa—his intelligence, his itching.

Life beyond the peaks that come together is as real as any other life. Not many men, however, have succeeded in going beyond the underground darkness to the luminous grottoes by way of fields of yellow minerals, enigmatic, phosphorescent, minerals of a fixed rainbow, cold motionless greens, blue jades, orange jades, indigo jades, and plants of sleepwalking watery majesty. And those who have succeeded in going beyond the subterranean darkness, when they return tell that they have seen nothing, and keep a constrained silence, letting it be known that they understand the secrets of the world hidden beneath the mountains.

The underground mist is not invincible, but it blinds men totally; it numbs their tongues, their feet, and little by little it empties their heads through their ears, their nostrils, blood pours from the ears and nostrils of those who resolve, come what may, to advance into the caves coiled underground like the viscous skins of snakes left empty, no snake is there, only the skin, there where the caves open out into lofty spaces vaulted like churches, further on their walls are soaked in drops of condensation, and still deeper inside they grow hot as if fires had been built within their silent cavities, there where the heat burns like chili powder, with a dry salt heat.

Those who resolve, come what may, to penetrate a few leagues beneath the earth, using ocote torches as their eyes, many leagues across lagoons covered with weevils of darkness into pleats crawling with grubs, abysses in which are buried towns whose sole companion is the oilbird's mournful song, and many, many more leagues through hordes of ants, termites and reptiles, creatures which may well be inoffensive in the clear light of day, but whose slightest movement causes terror in the darkness, and almost all those who get back alive return from their mysterious journey with their eyes hollowed round by deep black rings, their lips burned from smoking, their ankles weak with exhaustion, frozen, trembling. Have they been through a long illness? Have they been through a long dream? Had they had the eyes of forest animals, like the Curer-Deer of the Seventh Fire and the Coyote-Postman, to see in the darkness, they would have gone on undaunted to the luminous grottoes. Eyes of forest animals were the eyes of the curer and the postman, deer and coyote. The firefly wizards, descendants of the great clashers of flint stones, placed firefly grease in their pupils, in their little eyeballs of dewy glass, so that in the depths of the earth they might see the secret path down which they strode accompanied by hundreds of other animals, the shadows of grandfather animals, father animals come to bury tiny pieces of the umbilical cords of their children and grandchildren, born of the tribes, close by the heart of the snail, close by the heart of the tortoise, close by the green honey of the algae, the red nest of the black scorpion, the rattling echo of the wooden drums. They too, the children, the grandchildren, will come later, if life gives them leave, for the confrontation with their nagual, the animal that protects them.

Those who descend to the underground caves, beyond the peaks that come together, beyond the poisonous mist, go to meet their nagual, their animal protector, their other self, which presents itself to them alive, exactly as it is deep within the tenebrous dampness of their skin. The animal and person which coexist in them through the will of their progenitors at birth in a kinship still more intimate than the one between father and mother, brother and sister, separate themselves, to confront one another by dint of sacrifices and ceremonies to be performed in that vaulted, echoing world of darkness, just as the reflected image is separate from the real face. The postman and the curer have come down to witness the ceremonies.

Those who descend, and only those with eyes smeared with firefly grease can descend, half men, half forest animals, sit themselves down like human shadows in the dark grottoes, on

298

cushions of leaves or on the bare earth, abstaining from eating, drinking, speaking, greeting neither friends nor acquaintances, to cut all human ties.

Solitary shadows, black corpses with eyes whose pupils were lit thousands of years ago, gaze with indifference upon the desolate gloom wherein they dwell.

For nine days they endure this voluntary but maddening abandonment, from which some escape, haunted, to search for the sun, weeping, sobbing as they emerge from the caves in which, they say, they became lost. Only those who by force of calm courage exhaust their darkness, go on into the precious light.

Prepared by that long night of nine days of darkness and nine even darker nights, those who do not flee, having withstood this trial, pass on to a dimly lit grotto, shivering, nocturnal, themselves like a part of that darkness, like bats whose fur was darkness, dolls whose hair was darkness, shaken by the cold of death inside their woolen ponchos, beneath straw hats like the edges of rancho roofs, and they accuse themselves aloud of being made of mud, clay statues which their own thirst broke into pieces. They give voice to these laments as they clamber up and down the crags of the spacious, barely lit grotto wherein they move. Falling, jumping, sliding, wedged against the rocks, crawling face down on the cornices, elbows, fingernails, knees, all in order to run the ritual risk without falling into the horror of the abyss or the deep stagnant waters never seen by eye of woman. Fatigue makes them clumsy, at times they are short of breath, they open their mouths to ease their breathing, they vomit, some faint, others lose their nerve entirely and hurl themselves down the great ravines, the deep ravines, like falling leaves they take a long time before they fall to pieces on the rocks below. For four long days they go on with these clumsy gestures in this discordant dance, reeling like drunkards, clawing up lumps of earth that taste of roots to sustain themselves, relieving their thirst by licking at the damp sandstone rocks, moaning pathetically, the most virile of them, and the rest of them collapsed into a bottomless dream. The firefly wizards come to their aid. They announce that they are not men of clay, that those sad men of crumbling mud were all destroyed. In the night of deep aromas they wait for the sun. Those who endure. The precious light inundates them, penetrates their eyes, their ears, the million sponge-eyes of their open, joyful pores, until it soaks their hearts with red sand and returns from their hearts turned into a light which is not the light that surrounds what is vegetable, mineral, or animal, but the light that surrounds man, that has been inside man, the light that, since it is human, permits them to see the nagual separated from the person, to see the person just as he is and at the same time his image in the primal state hidden within him, to spring from within him into the body of an animal, to become an animal without ceasing to be a person.

A glittering flash of nacre, the clash of sun and man. Those who thus confront their nagual, outside themselves, are invincible in war and in love, against men and with women, they bury them with their weapons and their virilities, they own all the riches they desire, they make the snakes respect them, do not succumb to smallpox, and if they die it is said their bones are made of firestone.

A third trial awaits them. They climb high above cold forests sunk in vapors forming a white darkness which erases everything, like the black darkness of the caves. They move as though they were swimming through the leaves of ceibas and other trees whose branches weave a plain hundreds of green leagues long above the green of the earth stretched out below. An aerial plain suspended from branches over the face of the earth. A world of evaporating clouds, white orchids, static and motionless, with carnivorous orchids and vegetal beasts, green skin and gaping mouths with erysipelas, centipedes walking on hairs, maddened spiders, glittering beetles, fluid ropes of vipers which seem to be listening to cymbals as they sleep, lunatic gophers, raccoons that wash their food, honey bears, bleareyed sloths, pigeons whose nests stink of lime and feathers,

COYOTE-POSTMAN

aguamiel made from the honey of butterflies and dew trapped in mutilated bamboo branches, blood of vegetable cocks flowing in crests of fire, green fire of leaves with burning spines, ferns with long manes sleeping in curls, hives, swarms of soapy sound . . .

Four days they spend in this aerial plain suspended from the columns of ceibas high above the earth, those who passed from the black darkness of the caverns into the white darkness of the mist. Four days and nights without sleep, invincible, between the weavers of weariness and the vultures, the treetop leaves their only visible food, gestures their only means of talking, clinging to the branches as they move, heads bowed, snapped at the nape of the neck, without balance, their feet moving like hands, naked or half naked, laughing continuously with their genitals in the air. The light brings a chaste sleepiness. They grow drowsy. They scratch themselves. On the fourth day, as the sun turns to the West, the wizards announce that they are not men of wood, they are not dolls of the forest, and they grant them passage to the flatlands, where the maize in all its forms awaits them, in the flesh of their children who are made of maize, in the bones of their dead ones, who are skeletons of maize, powder of maize, in the flesh of their women, maize left to saturate for pleasure, because the maize in the flesh of a young woman is like the grain watered by the earth just as the shoot is about to rise, in the provisions which in that very place, after the ablutions in communal baths, they partake of to regain their strength: yellow-maize tortillas with eleven layers stuffed with black beans between each layer, one for each of the eleven days in the gloomy caverns, tortillas of white maize, round suns, with four layers and a filling of yellow flowers from the crookneck squash between each layer, for the four days in the earth evaporating; and tamales made of old maize, young maize, posoles, atoles, stews, and roasted sweet corn.

Arriving there, seeing all that, the curer and Señor Nicho, deer and coyote, shook their eight paws like plants pulled up

301

from the earth. The invincible ones, washed by the underground currents of rivers as icy as metal, having eaten, donning their ceremonial robes, set off in light canoes for the luminous grottoes.

My flint knife proclaims you! My hair combed with water! Me around you, I! Me around you, you around me! Tall and straight is the tree of the heavens and in it, everything happens, before it does on earth, victories and defeats, before it happens on earth, in the lake, in the heart of man! Your full hands, your green temples, your world between knees of water, flesh turned to flowers from kneeling down!

The first day, in a city of peasants with the roots of medicinal herbs, dawned to shield you against the bat so that you, sober and vertebrate within a medulla of melodious canes, with the blond hair of your sex upon your head, would be decapitated in full ripeness, among pyramids made from chains of serpents, the lunar fish, and the mist of those who have gone to disappearance!

Subterranean structures begin speaking without lips, a direct rigid voice propelling the song of the firefly wizards from the human throat into the booming cavity of those diamond-throated grottoes. The voice explodes, it is a petard opening out within the secret ears of the rocks, but the echo picks it up and molds it anew like clay, sculpting its modulations, until it is changed into a tinkling glass from which those who were not defeated at the bottom of the earth drink the ̍potable flight of birds, lest they be defeated in the sky.

The curer points his deer's hoof at Gaspar Ilóm, standing among the invincible ones. You can tell him by the amount of hot chili he eats, by his secretive eyes, and by the gray-white thatch on his head.

The Coyote-Postman, Nicho Aquino, looks at the chief of Ilóm among the invincible ones, as the Curer-Deer of the Seventh Fire explains:

"The conveyors of poison went up by night to bring him to death, in the midst of a celebration. His lips sucked the white poison from a gourd of cane liquor, little by little. La Piojosa Grande, his woman, flew away like cascading water when she saw that his lips were briny with poison. Gaspar would have killed her, but he saw the form of his son clinging to her back. Invincible as he is, he drank down the river to wash out the poison and returned with the chill of dawn, greater than death, in search of his men; but all that remained of them was their machete-torn corpses, tattooed with shots fired at point-blank range. Whereupon, pursued by the bullets of those who wanted him dead or alive, he threw himself back into the water, back into the river, back into the current, invincible, just as you see him now, among the invincible ones. I survived the massacre," the curer went on, a swarm of mosquitoes was flying close by his ear, "because I had time to turn back into what I am, to bring out my four paws, otherwise I would have been laid out there and then, made mincemeat of, like the other firefly wizards, who took the first machete blows as they slept, with no time to turn back into rabbits. That is what they were, rabbits, rabbits with maize-leaf ears. They were cut to pieces, but the pieces joined together again, the piece of each wizard which had stayed alive wriggled off to form one single wizard, a wizard made of the bleeding pieces of wizards, and with one voice, from the mouth of that strange being with many arms, many tongues, they launched the curses: Fire of the forest will destroy the conveyors of poison! Tomás Machojón and Vaca Manuela Machojón burned to death! Fire of the seventh fire will kill Colonel Gonzalo Godoy! The commander of the mounted patrol apparently burned to death in the Earth-shaker."

"Apparently?" said the coyote, who was looking for something to say, or rather, Señor Nicho hidden in the coyote.

"Yes. The firefly wizards, descendants of the great clashers of flint stones, condemned him to be burned to death, and in appearance the sentence was carried out, because the eyes of owls, fire with salt and chili, nailed him down pore by pore to a board, where he remained just as he was, just as he is, reduced horse and all to the size of a piece of sugar candy. He tried to kill himself, but the bullet crashed into his temple without wounding him. A little toy soldier, to carry out his vocation. Soldiers have the same vocation as toys."

The Coyote-Postman wagged his tail. To hear all that had happened long ago as though it were happening now, at the entrance to the luminous grottoes, among people disembarking from canoes gliding secretly to bring sustenance of copal to the invincible ones, present like dreams in all those rocks studded with precious stones, those who feed on perfumed smoke and on the flowers of the wind, those small flowers which leap off banks with just a tiny thread for a root, or are blown so that they rise and hang suspended in the inlaid diamonds and pearls endlessly rising and falling, magnetizing one another with the delicate feelers of dead butterflies.

"And after the curses, the fire," the curer rose with the solemnity of a deer, with a shake of his mouth ribbed in black around the white of his small teeth, "went out at one puff, as a light is blown out: the light of the tribes, light of the children in the loins of men who were as evil as the dry stony places that blaze with cold in winter and in summer blaze with the heat of the sun. In them and in their children and all their descendants the light of the tribes was extinguished, light of the children. Machojón, the first born of Tomás Machojón, the conveyor of poison, was turned into a star in the sky on his way to ask the hand of Candelaria Reinosa, and the Tecunes beheaded the Zacatones, who were pulled up from life like cut grass, descendants every one, children or grandchildren, of the apothecary who knowingly sold the poison he had used to put a wretched worm-eaten dog to death."

Flashes of sun among the trees, along the galleries, changed the decoration of the grottoes, now of emeralds, a mineral green which sank through an atmosphere of blue-green jade to the unreflecting green of the deep vegetal waters below.

There were so many things to ask, but because it was what most intrigued him, Señor Nicho, not without a sly coyote's nervous shiver running down his spine, ventured, "And the rock of María Tecún?"

"Your question, thick hair, sharp hair, is a stirrup for me to climb into my reply."

"Thick hair, sharp hair asks it of you, because much is told of María Tecún, of tecunas, those women who run away from home, and many are the men who have been lost on María Tecún Ridge," he took a long swallow of coyote saliva, an amalgam of tears and blowpipe breath for the howl, before managing to say, "and because that was the cause of my distress. I suffered what cannot be explained to anyone who is not both animal and human, as we are. I felt that my jealousy was forming great purple blood clots inside my head, until it stopped it up completely, and then poured out over my face, hot, and stuck to the outside, like a cancer stain. But underneath my jealousy were a few pustules of pity, and then I felt able to forgive her: poor thing, they gave her a 'spider-crawl' powder to drink. And it wasn't pity so much but a violent tickling in my throat which squeezed me until I vomited, while at the same time two circles, also of tickles, stuck to my nipples and sucked on them, and a circle of deep water coiled in my waist, and then not only did I feel able to forgive her, but to love her again in my secret desires, even taking pleasure from the idea that in her flight someone else might have known her, enjoyed her flesh, the luminous grotto within her, except that in the deep damp cave of her sex the jagged rocks move like animal roots. No one who is not an animal and a man can understand me. Now I know what happened. But to arrive at the sad consolation of knowing that she is dead—the dog was the only witness when she went out for water across a patch of grass and fell down a water hole—the things I had to go through: doubtless I bit defenseless animals, doubtless I frightened people in lonely villages, doubtless I howled by graveyards, doubtless I wound the tangled thread of my insanity on four paws around the rock of María Tecún, among the mists and shadows . . ."

305

"Let us leave the underground world, the road is short, the story long, and simple the explanation if we return to María Tecún Ridge . . ."

XIX

Señor Nicho Aquino could not go back to San Miguel Acatán. They'd have burned him alive just as the letters he was taking to the Central Post Office were burned by the wizards with black hands and firefly nails. After roaming far and wide, at times as a man, at times as a coyote, he turned up in a town which looked as if it were built on garbage. The truth, you could see it, was that it was built on top of lumps of old iron and planks, and columns of cement, and tree trunks stuck in the water of the sea, all briny and sticky, and stinking of malarial fever. Waterlogged shacks which you reached along rickety boardwalks and porches of rotting wood, some with glass windows which fell closed like guillotines, all with wire netting, and some others built right down on the bare hot earth, earth which stank of fish, with straw roofs and empty doorways like one-eyed men. Inside the houses a feeling of cats with catarrh. Iron stoves. Black cooks. They cooked with gasoline, though some houses had Spanish ovens of stones and mortar, with grates, and the food was cooked over wood or charcoal.

Cool weather, people there would say, but Señor Nicho felt he was roasting. He'd come down from the mountains, a fugitive from justice. To the crime of failing to take due care of official documents, a second charge was added: that he had murdered his wife, who had never been heard of again. The coast takes some getting used to. A woman who owned a shabby hotel that looked more like a hospital gave him lodging

306

for work as a messenger boy. Guest rooms decorated with flowered wallpaper long since faded by the sun. A hotel full of cats, dogs, poultry, cage birds, parrots, and a pair of macaws which shone like rainbows amid all that filth and served as lucky charms against fire.

Only one guest. An unknown guest. He walked off a ship every six or seven days, with a pipe in his mouth and his jacket folded over his white arm, a face ruddy with sunburn, blond, half lame. His napkin had to be changed after every meal, so he could clean his moustache, and it was Señor Nicho's job to serve him each course: soup, rice, meat, bananas, beans, and the odd peach in syrup. He found out that the man was a Belgian. What he could never find out, though, was why he kept going out to sea. He didn't fish. He didn't bring back contraband like the smugglers did. Just himself, his coat, and his pipe. In conversation with the hotel owner, the Boss-Lady, she told him she assumed he was measuring the depth of the ocean to see if English ships could enter, in case of trouble with England. The monotonous train of life, that could only be compared with the little train carrying truckloads of goods up and down the quay. A breath of fresh air in the evenings, smelling of fresh bamboo, well after the sun had gone down.

But Señor Nicho, who did a bit of everything—the only job I haven't done here is be someone's woman, he would tell the Boss-Lady—what he was used most for was for going twice, sometimes three times a week, depending on the orders, in a small launch rowed by a boatman, to the Harbor Castle.

Whereas along the coast on the side of the port and its boundaries there were palm trees with trunks reflected in the water like serpents rearing out of the sea, on the other side, looming in the liquid distance, just like a great oriole, was the Harbor Castle.

The Boss-Lady gave him a watch the size of a small turtle— the sea has its hours like all beasts, and grows to raging at night —which he fastened with a chain almost like a convict's to the second buttonhole of his khaki shirt, and its tick-tock vibrated in his breastbone until the bone got used to living between two pulsations, that of his blood and that of time. On either side, as the loaded canoe penetrated the sea to become sharpened, tapered, thinner than a stick, almost like a thread, the horizon went stretching away, spattered here and there by the heads and tails of sharks. Thrashing tails, bites, brute noises, turns and half turns in the silence of the water, beneath the silence of the sky.

Sometimes he would take a passenger, someone staying at the Hotel King who had come to an agreement with the Boss-Lady to rent the boat for a trip to the castle to visit one of the prisoners. In which case, Señor Nicho would take advantage of the paid trip to fill orders for the prisoners.

The prisoners in the Harbor Castle made a deep impression on Nicho Aquino, who was a highlander through and through, because being locked up there in the middle of the sea had slowly turned them all into aquatic creatures who were neither men nor fish. The color of their skin, their fingernails, their hair, the sluggish movement of their eyes, almost always fixed, their way of moving, of shaking their heads, of turning round, it was all fishlike, even when they showed their teeth to laugh. The only human thing about them was their shape and their speech, which in some of them was so quiet you might have thought they were opening and closing their mouths to let out bubbles.

In that Harbor Castle, fitted out as a prison, among those fish men, serving sentence for clandestine distilling of liquor, selling liquor without a license, perjury, robbery and contempt of court, were the criminals Goyo Yic and Domingo Revolorio. They were each given three years and seven months, not counting the time they spent in prison in Santa Cruz de las Cruces. The two compadres were the hotelkeeper's best customers for palm leaves to make hats. Day after day they sat opposite one another on two stones worn smooth even before they arrived, plaiting the palm fiber in an interminable ribbon which they rolled up until they had a good quantity and then sewed the hats, the Panama hats they made to sell by the dozen.

Every time Revolorio finished the gourd of a hat he would lean his elbows on his knees and looking at the sea would talk of having enough to make a hat the size of the sky. And as Goyo Yic twirled the finished hat on his finger, he would think about the thoughts which, as in some inverted fishbowl, would swim in it, from the tiniest fish to the shark which swallows them all up. The same thing goes for your head as for the sea. The big thought eats up all the rest. That fixed idea which is never sated. And the shark thought in Goyo Yic's head was still his wife and children, exactly as they were when they left him in the house that morning, alone, on the outskirts of Pisigüilito. All those years! He went round as a peddler right up to the time he was arrested, looking everywhere for her, and never heard anything, never had a scrap of news about her. His heart went out blindly, after all that time, to call her name, just as he went out of his house, blind in those days, shouting to her: "María TecúúúÚÚÚn! María TecúúúÚÚÚn!"

The prisoners. A hundred and twenty of them brutalized by eating and sleeping, and not doing anything. The sun dried out the atmosphere and the salt air they breathed kept them thirsty all the time. Fish without scales, smooth, moist, full. Those who went mad threw themselves into the sea from the towers. The water swallowed them up, followed by the sharks, and in the prison records a casualty was entered without a date. The date would be fixed when the dead man stopped eating, the day before some local bigwig came up from the town. Meanwhile the dead man went on eating for the benefit of the governor's pocket.

They were not special prisoners. They were forgotten prisoners. The prison overflow was sent there from time to time. A matter of luck. Sometimes they cleaned the cannons, an occupation which entertained some of them and irritated others. Cleaning old junk. Doing something pointless is worse than doing nothing at all. Candle-grease and rags until all the bronze was clean, with lions and eagles on its imperial coats of arms.

A strange notice engraved on a board with a red-hot iron

said: "IT IS FORBIDDEN TO TALK ABOUT WOMEN." From when did it date, that notice inscribed on a worm-eaten plank, dried out by the sun, the salt, wood which was almost ash? Some said that that printed order had sailed the seven seas on a pirate ship. In the castle's epic days the warning had been observed under pain of death. Once the garrisons had gone the crows arrived to pick out the eyes of the absent women who had been pictured there, without words, just by thinking about them. Now that place stinking of urine was the most deserted corner of the fortress.

"Lucky thing you weren't here when that notice was taken serious, compadre."

"What would they have done to me?" Goyo Yic asked Revolorio.

"Why, nothing much—a two-hundred-pound stone round your neck and a gentle push over the side."

"Let me tell you, compadre—"

"Speak, compadre, but not about women."

"The punishment couldn't have been for them that talked about their mothers, because I expect that was allowed, your mother comes before everything."

"You said it, compadre, and that's the very reason why they were forbidden to talk about their beloved mothers. No, the notice is wise, there's nothing more afflicting than conversations in which men bring the authors of their days out to dance. Soldiers grow weak when they start thinking happy thoughts about the past. They stop being soldiers and become little boys again."

A jailer with a face like a bent key came out to meet them and pointed to the clear sky, not a single cloud, and all the asphyxiating blue of the Atlantic Ocean.

"Now's the time to try and get a look at the other island. It's a big island. Eugrope, it's called . . ."

The compadres and the jailer climbed one of the towers. A small black dot on the sheet of the sea. Señor Nicho's boat returning to land from the castle. Señor Nicho exchanged the odd word with the oarsman. Juliancito Coy, though because of a speech defect he said "Juliantico," that was the oarsman's name. Naked, apart from a loincloth. He knew very little and he knew plenty. Very little learning and plenty launch. So Nicho Aquino talked to him. Juliancito showed his fish teeth and, combining rowing with talking, he breathed: Plenty shark here and out there on the land plenty alligators: us being what we are, we're food, these beggars want to eat us up. They climbed a ladder up to the quay, where the little Customs House was. Off Señor Nicho trudged with his bits and pieces, empty baskets and boxes, and the oarsman with his oar over his shoulder, each to his own house, if I saw you I don't remember.

"Compadre, the island of Eugrope," Revolorio said, pointing, and giving Goyo Yic a little dig with his elbow.

"Really, compadre? How did you manage to see it?"

The jailer, bushy-browed and moustachioed, wrinkled up his face and squinted to make out the island of Eugrope on the horizon. He couldn't see anything, but when he came down he said that if it wasn't the island of Cuba, it must be the island of Eugrope they'd caught sight of, well and truly caught sight of.

Five months Goyo Yic had left to serve, the same as his compadre, of course, when one day—he was sewing a hat someone had ordered—he heard his name called with all its letters at the entrance to the castle, among those of the new prisoners disembarking from a steamship, with a flag, soldiers, and a trumpet, whom the governor received according to a written list.

"Goyo Yic!" sang the governor, as he called the roll.

Compadre Poppa-Possum stopped what he was doing and went out to make the acquaintance of this man who must be some relation of his. At any rate he was his double namesake, in Christian name and surname.

A boy of about twenty, thin, with black hair, fresh-faced, bright-eyed, proud of bearing, was Goyo Yic.

311

Poppa-Possum asked him, "Goyo Yic?"

And the boy replied, "That's me. What can I do for you?"

"Nothing. I just wanted to meet you. I heard the name and came to see who you were. How was the journey? Tiring, I expect. Did they bring you on foot? That's how they brought us. But here you'll have time to rest, as much time as the dead men in the graveyard."

Poppa-Possum knew who the boy was the moment he set eyes on him. He shook his gray head slowly from side to side, next to the boy, eyes heavy with weeping that wouldn't come, words that choked up his throat. But mixed in with that bitter taste rising from his stomach to his mouth was a thread of hope, like a thread of sweet saliva: through his son he would learn what had become of María Tecún.

He went to tell compadre Mingo, and to ask him to say that most rare prayer, "The Twelve Emmanuels," which gives so much fortitude and such good counsel, the one that starts off with the first Emmanuel, Saint Caralampio . . .

Goyo Yic learned, through compadre Mingo, that Poppa-Possum Goyo Yic was his father. From the moment he saw him at the inner gate of the castle his eyes felt they had bumped into something that belonged to them, there where everything was alien and against him; but only now did he understand the reason for that feeling, which hitherto he had been unable to explain. And so he went and lay down to sleep at his side. If you can call it sleeping. It was the first night since he grew up that he had slept like that, protected by the presence of his father. Nevertheless, unconsciously, he closed his eyes without fear next to a man.

Poppa-Possum Goyo Yic inquired, fearful of what he might find out if he asked too many questions, of being left with his imagination like a balloon whose blue air has all been let out, but still he asked, what had become of María Tecún.

"When we left the house," his son told him, "she took us higher into the mountainlands, sure that our Tata would go down to the coast to look for us."

312

COYOTE-POSTMAN

"In the mountainlands where?" Goyo Yic asked.

"In the mountainlands, way up. We were there six years. Our Nana worked in the ranch house of a big hacienda. They gave her a rancho to live in and we all grew up there."

"With another tata?"

"No. No chance of that. There were a lot of us, and our Nana so ugly."

Ugly, repeated Goyo Yic silently. Ugly, ugly, and he was about to blurt out, "but she was beautiful, beautiful, a lovely girl," only he quickly remembered that he had never seen her, everyone just told him she was beautiful.

"Then we went back to Pisigüilito, we looked for my Tata, we looked all over for you, but you weren't there. Who knows, he's gone, we said, or he's dead, we said, sadly. Our Nana got married again. They said you'd fallen down a ravine looking for our Nana. Seeing as how you were blind."

"Who'd she marry?"

"A man who had a pact with the devil, and he must've, 'cause the strangest things kept happening in the house. There were always different men coming to see our Nana, and he used to find out, but he never hit them, he never went on at them, he never said anything. That's because they were only seeing if she was good, if she was doing right by him, with them traps."

"I'll say she was good!" Poppa-Possum exclaimed.

"Then we all ran away from home one by one, only the youngest one, Damiancito, stayed with her, and it was through him we found out the devil had fallen in love with our Nana. Least, that's what they said. He made her beautiful, clean, pretty, like one of them pictures in the pharmacy. But the man who married her wouldn't leave her side for a moment, and every time the devil turned up he sent him home with a beating: he really used to give him a thrashing, and the evil one couldn't do nothing, because that was the agreement—as long as our Nanita refused the other lovers my stepfather could hit them without them harming a hair on his head. And as my

313

Nanita wouldn't have anything to do with the devil, not even his picture, my stepfather could really give it him without Satan even touching him in return."

"What are you in here for?"

"For rebellion. They tried to make us work without pay, it ain't right, there's no justice."

Poppa-Possum Goyo Yic told his son how he'd wasted his life away searching for them along the roads and in the towns. First, the operation. Chigüichón Culebro restored his sight. Then his days peddling. Then the liquor fiasco and him ending up in jail. He'd been afraid she'd taken them down to the coastlands where there's that grub that makes you blind; but she'd used her head, thanks be to God, and although he'd lost his life, he hadn't lost his children.

Goyo Yic told him that his Nana, being more of a scrapper than most men, a pure guerrilla, had offered to get him out of the castle; but now he'd got a look at the place, with the sea so wild and all those sharks and everything, he would send word to her not to do it. The sea gets so rough at night.

"She'll come to see you first."

"Yes, she means to, and she'll bring me some things, a change of clothing."

"In that case, my son, let her come, and that way her own eyes will show her how dangerous the sea is, how jagged the rocks are, how cruel this accursed castle is."

"Will you see her?"

"Eh?" He made a doubtful gesture. "I'll see. Good thing she's not coming tomorrow, I'll have time to think about it. Anyway, let her come."

A curtain of dark clouds separated the coastland from the castle. A curtain of dark clouds echoing to the shudder of the thunder which followed lightning flashes painted like golden bramble bushes over the sea.

"At these times, my son, we don't even have the consolation of the sharks."

The wind roared. The rain lashed down. Waves as high as

314

churches rose and tumbled. The island and the castle got further away.

"Tata, I hope the island don't cut loose and get carried out to sea . . ."

"It might carry us to the island of Eugrope; only then you wouldn't see your lady mother again."

"Is there another island, then?"

"So one of the jailers says, the one they call Portuguese. But I don't think there can be anything beyond that blue current we can see. However much we try, we mountain folk can never imagine the sea, what it's like, like an animal."

Their hat-making also suffered with the bad weather. Without the sun your fingers won't work, they get stuck as though they too were plaited, immobile in the palm fiber, which gets too damp, so you have to put more effort into weaving it.

"Long-time prisoners, my son," Poppa-Possum said, changing the subject, "prisoners with tunnels of rheumatism in our bones, our hands unwilling, our legs so far gone they don't obey us. Pain becomes a pastime for us old folk."

The stormy weather beat furiously along the whole coast. Even in the deepest recesses of the castle, buried within walls five to six arm's-lengths thick, stone and mortar hardened by the centuries, it could be heard as if something very fragile, but at the same time very strong, had cracked at the base of the great rock. It was almost dark. The voices of the sentries, soldiers and prisoners keeping watch, drowned the naked scream of a human voice in the midst of the tempest. Soldiers and prisoners stared down at a boat, twisted and broken, at the mercy of the gusting squall.

It could not be reached. Nothing was found out. The prisoners went thin with dread, tiny, insignificant in the face of the overflowing elements. The waves were like flying axes, picks sinking into the deep, chopping up the sea, and foaming crests of water leaped at times like fighting cocks up to the dark, gloomy, silent towers.

The two Goyo Yics, eyes open wide, spent the whole night

315

in the rain-splashed darkness thinking the same procession of thoughts. They were reluctant to confide their apprehension, their alarm, their forebodings, but by midnight they could no longer keep silent, and anyway they couldn't get off to sleep. Their words flowed out of them like the barks of a dog which doesn't mean to bark and afterwards, when it does, is startled by its own noise. But no, it couldn't be, it couldn't have been her. First she'd come with the clothing for her son, Goyo Yic, and only then would they talk about getting him out of there.

"Unless that fellow in league with the devil has—" whispered Poppa-Possum Goyo Yic.

"No, Tata," replied Goyo Yic the younger, after a short silence, a long silence, at any rate, after a silence. "Folks are saying he's free again."

"What did you say his name was? Some names you can never remember."

"Benito Ramos, he's called . . ."

"So the devil's let him go."

"Yes, he set him free."

They pulled their blankets up round themselves and, after a word from one, a word from the other, they fell asleep. Poppa-Possum Goyo Yic let his hand fall somewhere over his offspring's body, so he would have a more comfortable sleep. Old blood and new blood from the same entrails, the old branch and a bud from that same branch in the midst of the storm.

Over at the harbor, the Hotel King, bedaubed with salt water, mosquito nets dripping, more like fishing nets. The Boss-Lady consulted Nicho Aquino with her eyes, about something Nicho Aquino clearly suspected but couldn't bring himself to turn into words within the cavity of his mouth, fearful that putting it into words would make it true, irreversible, a reality.

Pushed by the Boss-Lady's eyes, without opening his mouth, he decided to go up to the second floor. The winding staircase creaked beneath his feet. In a couple of steps, squeezing his hand along the salt-sticky banister, the little second-floor banister, he pushed open the door to the Belgian's room. Nothing. No one. Just his slippers, a ten-gallon hat—Señor Nicho fixed his eyes on that article, which he quickly calculated as a sort of inheritance due him under the kinship existing between master and servant—a candlestick with a half-burned taper, and a few matches.

Without the Boss-Lady asking, he said, "He ain't there."

"There. You see . . ." The Boss-Lady had her back to him when he went into the bar, she was standing by the counter. "I knew it . . . He got caught in the storm . . ." She leaned back and turned round, with an empty glass in her hand, "There. You see . . . You see . . ."

"But, is he in danger?"

"Not anymore, he isn't . . ."

The Boss-Lady hurriedly filled another glass with cognac and downed it.

"Oh, no need to worry, then . . ."

"If he went out in the boat he'll be out of danger by now, and if he didn't go then he ain't in danger either. I hope to God he's gone away to those mountains where they say there are minerals of gold."

The news of the boat wrecked at the foot of the Harbor Castle reached the Hotel King a few days later, by which time the storm was moving away up the Caribbean. That day the Boss-Lady finished off the bottle of cognac. Nicho Aquino uncorked it and took it to her room. She was lying in bed, naked to the waist, like an old mermaid. Nicho Aquino greeted her as he entered and took his leave as he left, but she didn't answer. She seemed to have gone mad. She didn't even notice that her breasts were hanging out for a stranger to see. Indeed, she scratched them without the least embarrassment. Sad breasts, weepy with salt water. The servant left the bottle and a clean glass on the bedside table. Butt ends of American cigarettes, smelling like perfumed crap. The Boss-Lady didn't see him, or made out she didn't, lost in a cloud of smoke. All she did was stretch out her nicotine-stained fingers to ask him to pass her another cigarette. When he went out Señor Nicho listened at the door. All he could hear was the glugluglug of the cognac going down her throat. Then he heard her getting up. She almost caught him at the door. She came out so quickly she overtook him at the top of the stairs. But she still didn't seem to see him. She gave heart-rending howls, blasphemed, insulted God in filthy language which made the servant's hair stand on end. The sea lifted its concave waves, like ears, and took what it heard to the bottom of all things, where God is.

The next day all was back to normal at the Hotel King. The storm had passed. Thousands of dead fish on the beaches. The trunks of the trees which went down to the sea's edge were bathed in marine substances, some of them mutilated, others jigging about roots and all like shipwrecked men with shoes on.

"Very dangerous," Señor Nicho remarked to the Boss-Lady, who now appeared with everything that was hanging out yesterday tucked away in her corset.

"Get on with the coconuts, and don't be such a coward."

"What do I seal them with when I've finished?"

"With rocket-maker's wax, black wax. That's how I made my money, selling these liquored coconuts. After cold weather like this the prisoners will give anything for a liquored coconut. You'll ruin everything with your anxieties, you will, act like a man. Everything in life is a risk," as she said this she was thinking of the boat smashed against the rocks below the castle, her man, "all very well you wanting to save some pesos to have your woman brought up from the well . . . You'll never get anywhere with your lack of nerve. Rich folks are rich because they take chances to rob other folk of their cash, trading, making things, you name it, after all, whenever a lot of money comes together in just one hand it's always a kind of robbery of the rest of us."

"But as coconuts are naturally cool and refreshing, who's going to believe I'm selling coconut milk? . . . Offering coconuts after a storm! What an idea, ma'am!"

318

"You grease the governor's palm: take a hundred pesos with you and slip it to him as you go in. Then shout, 'Coconuts! Coconuts!' The prisoners all know about it. When you see their eyes light up with gratitude you'll feel you ain't only doing good business, you're doing a good deed."

The coconut business was as solid as the coconuts themselves. They all bought a liquored coconut, every one of them. Instead of coconut milk the shells were filled, some with cane brandy, others with rum. The ones with rum in were more expensive. You needed to put down a few good mouthfuls of brandy or rum to relieve yourself of that sick feeling the storm left in your body and soul.

Domingo Revolorio bought one of rum, and took it off to offer compadre Yic a drink, though he made it clear it would have to be paid for, like that blasted flagon of liquor that landed them in jail. They both went through the pantomime of selling one another the drinks they took. Poppa-Possum explained their arrangement with the flagon to his son. "We sold cash down, two hundred gourdfuls at six pesos a time, it can't have been more because we spilled some on the way. Anyway, two hundred gourdfuls at six pesos each measure makes twelve hundred pesos. When we woke up in jail we didn't have a thing, and all they found on us was six pesos." The boy stared at them. The work of the devil. They tried it out with the coconut filled with rum, selling each swig at a peso a time. Yic, senior, paid Revolorio for one drink. He gave him the peso. Then Revolorio asked for a drink in return. He took it and paid him the peso. The same peso. And so on, until the coconut was finished: three drinks apiece. When they'd finished they should have had six pesos and all they had was the same lousy peso they started out with. Pure witchcraft. You sell cash down, you finish your product, and after all that you haven't even made cost, still less the profit you'd expected.

The days gushed sun, sun that in the Harbor Castle was like molten lead. Varmints suffocated by the heat came out to air themselves on terraces of sandy soil and grass the color of cobwebs. The prisoners gave chase, to throw them to the fish, with shouts of laughter as rats, lizards and mice fell into the clear blue-green water, transparent down to where the bottom began to turn dark like porcelain of penumbra with a jellyfish cold.

The garrison soldiers were forbidden to waste ammunition, and so they couldn't fire at the sharks, but oh, they were just itching to get their fingers on the trigger and paralyze, with one shot if their aim was good, one of the magnificent specimens of tropical shark swimming in shoals below, little bulls with fins like rainbow salamanders, tenacious, with double rows of pyramidal teeth. The blacks, two or three black prisoners, on days of great excitement, would dive in to take them on, like bullfighters, without knives, without anything, only the mockery of their slender nakedness. The negroes gave off the smell of dried mustard before they jumped into the watery ring. It's the stench of death that comes out in a man's fear, the jailers explained. However, the best marksman in the garrison was posted up in a tower with his rifle ready to fire at the sharks in case of danger, though it was said that on one occasion some years before he hadn't been able to see for the foaming waters and with one cat's spring a shark had carried off one of the black toreros. It was a brave spectacle, lusty and mysterious, and exercised such an attraction over the spectators that some fell into the water, breaking the incandescent swell, dives which went unnoticed, for although at other times they would have had everyone laughing, now there was no time for them, all attention being centered, magnetized, on the death-defying game the negro was playing out with the shark. What unexpected forms the human figure took up as it presented itself and evaded the shark wrapped in the youthful darkness of its marine shadow. The tenacious beast after the human rocket with a detonation of foaming bubbles along its arms, along its feet, unable to catch it. The dark mass of the shark undulated, stupid, compressed by the water, while the negro's varnished body shimmered, electrifying the spectators. In the expectant silence you could hear every drop of sweat falling from the

320

foreheads of the spectators into the liquid mirror below, and the blub, blub, bli, blub, be, blub of the rival bodies passing so punishingly close to one another that there was no time to think of what was not happening because by then the muscular ebony, with a laugh and a clacking of teeth, would lean out of the way of the shark which, tricked but not defeated, would swim rapidly downwards tracing a corkscrew of foam, to reappear in profile, wheeling back through rings of crystal which almost jingled as they clashed together.

The officers, the soldiers, the prisoners, returned to their own reality after the "shark show," hollow, opaque, their nerves pretty well in tatters, some looking as though they'd been in an accident, with twitching arms, or eyes like headlights.

Sea birds idly unplaited distances, winging with exaggerated difficulty, pitching themselves from way up to just graze the water and remount their flight, while flying fish leapt like pieces of chalk when someone bangs on a billiard table.

Goyo Yic came to him one very clear day and said, "Tata, there's my Nana."

"I hope you didn't tell her I was here."

"I told her."

"My God, why did you have to go and . . . I didn't want her to know. What did she say . . . ?"

"Nothing. She started to cry."

"And did you tell her I could see?"

"No. That I didn't tell her."

"Then I'll half close my eyes and you can lead me by the hand."

"She thinks you're still blind . . ."

María Tecún was still freckled, the straight threads of her red hair heavily flecked with white silken strands. She stepped behind the inner gate to wipe away her tears and blow her old woman's flared nostrils, and waited with a trembling of legs beneath her skirts for the blind father and his son to approach.

Poppa-Possum Goyo Yic went up very close to her, pretend-

ing to be blind, as if he were going to bump right into her, until
he did. She moved back a little, took him by the hand, and
stood looking at him with her small searching eyes trembling
beneath the fat tears springing from her lids.

"How have you been?" she said, after a moment.

"And you, how are you?"

"What are you in here for?"

"For smuggling. Because of a flagon of liquor I bought with
a compadre of mine to sell at the Santa Cruz fair. We lost the
permit and they shit on us."

"Imagine that . . . Us too, right, my son? They told us you
were dead, that you'd passed away. Have you been here
long?"

"I've been here—"

"Long?"

"Two years. I'm in for three."

"Holy Jesus!"

"And you, María Tecún, how are you? You married again,
I hear."

"Yes, Goyito told you. They declared you dead and gave me
permission to marry again. The children needed a father. A
woman's hand's no good on men. Men need a man and he
turned out good, thanks be to God—at least, he treated them
well. I left you . . ."

Goyo Yic made a gesture of irritation, unconsciously opening his eyes more than he should have, enough for her, though
she was immersed in her thoughts, to have noticed that the
pupils were clear, not like they used to be.

"Let me say it, the time has come for us to speak about it
before one of the children. I left you, not because I didn't care
for you, but because if I'd stayed we'd have had another ten
children by now, and we couldn't have coped; for your sake,
for their sake, for my sake. What would the kids have done
without me; and you with your eyes like that . . ."

"And didn't you have any children by your new man?"

"No, he's incapable. The wizards took away his power to put

322

his seed in a woman. A soothsayer told me. He took part in some Indian massacre and they put a curse on him, they dried him up inside."

"And what about me, if I had my eyes would you love me?"

"I might. But you wouldn't love me, because I'm real ugly, hideous. Ask your son. Though no mother is ugly to her own son."

"Nana," Goyo interrupted, laughing, "have you noticed anything about my Tata yet?"

"From the moment I saw him, but I've been pretending not to have. You wanted to hug me when you bumped into me, making out you couldn't see, Tatita."

Poppa-Possum opened his eyes. His pupils hesitated, and hers hesitated, before they met, came together, became fixed, the light of their gaze changing.

"How marvelous you've really got your eyes," María Tecún said, squeezing a piece of handkerchief in her hand, closed tight with emotion.

"But they've been no use to me until now, because I only wanted them to see you, and I searched for you, searched everywhere. I thought I'd recognize you by your voice, seeing that I didn't know you by sight, and I became a peddler, coming and going, talking to every woman I met."

"And would you have known me by my voice?"

"No, I don't think so . . ."

"Voices change with the years. Leastways, now that I hear you talking, Goyo Yic, you seem to be talking different from what you did before . . ."

"The same thing's happening to me with your voice. You used to have a different way of talking, María Tecún . . ."

Domingo Revolorio, whom Poppa-Possum Goyo Yic called over, came up to make María Tecún's acquaintance.

"Come on over, compadre."

"Godfather to a flagon that I took to the christening," Revolorio explained festively. "I wouldn't like you to think he had had more children, ma'am."

"That makes me your comadre, then."

"That's right, it does."

"Being as it was the flagon," Goyo Yic interrupted, he could scarcely contain the joy in his body, "she ain't so much your christening partner, compadre, as your drinking partner."

You could see the approach of evening.

The tinting of the sea, the tinting of the sky, the reddened clouds, and the motionless solemnity of the palm trees rising into the West. Here and there a boat inched across the distant horizon, which in a moment had taken on a dark violet color. The inner abstractedness of the deep waters, color of a bottle, increased the enigma of that moment of negation, of doubt before the night.

All that had been spoken and left unspoken had now been said. The idea of the younger Yic's escape was dismissed as too dangerous.

The old woman's jaw trembled as she said goodbye to her son. She snuffled. She tried not to cry, so as not to distress him. Her eyelids trembled. She wiped her nose nervously with her hand. Her freckles, her mouth pulled tight by grief, the wrinkles of her neck, her bosom without breasts. She turned and thrust her head into her son's shoulder. She would come again. Lucky she had brought something to sell. Six pigs. I'll get rid of them tomorrow, and come back and see you. Did she say it, or just think it?

Nicho Aquino came up with the Boss-Lady's watch in his hand, to inform the visitor it was time to return to dry land. They got into the launch, him with his bits and pieces, her with her sorrow, and the boatman began to row. Cool evening breezes cut into the hot air of the canefields moving out from the land. A gentle swell on the still yellow bay, surrounded by black palms, like a pool of golden turpentine.

Nicho Aquino asked the silent traveler, whose appearance was not so very agreeable despite the tender weeping now drying out on her face, "How much are you reckoning to get for the pigs?"

COYOTE-POSTMAN

"Depends. If maize ain't too high they might fetch a good
price, though the truth is pigs are selling well anyway this year.
Least, they've sold all right where I come from."

Juliancito, the boatman, straining away. His hair stuck up in
a peak on his head. His hungry Baby Jesus eyes reflecting the
dots of light shining in the navigating darkness of the port.

Nicho Aquino blurted out somewhat inopportunely what he
had been thinking ever since they sat down in the boat. He had
learned, because he overheard part of the conversation between the Yics and Revolorio in the castle, that that woman
was . . .

"So you are the famous María Tecún?"

"Would you mind telling me . . . ," what he said threw her
off balance, but she replied equably enough, "why famous?"

"Because of the stone, because of the ridge, because of the
tecunas," spluttered the postman of San Miguel Acatán, now
a nobody. The right hand of the Boss-Lady of the Hotel King,
and her lover; but a great nobody ever since the day he
stopped being a postman.

"So you've heard about the rock, too . . . Well, yes, that's
me—a stone there and a person here."

Señor Nicho was sailing on the sea with María Tecún, just
as he was, a poor human being, and at the same time he was
walking in the form of a coyote on María Tecún Ridge, accompanied by the Curer-Deer of the Seventh Fire. Two sharp-
haired animals cutting through the thick mist over the open-
pored earth surrounding the great rock. They were on their
way back from the luminous grottoes, where they had met the
invincible ones in caves of dead flint stone, keeping up their
conversation in order not to dissolve, the Curer-Deer in the
docile white mist of the ridge, so like death, and the Coyote-
Postman on the hot blue darkness of the sea, where he was in
human form. Had they not been talking, the Curer-Deer
would have been dissolved in the mist, and the Coyote-Postman would have returned completely to his real self, his human body sailing alongside María Tecún.

325

The bobbing of the boat made them more sociable. They were drawing near the miasmatic quay, stinking oily water, garbage.

María Tecún explained that her name wasn't Tecún, not really, but Zacatón, and Señor Nicho, who at the same time that he was sitting in the boat in the form of a man with María Tecún, was trotting up on the ridge with the curer in the form of a coyote, passed it on to the curer with a howl, did you hear that: she isn't María Tecún, she's María Zacatón, Zacatón!

The Curer-Deer of the Seventh Fire, who was so close to him—they were moving at the same pace as the famous white darkness of the ridge—dipped his deer's nose into the rough hairs of the coyote's ear to say with a crystalline smile of foam on his mournful lip, "You've a long way to go to become a seer, my friend the coyote. A lot of walking, a lot of listening, a lot of looking. Eat roasted quails, chew the umbilicus of white copal, and listen, until you become drunk, to the honey wine of the birds that fly above the green that sits up in the trees, which is the same as the green sitting up in the mountains. A seer you become the moment you stand alone with the sun up above you. And María Tecún, the one you say you see as though she were standing here before you, is not named Zacatón, which is why she is still alive: had she been of Zacatón blood they would have cut off her baby head in the decapitation of the Zacatones which I, the Curer-Deer of the Seventh Fire, ordered indirectly through the person of Calistro Tecún, when the mother of the Tecunes fell sick with cricket hiccups. The Zacatones were beheaded because they were the children and grandchildren of the apothecary who sold and knowingly prepared the poison which paralyzed the war of the invincible Gaspar Ilóm against the maizegrowers who sow maize in order to profit from the harvests. Just as though men made their women pregnant to sell the flesh of their children, to trade the life of their flesh, with the blood of their blood, that's what the maizegrowers are like who sow, not to sustain themselves and support their families, but covetously, to make rich men of themselves. But poverty pursues them, they don the ragged leaf torn asunder by the wind of impiety and their hands are like black crabs stained with ringworm, like the crabs turning white through being in the sacred caves."

"If it isn't María Tecún, and if it isn't María Zacatón, who is this stone, Deer of the Seventh Fire?"

For a moment Señor Nicho heard his voice drowning in the ruminant swaying of the gulf; but the curer's words took him back to the reality of the ridge as he replied that in that stone was hidden the soul of María the Rain.

"María the Rain, she will rise on high in the time that is to come!"

The curer opened his arms to touch the stone, returned to the human figure he saw in it, he who was also human, before dissolving in the silence forever.

"María the Rain, La Piojosa Grande, she who took flight like cascading water, running from death, the night of the last feast in the camp of Gaspar Ilóm! On her back she bore the son of the invincible Gaspar and was paralyzed there where she is, between the sky, the earth, and the void! María the Rain is the Rain! The Great Fleabag is the Rain! A woman whose body is air, only air, and tumbling hair, only hair, so much hair, on her back she bore her son, the son of Gaspar Ilóm, the man of Ilóm, she bore her son the maize, the maize of Ilóm, and she will rise on high in the time to come, between the sky, the earth, and the void!"

EPILOGUE

Lamplights maddened by the stings of mosquitoes, mosquitoes maddened by the lamplight glow. Mosquitoes, gnats, midges, sandflies . . . Señor Nicho's face fled to one shoulder, like the heel of a twisted shoe. The years. Weight and solitude of lead. Wrinkles curved like horseshoes hardly held up his jaw, an accursed bone always hanging, hanging irremediably. Flies. They got in his mouth. Spit them out alive. The Boss-Lady died of pernicious fever. Went black, like a scorpion. Her hair fell out the last time she combed it. Heir to the Hotel King and its sixteen thousand rats, Señor Nicho Aquino. Poppa-Possum Goyo Yic and María Tecún went back to Pisigüilito. She was widowed of her second husband, the false one. You only have one husband, all the rest are false ones. Benito Ramos, the one who was in league with the devil. Died of a hernia. So back they went to Pisigüilito. Drive in the uprights again and build a bigger rancho, because their married children had many children and they all went there to live with them. Wealth of men, wealth of women, to have many children. Old folk, young folk, men and women, they all became ants after the harvest, to carry home the maize: ants, ants, ants, ants . . .

Guatemala, October 1945
Buenos Aires, 17th May 1949

329

GLOSSARY

Achiote (from Nahuatl *achiotl*) The red or yellow dyestuff prepared from the pulp surrounding the seeds of the annatto *(Bixa orellana)*, used for coloring textiles, oils, cheeses, etc.

Amate (from Nahuatl *amatl*) A large tree *(Ficus glabrata)* which grows mainly by rivers or in wet, swampy places, with lustrous foliage and a figlike fruit.

Atole (from Nahuatl *atolli*) A drink or gruel made from maize meal, mixing in milk, salt, sugar and other ingredients as required.

Capulin A valuable Central American tree *(Prunus capuli)* which yields edible red fruits like cherries; the figlike seeds furnish a kind of flour, the sap is used in many native remedies, and the bark is employed in making wattle walls for ranchos.

Ceiba A large genus of trees within the silk-cotton family *(Bombacaceae)*.

Chayote (from Nahuatl *chayutli*) The gourdlike fruit of an annual vine *(Sechium edule)* of the same name, widely cultivated throughout Mexico, Central America and the West Indies, and eaten as a vegetable.

Chia Any of several species of sage, especially *Salvia hispanica,* cultivated for their edible seeds, from which a beverage of the same name is prepared by adding water.

Chichita A low, thorny bush *(Solanum mammosum)* whose name—roughly "titties"—is inspired by the shape of its yellow berries, which resemble breasts; the faithful have traditionally used them to decorate their hats on their return from the Esquipulas pilgrimage.

Chilacayote (from Nahuatl *tzilacayutli*) Any of several edible gourds common in Mexico and Central America, especially *Cucurbita ficifolia,* having a smooth rind and stringy flesh.

Chilate *Atole* to which chili—or, more recently, cacao—has been added; the Nahuatl *chilatl* literally meant "chili water."

331

Chilca A common bush *(Senecio salignus)* with yellow flowers and small, pointed leaves, which grows on roadsides and in woods; the roots, leaves and bark are boiled to produce a yellow dye.

Choreque A climbing plant *(Petrea arborea?)* which produces pink or blue flowers.

Chuj One of the Mayan Indian tribes, centered on the province of Huehuetenango in the western highlands of Guatemala.

Comadre Literally "co-mother"; specifically, a woman who has agreed to act as godmother to one or all of the children of a given matrimonial couple, and therefore enters into other formalized but close ties with them; more generally, the term is used to signify any intimate friend who may be relied upon for sympathy or assistance.

Comale (from Nahuatl *comalli*) A flat stone or earthenware dish on which tortillas are cooked, usually over a wood fire.

Compadre Literally "co-father"; see *comadre.*

Conacaste A large tropical American timber tree *(Enterolium cyclocarpum)* whose wood is much prized for building purposes; its fruits are shaped like the human ear, and the original Nahuatl *quaunacaztli* meant "ear tree."

Contrayerva Literally "counter herb"; a tropical American plant *(Dorstenia contrayerva)* whose aromatic root is a stimulant used as an antidote for poison and in treating other complaints such as burns.

Copal (from Nahuatl *copalli*) An aromatic resin exuding from the tree of the same name *(Protium copal)* in round or irregular pieces which may be red, yellow, black or colorless; it is used as incense in Indian churches, as a kind of chewing gum, and in making varnishes and lacquers.

Corronchocho A small bush found in the Guatemalan countryside, which produces pink fruits of the same name; similar to wild marjoram, with which it is commonly confused.

Coyole (from Nahuatl *coyolli*) A palm *(Acrocomia vinifera)* producing large bunches of fruits of the same name, which are small, round, yellow and aromatic.

Eloatole Atole made from the green ears of young maize *(elotes);* eggs and cinnamon are usually added.

Enchilada A dish whose base is the tortilla, dipped in a chili sauce, fried or baked, and stuffed with vegetables, meat, cheese and other ingredients, all of which are seasoned with chili.

Frijole Any kind of cultivated bean, but specifically the black seed of a variety of *Phaseolus vulgaris* which, pounded into a black paste and

GLOSSARY

served with tortillas, forms the staple diet of the Middle American
Indian.

Goat's-water A literal translation of the Spanish *agua chiva;* it is
water used by Indian women to moisten the maize dough and to
wash down the grinding stone; since it contains the residue from
the maize, it is given to domestic animals, particularly goats.

Guachipilin A large Central American timber tree *(Diphysa robin-
oides)* which yields a hard, fine-grained wood and a yellow dye.

Guarda, Guardabarranca A brown songbird, somewhat smaller
than the mockingbird, which nests in ravines and the trees which
grow in them; hence its name—literally "guardian of the ravines"
—which is itself a direct translation of the original Tzutuhil Maya
word.

Guarumo A tree with a thick trunk and leaves like those of the
papaya, to which various therapeutic qualities are attributed; guaru-
mos are invariably infested with yellow, stinging ants.

Guayacan The lignum vitae, a valuable tropical American tree noted
for its magnificent timber, white flowers and olive-shaped fruits; the
Spaniards believed its bark and resin cured all manner of diseases.

Guicoy A variety of squash used in several popular sauces and des-
serts of Guatemala.

Huipile (from Nahuatl *huipilli*) A rectangle of cotton with a hole in
the center for the head, worn as a dress or blouse—depending on
the length—by the Indian women of southern Mexico and Central
America.

Iguaxte A sauce made from pumpkin seeds roasted and crushed with
tomato and spices.

Ladino In Spanish America generally, a mestizo or half-breed who
speaks Spanish; in Guatemala, however, the term denotes any person whose speech and way of life are Spanish, that is, "European-
ized," even if racially he is mainly or entirely Indian.

Loroco A climbing plant *(Urechites karwinskii)* which produces sprays
of scented flowers; the edible seeds and the flowers themselves are
used in rice and tamale dishes.

Macho A stallion or studhorse; the male of any species; when used
in reference to a man, it implies the more extreme manifestations
of manliness, such as physical courage and sexual prowess.

Maguey An important American species of agave, whose fleshy
leaves yield fibers, narcotics, alcoholic beverages, etc.

Mamey The marmalade tree *(Mammea sapota)* or its perfumed fruit,

333

the marmalade plum; also the mammee apple or tropical apricot *(Mammea americana).*

Marimba A primitive wooden xylophone, of probable African origin, now Guatemala's national instrument, with bottle gourds of descending sizes suspended beneath the keys, which are struck with hardwood hammers tipped with rubber; the sound is most nearly like that of a fluid harp, and the instrument used to be played by up to eight men at a time.

Matapalo Literally "tree-killer." A variety of amate, commonly used as fodder, which grows parasitically on the trunks of other trees until eventually they wither and die.

Matasano A Central American tree *(Casimiroa sapota),* which produces a highly fragrant, edible fruit.

Nana The word used by Indians for "mother"; by extension, a respectful or affectionate form used to address any old woman.

Nance A tree *(Malphigia montana)* which bears a small yellow fruit of the same name, the size of a cherry.

Nixtamalero Venus, the morning star, so named because it appears at the time when the nixtamal (maize dough cooked overnight in limewater, to soften it) is removed from the fire.

Ocote (from Nahuatl *ocotl*) A resinous Mexican pine *(Pinus montezumae)* whose red wood is used to light fires; the torches made from its splinters are known by the same name.

Pacaya A small Central American palm (genus *Chamaedora*) whose large cylindrical fruits are edible when young, and whose leaves are used to decorate churches and houses on the occasion of public festivities.

Papaya The fruit of the tropical pawpaw tree *(Carica papaya).*

Petate (from Nahuatl *petatl*) A kind of mat, usually made of reeds, though sometimes of palm leaves; by extension, the material itself may also be called petate.

Pinole Maize roasted and ground, and used like pipian to garnish various meats, such as venison, chicken or iguana; also roasted maize flour or chia grains which are stirred into hot or cold water, alone or mixed with cacao, sugar, cinnamon or achiote, and drunk by the poor of Middle America.

Pipian A sauce used to garnish various meat dishes, made of oil, chili, tomato, onion, peppers, cloves, coriander, banana skin, salt and sugar.

Pita The maguey or its fiber.

Pitahaya The edible juicy fruit of several members of the cactus family, especially *Hylocereus undatus;* the highly colored flesh is full of black seeds.

Pixcoy A dark brown bird with a melancholy call which is considered an evil omen by Guatemalan Indians.

Posole (from the Nahuatl *posolli*) A dish made of meat, maize, hominy, garlic and chili.

Primavera A timber tree *(Tabebuia donnellsmithii)* with striking blossoms and a light, hard wood; often called the white mahogany.

Pulique A sauce made of red chili, cooked tomato, rice, breadcrumbs and achiote; first the sauce is fried, and then the meat, cooked separately, is added.

Ranchero Someone who lives in a rancho, usually as a peon on a large estate.

Rancho A crude hut or shack, usually of wattle and daub, in which Indians and poor Ladinos live.

Sancocho A stew made of meat, yucca, banana and assorted vegetables.

San Geronimo Formerly a well-known brand of cane liquor from the town of the same name.

Sarespino A variety of bush with long black thorns.

Suquinay A flowering bush whose fragrant blossoms give off a violent aroma, and whose leaves the Indians use as a treatment for stomach pains.

Tamale A basic Middle American dish made of maize flour mixed with meat, seasoned with red pepper, dipped in oil, and then steamed, usually in a wrapper of maize husks or banana leaves.

Tata The word used by Indians for "father"; by extension, it is used to address anyone who is old or in a position of authority.

Tipaches Disks fashioned from black wax, with which men and youths play various games for money.

Torero A bullfighter

Tortilla The principal element in the diet of the Middle American Indian; not the Spanish omelette, but a thin, flat, round cake of maize flour baked on a comale and used much as Europeans use bread.

MIGUEL ANGEL ASTURIAS

1899–1974

Miguel Angel Asturias was awarded the 1967 Nobel Prize for Literature. Born in Guatemala, he served in his country's diplomatic service, most recently as ambassador to France. His novels have been admired both for their re-creation of Indian mythology and for their indictment of economic, social, and political privilege.